WHY MEXICANS DON'T DRINK MOLSON

RESCUING CANADIAN BUSINESS
FROM THE SUDS OF GLOBAL OBSCURITY

WHY MEXICANS DON'T DRINK MOLSON

ANDREA MANDEL-CAMPBELL

Douglas & McIntyre
Vancouver / Toronto

For Andrea, Isabella and Scuby

07 08 09 10 11   5 4 3 2

Douglas & McIntyre Ltd.
2323 Quebec Street, Suite 201
Vancouver, British Columbia
Canada v5T 4S7
www.douglas-mcintyre.com

Library and Archives Canada Cataloguing in Publication
Mandel-Campbell, Andrea, 1969–
Why Mexicans don't drink Molson : rescuing Canadian business
from the suds of global obscurity / Andrea Mandel-Campbell.

Includes bibliographical references and index.
ISBN 978-1-55365-225-0

1. Competition—Canada. 2. Competition, International. 3. Business enterprises—Canada.
4. Corporate culture—Canada. 5. Globalization—Economic aspects—Canada.
6. Export marketing—Canada. 7. Canada—Commerce. I. Title.

HF3226.5.M35 2007   382.0971   C2007-900020-7

Editing by John Eerkes-Medrano
Copy editing by Ruth Wilson
Jacket and text design by Ingrid Paulson
Jacket photographs by Alex vs. Alex Photography
Printed and bound in Canada by Friesens
Printed on acid-free paper that is forest friendly (100% post-consumer
recycled paper) and has been processed chlorine free.

We gratefully acknowledge the financial support of the Canada Council for the Arts,
the British Columbia Arts Council, the Province of British Columbia through the
Book Publishing Tax Credit, and the Government of Canada through the Book Publishing
Industry Development Program (BPIDP) for our publishing activities.

"To those who urge upon us the policy of tomorrow, and tomorrow and tomorrow; to those who tell us, wait, wait, wait; to those who advise us to pause, to consider, to reflect, to calculate and to inquire, our answer is: No, this is not a time for deliberation, this is a time for action. The flood-tide is upon us that leads on to fortune, if we let it pass it may never recur again ... Heaven grant that it be not already too late; heaven grant that whilst we tarry and dispute, the trade of Canada is not deviated to other channels, and that an ever vigilant competitor does not take to himself the trade that properly belongs to those who acknowledge Canada as their native or their adopted land. Upon this question we feel that our position ... corresponds to the beating of every Canadian heart."

SIR WILFRID LAURIER, PRIME MINISTER OF CANADA, 1902

"We have met the enemy and he is us."

PORKYPINE, QUOTED IN *IMPOLLUTABLE POGO*, 1970

CONTENTS

INTRODUCTION

DAVID HOOD WAS leaving the American Bar in Düsseldorf late one evening when he was stopped by two stern-looking policemen, armed with AK-47s, demanding his identification papers in clipped Germanic tones. Startled, the Canadian businessman squinted in confusion, fumbling in the semi-darkness for his wallet as the stone-faced officers looked on in silence. But as soon as Hood pulled out his Canadian passport, the gun-toting police broke into broad grins, summoning up what appeared to be the only English words they knew, chiming in unison: "beer, hockey, Wayne Gretzky!"

Beer. What could be more Canadian? With its sturdy, honeyed depths, conjuring up images of ice-cold lakes, lumberjacks and rough-hewn beauty, it is one of the few things that seem to distinguish us from the rest of the world. As tightly bound to our still-wobbly sense of national identity as hockey, beavers, Mounties and medicare, it's the one symbol of iconic Canadiana we could arguably slap a label on and sell around the globe. And yet we don't. It speaks volumes that Canadian beer can capture the imagination of two policemen in Germany, the original purveyor of the barley beverage and home of Oktoberfest. Especially when just about the only place you can get your hands on a "cold one" is in Canada—and who knows for how much longer.

The Europeans may have invented the bitter ale, but nowhere are the conditions more ideal for brewing beer than in Canada. Consider its two key ingredients, water and barley: Canada is the largest repository of fresh water in the world and the second-largest producer of barley, its northern Prairie climes ideal for making high-quality malt. The country's reputation for superior beer has preceded it, while Canada's two traditionally dominant brewers, Molson and Labatt, bathing in their own self-perpetuated praise, have routinely disparaged their closest competition, American beer, as the brewing equivalent to Jamaican bobsledding. So why is it, when it comes to the global beer industry, that Canadian suds are like the dried-up foam left at the bottom of an empty beer mug?

In the 1970s, Molson was roughly the same size as Heineken, a beer dynasty based in the postage-stamp-sized nation of the Netherlands. Three decades later, the Dutch brewery is the world's fourth-largest, with 115 breweries in more than sixty-five countries. Heineken sells some 119 million hectolitres across the planet while its eponymous brand ranks fifth among global beer labels. In contrast, the venerable brewery begun by John Molson in 1786, some eighty years before Heineken was born, manufactures a meagre ten million hectolitres or so and doesn't claim a single brand among the world's top twenty. As Michael Palmer, a long-time beer analyst and president of Toronto's Veritas Investment Research, notes: "Molson literally spills more beer than it exports."

While the rest of the beer industry embarked on a global expansion spree in recent years, breaking into previously untapped markets like China and Russia, scooping up rivals and consolidating, Molson could barely bring itself to cross the U.S. border. Instead, it buried its head under the blanket of domestic security, selling off more than half the brewery to rival Australian and U.S. brewers in order to buy chemical companies and the Canadian hardware store Beaver Lumber. Dan O'Neill, Molson's outspoken former chief executive, admitted to the company's tunnel vision in a magazine interview as late as 2004: "When you look at the big brewers, you say Heineken—they were in a little tiny country, right? They recognized this need to get out many years before we recognized it. You look at

Interbrew,* same thing—they're in Belgium, and they go out. We just took too long to get out. So we're chasing the big guys."[1]

It's not like the Montreal-based brewer, whose extensive empire had once included steamships, a bank and even its own currency, didn't have the opportunity to branch out abroad. It had plenty. In the late 1980s, China's Tsingtao Brewery was insolvent and looking for an investor to inject $20 million into the company. It was a small price to pay for entry into what has since become the world's largest beer market. But Molson balked. "China was a long way away and putting $20 million into China was a dangerous thing to do then," says an individual familiar with the negotiations. "It was a time when Canada had a huge ability to be a really strong player in China...Molson was one of the best breweries in the world. Why weren't they going out and becoming world leaders?"

Andrew Stodart, the former international brand director for Black Velvet, was convinced that he could do for Molson what he had done for Canadian whisky in international markets. The liquor marketer was confident that Molson Canadian had all the makings of a global brand and approached the brewery's executives with a plan to break into Brazil and Russia. "I told them I could get Canadian launched in these markets as a premium-brand beer from Canada," says Stodart. "We could sell it as the most refreshing beer from the coldest place on earth." In Moscow, Stodart had potential customers lined up; a former Canadian from Halifax who owned a popular pub in the Russian capital was ready to actively plug the beer among his patrons. Molson would already have an important advertising platform that could easily segue into grocery store sales. But the brewer wouldn't bite. "They were too afraid to take the risk," says Stodart. "They felt they couldn't compete against the Heinekens of this world."

Molson finally did make its way to Brazil. The oldest brewery in North America and the last of its continental brethren to venture abroad, Molson bought Brazil's number two beer company, Cervejarias Kaiser, in 2002. But even then, it didn't dare to introduce its own trademark brand

---

* Interbrew subsequently acquired Brazil's Ambev and is now called InBev.

into the world's fourth-largest beer market. While bringing Canadian beer to Brazil somehow seemed absurd, Molson found nothing strange about peddling its Brazilian beer in Canada. Unfortunately, the Brazilian push was too little, too late, and Molson's disastrous South American foray would cost it the company and Canada another chance to make it into the multinational big leagues.

Just like Labatt Breweries, which was snapped up by Belgium's Interbrew in 1995 and is now just one more subsidiary within the world's largest beer empire, Molson was subsumed by U.S. brewer Adolph Coors. Carefully packaged as a "merger of equals," the Molson–Coors tie-up was in effect a "bailout," says Palmer, with the new entity's headquarters in Colorado and Coors brass in the top executive jobs. Just one month after the 2005 deal, the new Molson Coors announced it would push into Russia, flogging guess what brand? Coors. Not long after, Molson Coors jettisoned Cervejarias Kaiser, selling out for a song. It retained just 15 per cent of the brewery in the hopes that it could at least use Kaiser as a platform for launching guess what brand into the South American market? Coors.

Even back on Molson's home turf, the once ubiquitous Canadian brand may soon be a candidate for the endangered species list. I was in a Calgary pub during the first game of the 2004 Stanley Cup playoffs, which pitted the Flames against the Tampa Bay Lightning. The scene couldn't have been more Canadian: as giant-screen TVs broadcast the play-by-play from every corner of the bar, a waitress sporting a skin-tight T-shirt with "I love the Flames" stretched across her generous bosom waded through a sea of red hockey jerseys, a tray of beer expertly balanced on her fingertips. But I was hard pressed to find anyone actually drinking a Molson Canadian. At the table next to mine, a trio of mulletheads were squeezing quartered limes down the shafts of pale yellow Corona beers.

It is a damning indictment of Canadian global ambition that such a lightweight beer, from a country with little in the way of fresh water or barley, would become the fourth-best-selling brand the world over. Although Corona is not a favourite brew among discerning Mexicans, the beer associated with eternal sunshine and aquiline beaches is sold, along with the entire lime-squeezing ritual, in more than 150 countries. In Canada, Corona is the leading imported beer, a category that has grown by 500 per cent in the past decade, to represent 10 per cent of the domestic beer market. Still, the Mexican pale ale is not the most popular beer in Canada. That spot is reserved for those namby-pamby Americans, with Budweiser and Coors Lite, the number one and two beers respectively, taking some 20 per cent of the market in recent years.[2]

At the current rate of decline, Veritas's Michael Palmer predicts the once-mighty Canadian beer brands will cease to exist. "We will still have regional brewers, but the great national Canadian beer brands—the Exports, the Blues, the Canadians—they are going to go the way of the dodo," he says. "And it's their own fault."

How did this happen? More importantly, will the rest of Canada suffer the same fate as its beloved beverage and sink into the suds of global obscurity? Canadians have long peered into beer's pale golden depths for a reflection of themselves, and the state of the domestic beer industry should be a wake-up call to the perils of continued self-absorption in a globalized world. For what is happening in the beer industry is playing out across the economy, as Canadian companies—comfortable, complacent or crippled by government—are confronted with increasing competition, consolidation and the rise of new economic powerhouses like China, India and Brazil. And as with beer, it is a battle we are losing.

The loss of Canadian-headquartered companies with the potential to be global players is so common that it barely merits a headline—the same clutch of concerned citizens trundle out for a perfunctory lament before Bay Street bankers and lawyers are lured by the next get-rich-quick income trust. That Dofasco, the country's premier steelworks, would be tossed around like a football in a global tug of war—between the Europeans and an Indian billionaire who started out in 1976 with one steel mill in Indonesia—does not bode well for Canada's ability to harness the powerful levelling force of globalization.

If there is one area where Canadians have distinguished themselves in international business, it is mining. And yet look at the tragedy that has befallen what should be Canada's one uncontested world-beater.

It almost had a fairy-tale ending. After nearly a year of wrangling spurred by the planned merger of two Sudbury mining icons, INCO and Falconbridge, Vancouver-based Teck Cominco swept in like a white knight, poised to trump a takeover offer of the pair by American copper giant Phelps Dodge. Teck's brash $20 billion bid wowed the markets with its bold claim, so uncharacteristic for a Canadian company. During the few hours that it seemed Teck would prevail, CEO Don Lindsay declared: "I believe that it's important that there be Canadian champions on the world stage, and not just in mining."[3]

But before Lindsay had a chance to imagine what it would be like to head Canada's first and only "super major" mining company, his dreams were dashed by Brazil's Companhia Vale do Rio Doce, CVRD, and its eleventh-hour all-cash offer for INCO. Even before the world's largest iron ore producer sealed the deal, it announced that it would delist INCO from the Toronto and New York stock exchanges. As for Falconbridge, the Swiss–Anglo mining firm Xstrata swooped in with a $20.9 billion hostile takeover. The acquisition has launched what was, until recently, a little-known ferro-chrome business, with US$500 million in sales in 2001, into the elite Top Five of global mining companies with an enterprise value approaching US$50 billion. Just hours after assuming the reins, Xstrata cleared out Falconbridge's Toronto head office of senior executives, including almost its entire board of directors. While Toronto will be the headquarters for the company's nickel division, it will lose control over the former Falconbridge operations in seventeen countries, which are either being sold off or folded into the Xstrata empire.

Peter Munk, founder and chairman of Barrick Gold, the world's leading gold producer and, together with Teck, the only sizable Canadian miner left, lashed out at the Canadian industry's lack of leadership and vision. How, he wondered aloud, did the opportunity for a three-way tie-up between Teck, INCO and Falconbridge, and the chance to forge a global powerhouse, turn into an auction of the country's crown jewels? "This opportunity will never arise again in your generation and not in your children's generation to put together a group like that," Munk lamented. "That's when you've got to have the determination and the balls and the courage."[4] Within days, two of Canada's most historic, established companies were wiped off the map. "We are no longer a branch-plant economy," surmised John Gruetzner, a Beijing-based Canadian business consultant. "We are a non-headquartered economy."

Some people might say, so what? The nickel still has to be dug out from under the Canadian Shield, and somebody still has to forge the steel at Hamilton Harbour. Beer will always be brewed in Canada, even if it's Coors or Budweiser. If that's all Canadians aspire to, fine. But without head offices to hone management skills, to develop international networks and ultimately *to make Canadians responsible for their own destiny,* we become little more than "Mexicans with sweaters"—a quaint term coined by the American movie industry to describe Canadian film crews. Just as U.S. corporations set up factories south of the Rio Grande to take advantage of cheap Mexican labour, Hollywood sends its film production north so that it can hire lower-paid Canadian sound technicians and camera operators. The high-paid "talent," however—the star actors, directors, screenwriters and producers—are all still American. "Anybody who says head offices don't matter is dreaming in Technicolor," says Richard Haskayne, one of Canada's foremost corporate tycoons and chairman of TransCanada PipeLines.

Just ask Francesco Bellini. Born in the central Italian town of Ascoli Piceno, Bellini immigrated to Canada in 1967 and received a doctorate in organic chemistry from the University of New Brunswick. When the U.S. pharmaceutical firm he worked for in Montreal decided to move its offices to Boston, Bellini opted to stay put, founding BioChem Pharma in 1986. The pharmaceutical start-up developed 3TC, the first anti-HIV compound drug, which became the most-prescribed AIDS treatment in the world. Yet, despite the firm's tremendous success, it no longer exists; it was sold to Shire Pharmaceuticals of the United Kingdom in 2001 for $6 billion.

Within two years, the company's five hundred staff were fired and its once-impressive offices, located on a leafy high-tech compound in Laval, emptied. "They took the profit and destroyed the company," says Bellini. Also gone is the estimated $5 million a year BioChem used to donate to various charitable causes. "When BioChem was here, I don't know how much money I gave to local arts and the local university," Bellini says in his thickly accented English. "Now it's all gone."

For Bellini, who dreamt of creating Canada's first stand-alone pharmaceutical company, it's a huge disappointment. But he feels he had little choice: when he wasn't bending over backwards to convince skeptical local investors that a Canadian company was actually *good enough* to compete internationally, he was fending off stock market speculators who were pressuring him to cash in and make a quick buck. In 1998, several small bombs exploded outside BioChem's offices. Bellini thought it was the work of AIDS or animal-rights activists. In fact, the culprits were short-sellers looking to push the company's share price down so that they could buy the stock cheap and then cash in on their put options. "If you make a big discovery," Bellini adds, "local investors will push you to sell it, to do a venture with an outside company, because they want the profit right away. They don't realize that if you keep it, you can build something." Bellini was finally convinced to sell the company when he couldn't find anyone to replace him. Every potential manager he looked at "just wanted to ride the stock and get out."

Despite Bellini's frustration, the self-described "scientist–entrepreneur" couldn't help but get back in the game. In 2002, he took the helm of Neurochem Pharma, which is developing a treatment for Alzheimer's, pouring $25 million of his own money into the company. Bellini predicts it's only a matter of time before his new venture suffers the same fate as BioChem. "I guarantee this company is going to grow very high and will be sold off—puff," he says with a wave of his hand. "It's like you have a good hockey team, and every time you go to the arena the people boo and tell you to get out—or they don't come at all. Imagine playing to an empty arena." It won't affect Bellini, who has made a mint from the pharmaceutical business, but he worries about the big picture. "I win either way—I make my money and that's it, I go fishing. The problem is for the local economy, which is going to suffer."

It's too bad, because if Canadians were just willing to stick it out and have the confidence to build something of their own, they could be world leaders. As Bellini points outs, one year after Shire sold BioChem's vaccine unit, which at the time was one of the biggest in the world, for US$150 million, it was resold for approximately US$1.4 billion. "That shows we have good vision here, but we're not willing to support it," he says. It's a quality that the Italian immigrant acknowledges has always distinguished him from his fellow Canadians. He mortgaged his house so that he could buy more shares in BioChem, but "a Canadian would never do that," he admits. "I believed in what I was doing, and I believed that one day it would be a success. And for sure, I made a lot of money; my partners made money too, but much, much less. We could all have made a lot of money, the same amount, but I had a different attitude—you have to believe in yourself, and probably that's what Canadians lack."

But while Bellini is forgiving of his compatriots and grateful for the opportunity to pursue his dreams, Howard Balloch positively bristles at Canadians' constant need to second-guess themselves. Canada's former ambassador to China, Balloch left a twenty-five-year career in the civil service to open an investment boutique in Beijing. The crisply pressed, bow-tied diplomat is going head-to-head with bulge-bracket investment firms like Goldman Sachs and Merrill Lynch in one of the world's most sought-after markets. "My goal is to build the best little investment boutique, and I don't care who I'm up against," he says. "I'm going to win." What Balloch doesn't understand is why so few Canadians seem to share his boundless confidence. "Where's the belief that we can conquer the world? We're every bit as bright, we have smart people from all over the world who come to live here, we speak a multitude of languages, and we have natural resources," he charges. "What is it we don't have that means we can't compete? We should be on top of the world. We should be better than the Americans, faster than the Germans and more culturally conscious than the Japanese."

After watching "the earth's centre of gravity tilt" towards China in recent decades, however, there is one thing Balloch knows for sure: if Canadians continue to ignore these tectonic shifts, we will eventually fall through the cracks. The threat is all the more dangerous because it won't be a calamitous collapse, like that of Argentina, but a slow, stealthy slide that will sneak up on us while we snooze, our bellies still uncomfortably full after gorging on a feast of oil sands and high copper prices. "Life is too easy, and Canadians are happy in their kind of graceful decline. We are determined to become the Argentina of the twenty-first century," says Balloch. "We're not under threat, we'll just lose a little market every year, get a little smaller, another country will pass us on the scale and we'll lose another hockey team."

It's a far cry from Sir Wilfrid Laurier's bold pronouncement that the twentieth century belonged to Canada. From Laurier's vantage point, over-seeing a golden age of economic prosperity, an influx of immigrants eager to carve out a new life for themselves and the building of the country's second transcontinental railway, Canada's potential seemed to know no bounds. But like a locomotive that has run out of steam, Canada's promising future has lost its momentum, sapped by decades of disastrous government policy and a complicit citizenry. Somewhere along the way, we lost the faith in our-selves and, with it, the opportunity that was ours for the taking. Now, left without the necessary tools—multinationals—for negotiating in a globalized world, we are in danger of becoming collateral damage.

A growing number of Canadians see the danger. Gary Comerford is one of them. Working as a branch manager for Canada Permanent Trust in Hamilton in the mid-1970s, Comerford concedes his most serious con-cern was whether a personal loan or mortgage went bad. "My world was the mountain in Hamilton," he says. "It was a very limited, very parochial view of the world." Thirty years later, as a vice-president with Sun Life Financial, spearheading the insurer's entry into the Indian market as well as working on its entry into China, Comerford admits his perspective has been irrevocably altered. "It has become clear and unmistakable in my mind that you have to operate on a world platform. Speed to market and quality of execution: that's what protects jobs, that's just the reality," he says from his Toronto office. "That micro world that you want to live in, the world of protecting what you had in the past, you realize is a fleeting thought. It's like keeping a butterfly in a bottle; it's beautiful and you want to keep it there forever, but if you keep it in the bottle, it will die."

It's time to set the butterfly free. To do that, Canadians will need to smash through a lot of myths that we have constructed about our-selves—myths about how the world operates and our place in it. We need to stop thinking of ourselves as victims and become "more than an expression of geography." It's time to boldly embrace who we are, and not just behind the comfort and security of our drawn curtains. Canada and Canadian companies need to learn how to *brand* themselves, and not only to their home audience but to the *world*. As one frequent traveller to China put it: "There is a Starbucks opening on every corner in China—they have a great brand. Canada doesn't have a brand."

Molson had a brand. But the company never really believed in it. If it had, its breakthrough "I am Canadian" ad campaign would have become a rallying cry for taking on the world instead of a tired rant predicated on, as one marketing expert observed, a "single-minded, almost simple-minded patriotism."[5] By opting to coast on a cheap appeal to Canadian pride while selling its beer in ugly old brown bottles, Molson chose easy profits at home over global conquest. It was a formula that was doomed to fail. "They had such a short-term emphasis on profit that they fucked their long-term prospects," says Michael Palmer of Veritas. Molson, concluded one newspaper columnist, inevitably became "trapped in its own marketing impotence."[6] The question is, will the rest of Canada make the same mistake, or will it find a new anthem?

In 1998, while working as a reporter in South America, I took a trip to Patagonia. Having crossed over the border from Chile, I had made my way to the windswept coastal town of Rio Gallegos in Argentina. Walking into a souvenir shop on the town's deserted main strip, I noticed there wasn't much to buy and I soon found myself talking with the store's disconsolate owner. As he observed his empty shop, a layer of dust covering the leather boots and crude silver knick-knacks, he bitterly lamented the dire situation his country was in, made all the more evident when compared with the boom in neighbouring Chile.

Argentina produces more than twice as much wine as Chile and is believed to have even richer mineral deposits. Yet it is Chile, a tiny sliver of a country that is almost completely consumed by mountainous terrain and uninhabitable desert, that has emerged as the economic dynamo, while Argentina, a vast expanse of unmined opportunity, remains a backwater. "You know what the Chileans have that we don't?" said the shopkeeper. "They know who they are."

It's something Canadians might do well to think about. At the time, Molson's "I am Canadian" seemed to sum up the country's essence. But on reflection, do we know what it really means?

PART ONE

WHY WE CAN'T COMPETE ABROAD, OR WHAT HAPPENED TO OUR COJONES?

1 | TIME TO WAKE UP

> "Canada is the most comfortable country in the world. You are nice people, but you are not a trading nation."
>
> **BORIS ROUSSEFF, EUROPEAN TRADE EXPERT**

IT'S 3 PM and the patio of El Coronito restaurant in downtown Mexico City is quickly filling up with businessmen in dark suits and open-necked dress shirts meeting for lunch. The smog that normally hangs over the Mexican capital like a dusty grey-brown shroud has temporarily lifted to reveal a cloudless, azure sky. A bright white sun beats down on tables cluttered with bottles of pale beer and tequila shots, its rays refracting in the mass of glass and crystalline liquid, creating a dazzling glare.

Bruno Perron orders his usual *michelada,* a Mexican beer doused with chili and a squirt of lime, before reaching for a tortilla and filling it with a mixture of melted cheese and chorizo. If it weren't for the slight French inflection in his otherwise flawless Spanish and the Quebec licence plate on the SUV he drives like a demon through the city's crumbling streets, he could easily pass as Mexican.

Originally from the small Quebec town of Thetford Mines, Perron moved south more than a decade ago. He had just finished university and had a job offer from a large mutual fund company. But somehow, perhaps after watching his hometown, one of the world's largest producers of asbestos, go from boom to bust, he figured he needed a competitive edge over the three thousand other students in his graduating class. The much-vaunted North American Free Trade Agreement, NAFTA, was just being signed. The twenty-something figured that if he learned Spanish and got a handle on the Mexican market, it would give him an advantage when he eventually moved back to Montreal.

"Looking ten years ahead, I thought Mexico was going to be important," says Perron. "Unfortunately, it is not as important as I thought it would be."

Far from it. More than a decade after NAFTA was signed, the road paved into the dense, jumbled market is largely deserted. While Americans, Europeans and Asians have piled in to sell product to Mexico's young and underserved population or outsourced manufacturing to take advantage of lower labour costs, Canadians have eschewed Mexico's arid northern industrial parks and rutted city streets for the silky-white sand beaches of Cancún.

Canadian business, either baffled by Mexico's seemingly inscrutable business culture, leery of corruption or dismissive of its still developing market, has largely opted out. While bilateral trade has tripled since 1994, Canada sells a scant 0.7 per cent of its merchandise goods to Mexico. As of 2005, Canada had invested a measly $3.1 billion, equivalent to less than 1 per cent of its worldwide assets[7] and a drop in the bucket compared with the more than $130 billion in foreign investment that has poured into Mexico since 1994.

It is not as if the Mexicans didn't want Canadian investment. In fact, as they launched the largest sell-off of state-owned assets in Mexican history in the late 1980s and 1990s, they actively courted Canadians. Modest, manageable and politically neutral, the Canadians offered a middle road between powerful American interests still tainted by a history of war, annexation and economic imperialism and the powerful clutch of Mexican families whose sprawling, interwoven conglomerates dominate the economy. But there were few bites.

One Canadian banker recalls how he was approached by a Mexican cabinet minister looking to unload a vast copper mine in northern Mexico.

The government was anxious to keep the mine out of the hands of Jorge Larrea, a hard-nosed tycoon who already controlled a number of privatized mines and railroads. Canada seemed like an obvious candidate. "The minister told me price was no object," said the banker, who set up meetings with Canadian mining companies Noranda and Falconbridge. "The Canadians didn't even want to look at it," he said. In 1991 Larrea acquired the mine—Cananea—turning it into a springboard for his company, Grupo México, which went on to buy mines in the United States and Peru and is now the world's fifth-largest copper producer. As for Noranda and Falconbridge, they no longer exist, having been acquired in a $20 billion hostile takeover by Xstrata and subsumed into its sprawling empire.

In 2001, President Vicente Fox took the unusual step of inviting twenty Canadian energy companies to his private ranch in a bid to coax them into investing in the creaking Mexican energy sector. His country was ramping up its industrial production and was in dire need of new energy capacity. The Canadians, mid-sized and without the political baggage of the Americans, seemed like the perfect fit. "There were twenty guys at the ranch—and only three went in," said Michael Stewart, former president of B.C.-based Westcoast Energy International and one of the guests.

Of the three, including Westcoast, only the Alberta energy utility TransAlta is left. "People view Mexico as a wild, unsophisticated country, but parts of it are much more sophisticated than Canada, and some parts are much better to do business in than some parts of Canada," said Stewart from his Calgary office. "You would think people in this town should look there. You can fly to Mexico City in the same time it would take you to get to Halifax—and the food's better. But it's tough to get people interested—they're put off by the bureaucracy, the language and the built-in biases of what they think they can and cannot do."

It's the same story in banking. Canada's Scotiabank and Bank of Montreal (BMO) were among the first foreigners to make careful inroads into Mexico's tumultuous financial sector. Mexico's banks had been nationalized in the 1980s and then reprivatized in the early 1990s before a currency crisis in 1994 prompted the collapse of the entire financial sector. In a cautiously astute manoeuvre, BMO swapped Mexican sovereign debt in 1996 for a minority equity stake in Bancomer, the country's number two bank. The move was expected to position BMO, which already owned Harris Bank in Chicago, as the pre-eminent NAFTA bank. Instead, at the height of a foreign feeding frenzy in the sector, including the massive US$12.5 billion purchase by Citigroup of Mexico's largest bank in 2001, BMO pulled out of Mexico.

David Winfield, Canada's former ambassador to Mexico, was on the board of Bancomer at the time. He tried to persuade BMO to buy the bank. "They could have done so much better, and so much better throughout the Americas. BMO was well positioned with Harris Bank in the United States, and Bancomer was exceptionally well positioned to do Hispanic banking."

Instead, Tony Comper, BMO's president and chief executive, "was persuaded it was too big a risk and too expensive," says Winfield. "I think it was the wrong decision. But it required a visionary to see there was a business opportunity there." Comper, who was tapped for the "Don Knotts Award for Meekest Ambition" by *National Post Business* magazine, sold out to the Spanish, who along with the Americans and the HSBC Group dominate the amazingly profitable sector, which boasts returns of over 20 per cent.

It is not as if there are no Canadian companies in Mexico. Scotiabank survived the currency crisis to see its wildly profitable Inverlat subsidiary, which represents just 6 per cent of the Mexican market, contribute 11 per cent to the bank's bottom line. A number of Quebec companies, like Bombardier, Quebecor and Transcontinental, have also made the trek. In many cases, however, companies such as auto parts maker Magna "were dragged down" by their clients. Others tried, but were unable to penetrate the market. "When I compare the number of Canadian companies going through my office and the rate of success, it was very, very low," says longtime Mexico hand and former Scotiabank executive Pierre Alarie. "We missed the boat everywhere."

Troy Wright, former president of the Canadian Chamber of Commerce in Mexico and the managing director of Inverlat's capital markets division, admits Canada's track record has been patchy. "The Europeans—Spain,

France, Italy—have been aggressive. It's an attitude you don't see in Canada. The U.S., when they see an opportunity, they attack," says Wright. "Canadian companies take the cautious route or no route at all."

To be sure, there are plenty of risks in doing business in Mexico, and Canadian companies are justified in being cautious. Although conditions have improved significantly, Mexico remains rife with corruption and its democratic institutions are still a work in progress. Yet, it is not the tenuous rule of law or language barriers that seem to most flummox Canadians. As Ambassador Winfield recalls a businessman telling him: "Why should I go to Mexico if I can't even drink the water?" One Canadian government bureaucrat explained the dilemma this way: "How do we get Canadian companies more engaged in Mexico and not get diarrhea?"

ARMCHAIR TRAVELLERS

At first blush, the delicate constitution of Canadian companies seems incongruous with the country's claim to be one of the world's great trading nations. Despite representing 2.5 per cent of the world's economy and just 0.5 per cent of its population, Canada is the world's eighth-largest trader, a feat that has secured its place in the elite group of eight most-industrialized countries, the G8. Over the past two decades Canadian trade has expanded exponentially, from 44 per cent of GDP to 72 per cent, making it the most trade-reliant country of the G8.

But while some $1 million in merchandise trade criss-crosses the Canada–U.S. border every minute, cementing the world's largest single trading relationship,* Canadian "trade" rarely ventures beyond the cozy confines of the northern United States. When it comes to the rest of the world, Canadians are armchair travellers, rarely roused from the familiar contours of the "intramestic" American market to seek their fortune in foreign lands.

---

* Canada–U.S. trade represents the world's largest cross-border exchange between any two nations, but trade between the United States and the European Union is larger.

Canadians may be trading with, and investing in, the rest of the world more than ever before, but the record to date reveals, if anything, that they are the antithesis of true traders. In every major market from Brazil to China, Canada is facing ever-widening trade deficits as its market share continues to erode under the strain of increased global competition. In 2005, Canada racked up a record $44 billion trade deficit with the rest of the world, and with the odd exception of countries like Lebanon and Sri Lanka, its only trade surplus was generated from just a single country: the United States. As Pierre Alarie, a Canadian veteran of international markets, observed: "If Canada were beside Bosnia instead of the United States, we'd all be bankrupt."

When it comes to foreign direct investment (FDI), Canada musters the lowest level of outward-bound FDI in the G8 and remains largely absent from the current global push into developing markets. While it's true that Canada is now a net exporter of FDI for the first time in its history, it's also true that the third-largest recipient of Canadian foreign investment is Barbados, an offshore tax haven and post office box for dozens of Canadian banks and insurance companies.* According to Statistics Canada, an estimated $88 billion, close to a quarter of Canada's overseas investment, is parked in similar tax havens in Ireland, Bahrain and the Caribbean.[8]

"Canada's trade and investment market share has been falling, falling, falling, year after year, with few exceptions, since the end of the 1970s," says Glen Hodgson, chief economist at the Conference Board of Canada. The dismal showing comes as little surprise to the rest of the world, which by now has become resigned to Canada's cursory attempts at international business and seeming unwillingness to wade in and take the time and energy to actually *cultivate* trade. "You are nice people," says Boris Rousseff, a European businessman who has worked closely with Canadian companies, "but you are not a trading nation."

---

* Barbados, Ireland and Bermuda hold the third, fourth and fifth spots respectively for top Canadian investment destinations, followed by France and the Cayman Islands in the sixth and seventh positions.

A quick tour of world markets reveals Canada's declining and increasingly peripheral position. In Europe, long considered a second home for Canadian goods and investment, "Canada's turn seems to have passed," says one European diplomat who has worked to enhance two-way trade. Canada's share of European Union (EU) imports declined by a third between 1990 and 2002. While Europe has been a beachhead for some of corporate Canada's most aggressive international forays, including Alcan's $4 billion acquisition of French aluminum giant Pechiney in 2003, Canadians on the whole have taken a laissez-faire attitude to Europe. As the Americans and Japanese scramble for position and the EU becomes increasingly preoccupied with its growing membership and the rise of China, Canadian companies have hung back like awkward teenagers waiting to be asked to the prom. Europeans, as a result, are often left scratching their heads, wondering why the Canadians bother showing up at all.

"Canadians are perceived as very friendly, but we don't know what they are up to. What are they here for? What do they want to achieve? They don't make any effort. They wait, like in the old days when women expected to be approached by men," said one European businessman. "Things have changed. Even women don't go for that anymore." Apparently, neither do the Europeans. "We can tolerate that attitude from the U.S., but not from an average-sized country like Canada. You are bound to lose."

Nowhere is Canada's losing record more evident than in Latin America. In a rare burst of foresight, the Canadian government led a series of Team Canada trade missions to the up-and-coming region in the early 1990s in a bid to pre-empt American hegemony by parlaying Canadian goodwill into a first-mover advantage. As a result, Canada signed a free-trade agreement with Chile in 1996, six years before the United States did. Nevertheless, Canadian exports to Chile have stagnated to 1994 levels, as they have in almost every country in the region.

At the same time, Canada's trade deficit has grown. All told, it exports less than 1 per cent of its merchandise trade to South America and the

Caribbean. The lacklustre trade has been mirrored by a mass exodus of some of Canada's biggest companies, including Bell Canada's (now defunct) international wing, BCI; Quebec cellular group Telesystem International Wireless; Alberta pipeline companies Nova Gas and TransCanada PipeLines; and even Scotiabank in Argentina. Many left the region with their tail between their legs.

Canada's biggest retreat has been in Brazil. Exports to the sprawling country have been declining since 1997 as a $300 million trade surplus was converted into a $2 billion deficit in 2005. Sales to the world's fifth-most-populous country represent just a quarter of 1 per cent of Canadian exports.

James Mohr-Bell, executive director of the Brazil–Canada Chamber of Commerce, says two-way trade, while edging up in favour of Brazil, remains "ridiculously low." The Brazilian businessman has watched in frustration as Canadian companies remain "on the sidelines" while other foreigners, shrugging off currency devaluations and political volatility, have snapped up privatized state assets and invested in infrastructure projects. Although Canadian direct investment has cautiously expanded from $6.7 billion in 2000 to $8 billion five years later, overall foreign direct investment in Brazil has ballooned from US$40 billion in 1992 to over US$236 billion[9] a decade later. "Canada has lost a lot of position. It used to be the sixth- or seventh-largest investor in Brazil, now it's twelfth or fifteenth," says Mohr-Bell. "As far as Canada is concerned, Brazil has just been forgotten, left aside. It was never exploited by Canadians to its potential."

But perhaps the most worrying omission in the Canadian trade calculation is Asia. By mid-century, the region is expected to be home to three of the world's six largest economies, yet Canada is barely a footnote in what is being touted as a historic changing of the economic guard. Canada's share of Asian imports has almost slipped off the charts, from 2.88 per cent in 1988 to 1.06 per cent in 2004 in the wake of near-negligible exports and ballooning trade deficits. In 2004, Canada trailed Chile as the eighteenth-largest foreign investor in Southeast Asia.

While shrinking exports to Japan, a long-time trading partner, and Korea are cause for worry, it's the seeming indifference to China that's most alarming. As the world scrambles to feed China's ravenous economic appetite, Canada directs less than 2 per cent of its exports to what has been the globe's fastest-growing economy for the past decade. Not surprisingly, Canada lags behind every other major country in export growth to China.[10] In fact, in the first half of 2006, exports actually contracted by 8 per cent compared with the same period in 2005.

Canada's meagre and diminishing share of Chinese imports is matched by minuscule direct investment. By 2005, Canadian investment in the world's most populous country barely topped $1 billion, representing 0.2 per cent of all Canadian investment abroad and nowhere near the $11 billion of Canadian money socked away in the Cayman Islands. At the same time, foreign investment in the Middle Kingdom has shot up by a phenomenal US$356 billion[11] between 2001 and 2006.

The anemic performance even caught the attention of James Wolfensohn, the former president of the World Bank. During a speech at the Montreal Board of Trade Conference in 2004, he carefully admonished the country for not taking "as significant advantage of that extraordinary market as you might." Howard Balloch, Canada's former ambassador to China, is decidedly less diplomatic in his assessment of the country's limp efforts. A trace of impatience ruffles his otherwise cool, bow-tied demeanour when asked why Canada still lingers at the water's edge while the rest of the world takes the plunge.

"The Japanese recognize their presence in China is vital to their own economic existence. They are huge investors. The Germans are all over China. General Motors is investing billions. Where are the auto parts companies? This is supposed to be our flagship industry. There is a housing boom and heavy demand for wooden flooring—where are Canadian forestry products? The Scandinavians are bringing in their wood and wood from Siberia and making furniture and shipping it to North America. Where are our furniture companies?" says Balloch. "Look where we are supposed to be strong in Canada. Why are we not there?"

A MATTER OF PERSPECTIVE

That question is at the very heart of this book. The next few chapters deal with the reasons why Canadians so often fail to make the leap from hometown success to global conquest. The answer is a complex one, the product of a unique confluence of history, geography and culture that has made a powerful impression on our collective imagination. At its most elemental level, it's about perspective.

Canadians seem to view the world through a fish-eye lens. Their immediate surroundings are dramatically overemphasized, to the point of distortion, while the backdrop—the outside world—appears dwarfed and distant. But just like the view from a fish-eye lens, the extreme wide angle is an optical illusion, fashioned through the careful engineering of optics and lenses to trick the mind's eye. And we've been fooling ourselves in this way for a long time.

The effect can perhaps best be observed in Vancouver. Nowhere in Canada does the country's natural bounty loom so large. The city's downtown boardrooms offer panoramic views of majestic mountains, lush forests and shimmering bays. The gaze of Vancouver, a coastal city with a natural harbour, is cast away from Canada, towards the Pacific Ocean and the Orient beyond. Yet the "Gateway to Asia" appears truncated, its wide, luxuriant pathway suddenly subsumed into a blurred, distant horizon.

Despite the phalanx of glass and steel high-rises crowding the downtown skyline and a bustling port, Vancouver is essentially a "bedroom community," says John Wiebe, head of the GLOBE Foundation, an international consulting group, and the former president of the Asia Pacific Foundation of Canada. British Columbia, while leading the country in exports to Asia, remains among the least export-oriented provinces in Canada.* Why? Because the West Coast, like much of Canada, has never had to adjust its depth of field. As long as the foreground was in focus, the backdrop wasn't all that important.

---

* Only Prince Edward Island and Nova Scotia fare worse.

Michael Novak, an executive vice-president with Quebec construction giant SNC–Lavalin, calls this phenomenon "the Canada syndrome." Its origins and continued propagation can be traced to two key factors: an abundance of natural wealth that provided Canada's tiny population with one of the highest ratios of natural resources per capita in the world; and the United States. Taken together, these two factors form the basis of a quick and easy trading recipe that some argue would spoil any cook from tackling more ambitious confections.

Some 85 per cent of Canadian-made goods need travel no farther than a few hundred kilometres, into a market that is often no more difficult to trade with than some Canadian provinces. Without the natural barriers of language, culture or distance, an estimated 90 per cent of Canadian exports to the United States are shipped to buyers on an open account, without a contract. "We've had it easy. We've got lots of resources that we could sell easily to a market that spoke English and was close by," says Carin Holroyd, senior research analyst at the Asia Pacific Foundation of Canada in Vancouver. "We haven't had to work very hard."

What makes it even easier is that Americans and other foreigners are doing most of the heavy lifting for us. Historically Canada has one of the highest levels of foreign ownership in the developed world,[12] with more than half of its manufacturing base and 42 per cent of its oil, gas and coal mining industry currently in foreign hands.[13] According to a Statistics Canada study, foreign affiliates represent just 2 per cent of all Canadian-based exporters yet account for an incredible 44 per cent of all exports. Of that, some 70 per cent is intra-industry trade—goods of a similar nature that are being imported and exported.[14]

What does that mean? That Canada's three leading "exporters" are the Big Three American car manufacturers—General Motors, Chrysler and Ford—which manufacture cars in southern Ontario and ferry them across the border. In Ontario, Canada's most export-oriented province, 53 per cent of exports are generated by foreign affiliates.[15] The automotive industry represents nearly a quarter of the country's total merchandise exports. "If you take out automotive," says Bob Armstrong, the former president of the Canadian Association of Importers and Exporters, "what are we really selling?"

In a word—commodities. While more sophisticated Canadian exports of things like software and airplane parts have grown over the past two decades, more than half of the nation's foreign sales still come from oil and gas, lumber, chemicals, fertilizer, grains and potash. Unlike value-added manufactured goods, which must be actively peddled and pushed into new markets, commodity prices are largely set by world markets, and the buyers, more often than not, come to you. Take Canadian exports to Japan, for example: an estimated 75 per cent of this trade is controlled by Japanese trading houses with offices in Vancouver and Toronto. Those same trading companies are also behind much of Canada's trade with China—and even China's state grain trader has an office in Vancouver. "There aren't many Canadians actively seeking a market," says John Wiebe. "Commodities are so hot, you don't have to sell. If you've got pulp, there's a buyer at your door. Our companies don't have to go out and spend a lot of time in China. You don't see the commodity guys out there very much peddling product, and we don't sell a lot of other stuff."

As a result, between cars, commodities and the U.S. market, Canada not only never has to go the extra mile to sell its goods, but is caught in a strange paradox, wherein, as Carleton University trade guru Michael Hart points out, "Canada has become a trade-dependent economy without a deep-seated trading culture."[16] With the rest of the world knocking on their door, says one government trade promoter, Canadians could afford to remain "nice and kinda dozy," eschewing the hardscrabble edge of hungrier, less-endowed countries while never being forced to develop a homegrown global trading base.

"We are major traders, but not really. We are really sellers into the global marketplace," says Jayson Myers, senior vice-president and chief economist of Canadian Manufacturers & Exporters. "What's the difference? Sellers are just told how much to produce and the market is made for you. A major trader is out there developing his own market. We don't have a lot of companies doing that in Canada."

Myers estimates that with 60 per cent of Canada's trade being intracorporate and 30 per cent taken up by energy, raw materials and commodities, only 10 per cent of the economy is made up of companies with the impetus to actively develop markets. The problem is, they are overwhelming small and medium-sized enterprises (SMES), which lack the financial stamina to withstand expensive international forays and the motivation or mindset to manoeuvre in more complicated foreign markets.

In fact, most SMES do not even *think* about exporting. According to a poll taken by the Canadian Federation of Independent Business in 2004, an astounding 51 per cent of respondents didn't sell abroad because their products or services were "not exportable." A report by the Toronto-Dominion Bank quickly jumped on the finding, asking: "In this day and age, what isn't a global product?"

All told, less than a fifth of small businesses, which account for 99 per cent of all Canadian companies, actually export. Even fewer do so regularly. Myers calculates just 3 per cent of SMES are "active exporters," engaged in producing and servicing goods in and for foreign markets. According to Statistics Canada, a meagre 1.5 per cent of small business exporters account for 75 per cent of all exports by SMES.[17] In other words, the vast majority of SME "exports" are one-off, opportunistic and usually unsolicited sales, worth a few thousand dollars at most. For many companies, concedes one business owner, exports are just "extra gravy."

In the absence of a sustained and focused export strategy, companies tend to take a haphazard, scattershot approach to international business that rarely hits the bull's eye. Two key challenges seem to particularly plague Canadian firms: a failure to follow up on new business leads, and an almost debilitating aversion to risk. Both are anathema to operating in globally competitive markets. Canadian companies, says Michel Charland, director of Industry Canada's International Trade Centre in Montreal, "lack the preparation, the vision and the commitment" to venture into the choppy seas of international business.[18]

When they do venture forth, the results tend to be disappointing, both for Canadian companies and for many foreigners who, given the choice, would prefer to do business with Canadians. Instead, the tepid and at times amateurish approach has left many perplexed and even irked by Canadians' stubborn insistence on being the wallflowers of international business. "At home they are as efficient as Americans, but when they go abroad and are doing international business, they are shy, withdrawn and inward looking," says Boris Rousseff, who as executive director of the Canada Europe Round Table for Business has worked for two decades trying to better familiarize Canadian companies with Europe.

But while some foreigners interpret this indolent attitude as laziness or even arrogance, others insist it is a mask to deflect the colonial mindset that still pervades Canadian thinking and colours the nation's ambitions. Weaned on the British Empire and then overshadowed by the United States, Canada has spent most of its young existence trying to convince a vast and disparate Dominion that it too has a manifest destiny. Still ill at ease in the makeshift union and too preoccupied with its own reflection, the country seems to lose its conviction when it strays too far from home. "We are timid about nationality, and [therefore] we are timid about trade," says Michael Novak of SNC–Lavalin, the country's only global engineering and construction firm.

Many people involved in international business pin at least part of the blame on an overweening government that has often been the only common connection in the country's bid to become more than an expression of geography. Like an overprotective parent, the state has nurtured dependence and sheltered business from risk, often throwing up obstacles that discourage companies from spreading their wings, either by weighing them down with burdensome regulation or by protecting them from competition.

When companies do fly the coop—often at government urging—their path has been paved with government funding to pay for everything from plane tickets to hotels. In many cases the money was ostensibly a loan, but both parent and child knew it did not have to be repaid. In recent years, the federal government has become stricter with the purse strings, but behavioural patterns and expectations, ingrained over decades—sometimes centuries—remain largely unchanged.

At Ontario Exports, the export promotion arm of the provincial government, potential exporters are shepherded across the border on trade missions to Buffalo. While on these exotic trips, companies expect the government to find contacts, set up meetings for them and even pick up the tab. "We call it handholding," said one official, recalling a junket to the southern United States to attend a trade fair. A month later, the provincial official received an angry call from an American distributor who had been trying to contact two Canadian companies that attended the fair. Frustrated after they did not return his repeated calls and emails, the American phoned the provincial government and asked: "Are you guys serious about doing business or not?"

COASTING TO IRRELEVANCE

"Not so much," seems to be the answer. And why should Canada be concerned? It has done fairly well by mining tried-and-true veins of wealth and opportunity. By cutting down trees, pumping oil and assembling cars, the country has attained one of the highest standards of living in the world. Do we really need to be jumping on planes, eating strange food and scarfing down Imodium pills to drum up more business?

According to Thierry Vandal, the chief executive of Hydro-Québec, we don't. In the 1990s, the government-owned utility made an aggressive push into Asia, Africa and Latin America, but despite its domestic know-how, the costly venture floundered and its newly minted international division was disbanded. Luckily, the utility, which boasts the largest installed capacity of hydroelectric power in the world, has enough work in Quebec to keep it busy for the next fifteen years. "You don't chase the hard stuff if there's easy stuff. You pick low-lying fruit first," says Vandal. "We don't need to be chasing international at this stage. That'll come in maybe twenty or thirty years."

Vandal says he's "not convinced" that putting off foreign forays by a few decades will put Hydro-Québec at a disadvantage to global rivals like Germany's E.ON and Gaz de France, whose tentacles already stretch

29

around the globe. Maybe. But what if he's wrong? As of 2005, Quebec had become a net *importer* of energy. What if the utility's copious projects were suddenly put on hold, let's say by environmental concerns or opposition by Aboriginal groups, in much the same way as its Great Whale project on James Bay was stalled in the 1980s? And don't forget that Hydro-Québec is the most indebted company in Canada, with $32.5 billion in long-term debt.[19]

Would the state-run utility know how to operate in an international context? Its less than stellar performance outside of Quebec would indicate that, at the very least, it would be at a disadvantage in a global market that is not only getting more and more competitive but is dominated by countries and companies that conduct business in a vastly different way from Canada and the United States. With just fifty companies in Canada accounting for half the country's exports[20] and little in the way of foreign investment, one could argue that the great majority of Canadian companies are in the same boat.

Joseph E. Martin, an executive in residence at the University of Toronto's Rotman School of Management, likens the situation to the historic 1972 hockey series that pitted Canada against the Soviet Union. The Canadians, who fancied themselves the best players in the world, were surprised to find that their blunt force and power could be so easily deflected by the discipline and dexterity of the Russians. What was expected to be an easy win turned into a hair-raising comeuppance for the Canadians, who only barely squeaked to victory with a last-minute goal. "We have a wrong sense of what is going on [in the world] because we have never tested ourselves against the rest," says Martin. "You need to be out there testing yourself and competing. Otherwise, you won't know how good the other guys are."

We are already starting to find out. In the United States, Canada's share of imports has been steadily declining from 19 per cent in 1999 to 17.2 per cent in 2005 as exports from China flood into the American market. In contrast, China's share of U.S. merchandise trade has skyrocketed from 3 per cent in 1990 to 14.6 per cent in 2005. Already the second-largest

exporter to the United States after edging out Mexico, China even temporarily pushed Canada out of top spot in July 2005.* It is only a matter of
time, say observers, before Canada is permanently unseated as America's
biggest trade partner.

China's rising prominence in the United States is perhaps the most
tangible indication of its emergence as a global powerhouse and its pivotal
role in the ongoing revolution sweeping the global economy. The World
Bank estimates that by 2050 the developing world will represent 40 per
cent of global GDP, up from 18 per cent.[21] Goldman Sachs, the U.S. investment bank, predicts the future membership of the G8 will be almost
unrecognizable from the current line-up: Brazil, Russia, India and China
will eclipse all other major industrial countries in size, with the exception
of the United States and Japan.[22]

In this new scenario, the United States will no longer be the global
behemoth that it has been. As David Emerson, Canada's then minister of
industry, noted in 2005: "It's slowly dawning on most of us that something we took for granted for decades—the global dominance of the
United States—is under threat."[23] That does not bode well for Canada.
Between 1993 and 2004, the vast majority of new export growth—more
than 92 per cent—went to the U.S. market.[24] At the same time, if it
weren't for energy and cars, Canada's enviable trade surplus with the
United States would quickly evaporate.†

As the United States seeks greater trade ties with the rest of the
world—it now has free-trade agreements with at least seventeen countries—
and more competitors gain the field, Canada, a small, trade-dependent
country with scant on-the-ground experience, will have little alternative
but to bone up on Mandarin and maybe start returning some of those
unanswered phone calls. "At some point we will have no choice but to go

---

* This calculation is based on the European Union being treated as separate countries
rather than a single bloc.

† In 2004 Canada racked up a record trade deficit of $11 billion in automotive trade with
non-NAFTA countries.

out. There is a huge chunk of the world we know nothing about," says Prem Benimadhu, a research director with the Conference Board of Canada. "The growth will be in Asia, and they have a different way of doing business."

But while those involved in international business see the writing on the wall, they are not convinced that the vast majority of Canadians are getting the message. Back in Vancouver, trade commissioner Bill Johnston has his doubts. From his corner office, the veteran federal trade commissioner surveys the sparkling high-rises and ocean beyond with an air of blithe resignation that betrays his disappointment. For years he has been trying to coax Canadian companies to trade in their cushy domestic berth for more distant shores.

"They call it the sailboat mentality," shrugs Johnston. "Why would you get on a plane and fly halfway around the world to have tea with a bunch of strangers when you could spend the weekend on your sailboat or at the cottage?"

Across the country, Stanley Hartt's Bay Street office in Toronto affords a very different view. His exclusive eleventh-floor perch looks out on the glass and steel towers that form the vertebrae of the country's financial spine. But the Montreal-born lawyer, former deputy finance minister and now chairman of Citigroup Global Markets Canada is gripped by the same sense of foreboding. Every day, he says, Canadian companies pass up opportunities to trade and invest just across the border in the United States—never mind Asia.

"We have a chance to buy large U.S. companies and we don't. We think it's too big and we don't want to bet the company, so we tend to creep back to the Canadian market. It's a market we know and feel comfortable in, and we're not hard pressed," he says. "We are very happy to coast. There's such abundance here, we've decided to pump it out and sell it. Who needs to do value-added when you can just stay home and have a nice life?"

The pervasive sense that "everything will be okay" has even raised alarm bells in slow-moving, navel-gazing Ottawa. Within the well-insulated offices of the bunker-like Lester B. Pearson building—home to the ministry of foreign affairs and international trade—senior bureaucrats have coined a phrase to describe the growing danger of continued unconcern: complacency risk.

Nowhere has that risk become clearer than in the case of Japan. The world's second-largest economy, the Land of the Rising Sun has been a target of Canadian efforts to diversify trade for nearly half a century. Those efforts reaped little return, until a housing boom in the 1980s sparked a massive demand for Canadian lumber. Canadian exports, led by wood products, peaked at $13 billion in 1995 before a banking crisis in Japan plunged the country into a decade-long recession. Canadian sales to Japan followed suit, contracting 26 per cent in the last decade.[25]

It is easy to blame Japan's economic woes for the precipitous decline. But while forestry products companies turned their attention to the thriving U.S. market, the Swedes, Finns, Russians and Southeast Asians have been filling the void the Canadians left behind. By 1997, the Scandinavians, with only a couple of years in the Japanese market, were exporting 1.8 million cubic feet of lumber—a feat that took their Canadian counterparts decades to achieve.[26]

As a result, Canada's share of Japanese imports is half what it was in 1989. "We could have been raising exports all along, but instead we turned away," says John Powles, a Vancouver-based trade consultant. "Nobody ever thought of turning around our advantage and developing a strong sales team. So the Japanese went elsewhere. And we let it happen.

"We could have been much more competitive if we had put the effort in," adds the long-time Japan hand. "But the U.S. was strong, so we shrugged our shoulders. Then the softwood lumber dispute with the United States happened, and the Japanese market was lost to Scandinavia."

Canada appears set to suffer a similar fate in Europe, the country's only other significant export market outside the United States. Its declining market share is being eroded by the addition of twelve new member countries to the EU. The new entrants, many of whom have low labour costs, educated populations and undeveloped resources, compete head-on with Canadian goods, ranging from lumber to car engines. Many predict that without a concerted effort, Canada will be completely cut out of the EU. "Trade is going down," says transatlantic trade consultant Boris Rousseff. "Canadians would have to make an enormous effort to change the tide. Or they can just sell 100 per cent of their goods to the U.S."

As Canada has already learned the hard way—softwood lumber and the ban on Canadian live-cattle exports are the most recent examples— complete reliance on the United States is neither smart nor sustainable. "I don't think we can live off the U.S. forever, and it's very dangerous to think we can," says Lorna Wright, an associate professor of international business at York University's Schulich School of Business. "As a country you need to be diversified. If an individual company is at capacity, selling all its widgets to Buffalo, that's fine. But as a country, if all your companies are selling all their widgets to Buffalo, then Buffalo can hold you to ransom."

A NEW MAGNETIC NORTH

For many observers Canada, inadvertently or by omission, has already decided its fate. Without the disposition, appetite, marketing skills or, in many cases, the companies to go global, Canada is simply not cut out to be a global trader. "Canadians are not equipped to work on the world stage," says Edy Wong, director of the Centre for International Business Studies at the University of Alberta's School of Business. Fred Lazar, professor of strategy at York University's Schulich School of Business, concurs: "We are able to survive because the market has been given to us. The U.S. is easy and close. We haven't developed the links elsewhere, and we don't know how."

Others fervently believe that Canada can and should have a place at the global table. Some are battle-hardened trade veterans who, despite years of disappointment, stubbornly refuse to give up hope. Some are Canadian professionals, entrepreneurs and chief executives who have gone abroad and flourished. Some are new Canadians, who, grateful for the country's stable business climate and still hungry, see opportunities instead of obstacles. "The world should be our oyster," says Ian Mallory, a Calgary-based venture capitalist. "Until now it's just been easier to do nothing, live off the taxes from our natural resources, work 9 to 5 and go to the cottage."

Canada has been chewing on this particularly gristly tidbit of truth for decades. Prime Minister Pierre Trudeau's infamous "Third Option" of the 1970s was the outgrowth of half-hearted efforts to wean ourselves off the United States and expand our trade ties with the rest of the world. For the most part, however, our global coming of age has yet to be realized— paralyzed, it seems, in a kind of arrested development. But, as I will argue in this book, the Third Option, if it's done right, is not the chimera it has come to represent.

Given what Canadians have been able to achieve at home, in such a harsh and unforgiving climate, going abroad is eminently doable. If we can build ice roads across hundreds of kilometres of barren, treeless tundra that are able to withstand the merciless pounding of thousands of transport trucks as they make their way from Yellowknife to the diamond mines just south of the Arctic Circle, then we can do anything. It's a matter of first *wanting to,* and then familiarizing ourselves with the new topography.

But if we are to get our proper bearings, we will need a new compass, one that is more accurately attuned to the global marketplace. This new compass must be able to adjust for distortions in the domestic economy that often throw off our readings of global competition. It must also include a recalibrated Third Option, one in which trade with the rest of the world is not meant to temper Canada's reliance on the United States but exists on its own merit and for its own sake. By this measure, international trade and investment is the new magnetic north.

Practically speaking, that means not only significantly increasing the number of companies involved in international business, but also enhancing the quality and quantity of that business. It's a problem that goes beyond small and medium-sized enterprises. According to *Canadian Business* magazine, the country's top 500 listed companies generate a minuscule 1.91 per cent of their revenue from foreign markets.[27] "We just don't think in a worldly way," says Bob Armstrong, a former president of the Canadian Association of Importers and Exporters. "We need a shift in attitude."

That shift entails more than simply making the leap from the United States to the rest of the world. It also requires a fundamental rethink of *how* to conduct business abroad. "We don't have a vision of the world that lets us think outside the box," says the Conference Board of Canada's Prem Benimadhu. If companies and government are to avoid repeating past failures, they will have to approach overseas markets with a new understanding and respect, as well as have a strategy in place that capitalizes on their competitive advantages. "If ever there was a time for Canada to have both a North American strategy and a long-term, non–North American strategy, it is now," writes Wendy Dobson, professor at the University of Toronto's Rotman School of Management.[28]

If not, Canada will be forced to contend with the flip side of complacency risk: irrelevance. Stanley Hartt fears it is already happening. He recalls flying down to New York in 1998 to see whether Salomon Smith Barney's corporate chiefs would be interested in acquiring Nesbitt Burns, the investment banking and brokerage arm of the Bank of Montreal, which would have likely been spun off if a planned merger between BMO and the Royal Bank were to proceed. Salomon's management immediately dismissed the suggestion as "crazy." Why would they bother buying a Canadian broker with a return on investment of 15 per cent, they asked, when they could get 25 per cent in emerging markets?

"When the leading financial institutions talk about countries in which they are making investments and building and growing, Canada is not on the list," says Hartt, noting that foreign-ownership restrictions on banks and insurers are a large part of the problem. "The real danger is when foreign investors say, 'Why do we bother with Canada?'"

Back at El Coronito in Mexico City, the sun's white glare highlights the green flecks in Bruno Perron's hazel eyes. It's so bright, waiters scramble to unfurl a patio awning dusty with the accumulated detritus of a large, teeming metropolis. The Quebec native absent-mindedly brushes off the flakes of grit that drift down onto our table. He, like others who have ventured down here, has gotten used to seeing beyond the city's smoggy veil.

At the age of thirty-eight, Perron now heads up his own multi-million-dollar import–export outfit with offices in Canada, Vietnam, Hong Kong, Shanghai and India. When asked what advice he would give his fellow Canadians, Perron contemplates his chili-spiked beer for a moment before taking a swig. "Wake up," he says with an air of exasperation.

2 STEEL DINOSAUR

> "There is not a part of the country where people are not feeling
> the dramatic changes as a result of globalization. The question is,
> where does Canada fit?"
>
> **PERRIN BEATTY, PRESIDENT, CANADIAN MANUFACTURERS & EXPORTERS**

WALKING DOWN Barton Street in Hamilton's east end for the first time is
like stepping into an old *Star Trek* episode in which the crew is beamed
down to a lost civilization. Its once impressive structures are eerily vacant,
slowly mouldering under the weight of eons of neglect. Everything appears
frozen in time, as if the unsuspecting population had no warning before
disaster struck. Once-luminous neon signs hang disconsolately, rusting
and faded, while the door to an abandoned barbershop swings open. At one
shoe store, the smell of mould is so strong it penetrates the glass store-
front. The walls of the half-empty display cases are peeling, and the shoes,
scattered at unnatural angles or hanging perilously from half-dislodged
hooks, are covered in dust and discoloured by the sun. The only ostensible
signs of modernity are fast-cash depots, numerous Tim Hortons shops
and a few down-at-heel bargain-basement stores, one fittingly dubbed the
"Last Chance Outlet."

It wasn't always like this. Barton Street used to be the swanky shopping district for the well-paid blue-collar workers who found jobs in the
hundreds of factories that sprang up along the shores of Hamilton Harbour.

At first a beachhead for textile mills and foundries started by waves of new immigrants, the border town with the best port on Lake Ontario soon became the capital of the country's steel industry and a favoured spot for multinationals looking to set up branch plants in Canada.

By the 1950s, Hamilton was a boomtown. The heaving blast furnaces and black-plumed smokestacks were signature signs of progress that formed the bedrock of a thriving industrial hub. Railway freight cars criss-crossed the city's east end, and the port hummed as factories churned out everything from agricultural equipment and household appliances to Studebaker cars and Life Savers candies. During the halcyon days, Steel Town, as it became known, was home to corporate heavyweights like Procter & Gamble, Westinghouse and General Electric and was the country's uncontested manufacturing and industrial capital. It was a proud, can-do kind of place.

But in less than a generation, the steely foundation that girded the city to the country's industrial engine seems to have crumbled like cardboard. The once-thriving east end looks more like a "war zone," says Rolf Gerstenberger, a veteran steelworker who has watched as factory after factory closed up shop, their rusted-out, soot-stained remnants the only clue to the city's former glory days. The gradual decline that began in the early 1980s continues inexorably to this day. In recent years, Camco, one of Canada's few remaining appliance makers, Slater Steel and jeans manufacturer Levi Strauss & Co. have all closed their plants, shedding thousands of jobs.

"When I started thirty-two years ago, it was the industrial heartland," recalls Gerstenberger. "There were probably twenty factories with over a thousand people in each one—Stelco, Dofasco, Firestone, Westinghouse, International Harvester, Otis Elevator. The kids just went from one factory to the other until they found one they liked."

"Well, that is all gone," he says. "I don't know what the kids are going to do—McDonald's or something—because there's no place else to go."

Even the mighty steel industry, the city's heaving heart and last hope, is a hollowed-out shell of its former self. At one time, Stelco and Dofasco, the two big steel companies, employed more than thirty thousand people in their hulking steelworks overlooking the bay. But in the past two decades, financial crises and downsizing have whittled the workforce down to twelve thousand. In 2004, Stelco filed for bankruptcy protection and, after a $100 million provincial bailout, emerged much downsized and largely owned by New York hedge funds. Dofasco now has European minders, the concession prize in a high-stakes tug-of-war for global steel domination.

Although the two companies were very different—one profitable, one not—neither could avoid the whirling juggernaut that has laid waste to so much of Hamilton: globalization. In its latest incarnation it is convulsing the steel industry through a combination of massive new capacity in low-cost countries like Russia, Brazil and China and the creation for the first time of global behemoths in the historically fragmented steel sector. The new paradigm, which redefines the winners and losers in the industry, is dictated by size, low cost and global scope. On each count, the Canadians came up short.

China alone now represents more than a quarter of worldwide steel capacity, adding the equivalent of Canada's entire production every year.[29] This unprecedented ramp-up coincides with the mega-mergers of several steel industry leaders. The Netherlands-registered Mittal Steel, headed up by Indian-born billionaire Lakshmi Mittal, emerged from obscurity to become the industry kingmaker, acquiring U.S. steel assets before making a stunning US$38 billion hostile bid for its number two rival, Europe's Arcelor SA. The merged powerhouse, Arcelor Mittal, is far and away the world's largest, representing 10 per cent of global steel production. As part of the deal, Mittal was to offload Dofasco, which was in the midst of being acquired by Arcelor, to a rival contender for the Hamilton company, ThyssenKrupp AG. At the time of writing, however, the sale was being blocked by Arcelor shareholders and Dofasco's fate remained unclear.

It's a stunning reversal of fortune for the two Canadian industrial icons that enjoyed a privileged position supplying steel to the United States, the world's largest automotive market. The two were arguably well positioned to be players instead of pawns in the global steel shakeout, yet both failed to capitalize on their advantage. While Dofasco carved out a lucrative niche as a value-added steel producer, it, along with its more commodity-oriented cousin, Stelco, never dared venture far from home. Other than Dofasco's minor incursions into the United States and Mexico, the two were decidedly domestic, each rolling out five million tonnes of steel annually, a drop in the bucket compared with Mittal's 115 million tonnes, furnished by furnaces from Indonesia to Kazakhstan.

"If you were going to name a Canadian national champion, the steel industry would definitely be one. It is one of the few industries in which Canadian producers, taken together, were actually stronger than American producers," says Peter Warrian, a senior research fellow at the University of Toronto's Munk Centre and an expert on the Canadian steel industry. "But they didn't conceive of anything beyond the North American market. It was a failure of imagination."

It's not as though Canadians didn't have the chance to expand abroad. In the 1980s, Stelco turned down a sweetheart deal to buy a bankrupt Chinese steel company, Maanshan, for next to nothing. "They thought it was too far away and they would have had to manage it," said a person familiar with the deal. Maanshan has since been restructured and is the world's twenty-sixth-largest steel producer, with a production capacity nearly double that of Stelco. "They could have bought Maanshan, revived their technology division and been one of the world leaders in steel production if they'd kept going," said the source. "We had the world's best steel industry from the point of view of technology and quality. Why is it a bunch of guys from Korea or India ended up being the world leaders?"

Brazilian manufacturers, who have yet to get their domestic automotive industry off the ground, definitely recognized Canada's competitive advantages. Considered among the world's most antiquated steel industries less than two decades ago, Brazilian producers are now among the most modern, led by the likes of Gerdau SA. That company's first foray outside of Brazil was into Canada, where it acquired a steel mill in Cambridge, Ontario, which was followed by another in Selkirk, Manitoba, in the late 1980s. Now with operations in seven countries, Gerdau has gone from being the world's 54th-largest steel company in 1997 to 14th in 2006, surpassing 51st-placed Stelco. In Canada, its Gerdau AmeriSteel subsidiary ranks as the country's 75th-largest company. Stelco is 131st.[30]

The decision to stay home, however, is costing more than just a few rungs in the corporate rankings. The failure to retool Hamilton's fading industrial and manufacturing muscle is reflected in the lifeless shop windows along Barton Street. A metaphor not only for the dwindling fortunes of Steel Town but for much of Canada, the strip is a relic of times past, an almost miraculous effort to stave off decades of changing tastes and trends.

Sadly, the once-modish facades are not monuments to former glory days. Boarded up and decrepit, they have become the most visible signposts of the entrenched poverty and gritty hopelessness that is gripping what was one of the country's most vibrant cities.

Wayne Marston's eyes well up with tears as he recalls the scores of immigrant families holed up in tiny apartments on the city's dilapidated northern fringe. The president of Hamilton's Labour Council, Marston describes how the overcrowded living conditions force children to sleep in discarded refrigerator boxes. Unlike the newcomers who came before them, these immigrants don't have well-paying factory jobs. They are forced into low-wage jobs cleaning offices, driving taxis or working in fast-food restaurants.

Unable to make ends meet, these newcomers have swelled the ranks of the working poor and pushed the city's social services to the brink. The use of food banks in Hamilton has skyrocketed, and homelessness has more than doubled. Hamilton's inner-city core is among the poorest in the country. In some areas, like Barton Street, two thirds of the residents live below the poverty line. As teenage pregnancy, high-school dropout rates and illiteracy reach critical levels, the city is staring down the intractable barrel of generational poverty.

"We have been bleeding jobs continuously, and replacement jobs have not been the rewarding ones," says Marston. "Fifteen years ago people thought the food banks were a temporary institution. Now it's not just the unemployed who use them, but the working poor—they can't make it."

From the looks of things, the situation isn't going to improve soon. A quick perusal of the city's top fifteen employers shows that the overwhelming majority of jobs—three quarters of them—are in the public sector, either in hospitals or schools or in the municipal, provincial or federal governments. Outside the two steel companies, there is scant evidence of any real wealth creation. According to Paul Johnson, director of the city's recently created poverty task force, some of the biggest job growth has been among welfare support services and, of course, Tim Hortons, which now has more than four hundred employees in the city.

"We are just buying time," says Johnson. "What happens to Hamilton when another recession hits? We're treading water, and yet we're in the best economic times we can remember. The only thing we know for sure is, it will come to an end."

CHINA CHANGES THE WORLD

Bolton is not far from Hamilton, maybe fifty kilometres north, one more watermark in the sprawl of featureless highways and cookie-cutter housing developments that ooze from Toronto like an oil spill that can't be contained. Once an expanse of farmers' fields, this suburban enclave is home to Husky Injection Molding Systems, the biggest game in town and a rare gem among the sparsely populated ranks of homegrown manufacturers.

Tucked in behind a thick wall of vegetation, Husky's leafy compound couldn't be more different from the heaving industrial miasma of Hamilton. To encourage environmentalism as well as efficiency, the company provides a fleet of yellow bicycles to commute between each of its well-manicured manufacturing complexes. Instead of entering a stuffy boardroom, visitors are led into the "Imagineering Room," a bright, sky-lit space, adorned with woodsy paintings and country-style furniture meant to encourage creative thinking.

The architect of this carefully constructed sanctuary is Robert Schad, a German-born entrepreneur who came to Canada in 1951 to escape war-ravaged Europe. A toolmaker by trade, Schad turned his garage tinkering into a world-beating company. Husky is the leading manufacturer of high-end equipment used to make plastic mouldings for everything from pop bottles to auto parts. With sales of more than $1 billion, Husky has offices in almost thirty countries and factories in Canada, Luxembourg and Shanghai.

But while Schad built his empire on an unflagging credo of "automate or die," a recent trip to China convinced him that that credo is not nearly merciless enough. "China changes the whole world. The drive for speed, the quick decision-making, it's really a very ruthless business approach," he said during an interview in the Imagineering Room before retiring as Husky's chief executive officer in 2005. "If you don't compete in China, you will not compete globally. It's a benchmark now of global competition."

Convinced of China's pre-eminence, Schad pulled his twelve-year-old son out of Toronto's prestigious Upper Canada College so that he could be home-schooled in Mandarin. Yet, despite Husky's international reach and its reputation as the Cadillac of its class, the company's revenue plunged 15 per cent in 2004.[31] Schad admits that Husky will be able to maintain its technological leadership "only for so long."

With the company's carefully tended garden ruffled by the rumble of competition half a world away, the salad days of after-work massages, a company fitness facility and a daycare centre are numbered, warned Schad. "There's a certain entitlement attitude here. We're going to close some things down, make it tougher," he said of plans to introduce rigorous performance evaluations. "We can't afford to live in an oasis here and let things go by. We have to compete."

What Schad is up against is a daunting combination of technology, transportation and hundreds of millions of hard-driven people willing to work twelve hours a day, six days a week, assembling everything from toys to televisions for pennies an hour. The promise of low-cost production and global reach has lured the world's leading multinationals to China's shores while awakening the Middle Kingdom to its own global aspirations.

The one-time sleeping giant is now flexing its muscle, building home-grown multinationals like Huawei Technologies, an electronics equipment maker, which can afford to employ thirteen thousand highly educated Chinese engineers, roughly equivalent to Nortel Corp.'s own R&D staff, but paid one third the salary. The company, which didn't exist before 1988, is scooping up multi-million-dollar supply contracts from Oman to Brazil and has quintupled in size since posting sales of US$1.8 billion in 2000. In 2005, Huawei racked up revenues of US$8.2 billion, including US$4.8 billion in exports, and at its current rate of growth is on track to surpass the once mighty Nortel in a matter of years.*

This new template, being forged by the likes of Huawei, Gerdau and Mittal, turns on its head the groundings of much of the world's economic compass. It redefines the concept of what is a commodity, reconfigures global trade patterns, blows away comparative advantage and defies the idea that proximity to market, a long-cherished Canadian advantage, matters. "The world is small and the world is flat," says Jack Gin, chief executive of Vancouver-based Extreme CCTV, which exports surveillance cameras around the world. "It's scary. It's scary if you've got kids."

The future, many believe, is looking decidedly grim for Canada, still sleepily ensconced in its makeshift domestic haven. Branding itself as the world's cheapest industrialized country,[32] Canada has opted to compete as a low-wage alternative to the United States, instead of capitalizing on scale, scope or innovation. As a result, all its advantages—from its cherished car industry to its storied natural resources—are now in the direct line of fire from China and other ambitious upstarts such as Mexico, Brazil and India.

Take the $100 billion automotive sector, the bread and butter of Canadian industry. The Big Three vehicle manufacturers, General Motors (GM), Ford, and DaimlerChrysler, on which the Canadian industry overwhelmingly depends, have been hemorrhaging money and jobs in recent years as they struggle to compete against more popular imports and more efficient rivals. But while massive plant closures and job cuts were

---

* In 2006, Huawei landed a five-year, twenty-one-country contract to supply Vodafone, the world's largest wireless operator, with handsets based on third-generation technology.

announced in the United States and Canada in 2005 and 2006, China is attracting investment by the buckets—including from GM, which admitted that its Chinese unit was the only bright spot on the company balance sheet. China, a nation that once produced fewer cars than Australia, is expected to account for half of all new global vehicle-making capacity in the coming years. Already ahead of Canada, which since 1999 has slid from being the world's fourth-largest vehicle producer to the eighth spot today, China is set to overtake Japan as the globe's number two manufacturer by 2010.

The vehicle makers, along with a host of upstart domestic manufacturers, are drawn not only by the hundreds of millions of carless Chinese but by the country's potential as a global export base. In 2005, Honda delivered its first made-in-China cars to Germany. DaimlerChrysler quickly followed suit, inking a joint venture with China's Chery Automobile Co. to export Chinese-made subcompact cars to Europe and the United States by 2008. In what the *Financial Times* described as "the start of an unstoppable shift in the global automotive sector,"[33] China's Geely, which already ships cars to thirty-four countries in the Middle East, Africa and South America, will begin exporting hundreds of thousands of cheap compact cars to the United States sometime between 2009 and 2011. For Canada, which ships 92 per cent of its domestically manufactured cars and parts to the United States, the implications are huge.

"China is a time bomb," says Jim Stanford, economist with the Canadian Auto Workers union. "There is no way we will be able to compete once they get the infrastructure. They will be able to export vehicles and sell them for half the price."

While Chinese car manufacturers, still grappling with design and quality issues, have been forced to temper their export ambitions, not so for the auto parts industry. China is looking to become the world's low-cost parts producer, with a stated goal of exporting US$100 billion in parts by 2010, up from US$5.6 billion in 2004.[34] The country's largest manufacturer, the privately owned Wanxiang Group, which counts GM and Ford among its customers, has built up an international supply chain with stakes in more than one hundred companies, including dozens of overseas parts makers in the United States, United Kingdom, Germany and even Canada. At the same time, Germany's Volkswagen announced plans in 2006 to increase its exports of Chinese-made car parts from just US$100 million to US$1 billion, while Ford announced that it was set to double the value of components it sourced from China to US$3 billion in 2006. "There will be a permanent shift of certain component manufactures," says Felix Pilorusso, a Toronto-based auto industry consultant. "It's already happening."

The inevitable tug towards lower-cost areas of production is even uprooting the natural-resource industries, supplanting Canadian salmon with Chilean sea bass and softwood lumber with Latvian spruce and Brazilian loblolly pine. Massive new pulp mills in South America, Eastern Europe and China are not only tapping into fast-growth forests and low-cost logging but are fundamentally changing traditional trading patterns, says Clark Binkley, a forestry industry expert and former dean of the University of British Columbia's Faculty of Forestry.

Until very recently the forestry industry was segregated into three regional trading blocs, which flowed north–south. Canada supplied the United States, Scandinavia sold to its more southerly European neighbours and Russia exported to Japan and Korea. But as production ramps up, particularly in the southern hemisphere, new "variegated" trade patterns are developing, says Binkley. New Zealand is now supplying the United States with wood, and Brazil is selling pulp to Europe and the United States. "Global trade is emerging," he says, "and there's a lot more opportunity for somebody else to be the lowest-cost producer."

Canadian softwood lumber producers learned that lesson the hard way when the U.S. government, under pressure from its domestic industry, slapped import quotas on Canadian wood. Both the Americans and the Canadians assumed the quota would constrict supply, pushing prices up to the benefit of both sides, says Binkley. Instead, it opened up a window of opportunity for a slew of imports from Brazil to Estonia. The newcomers managed to grab a chunk of the market, keeping prices down.

And even though the original quota system is gone, the newcomers are not. European imports, virtually non-existent a decade earlier, reached record highs in 2005, accounting for nearly 5 per cent of U.S. sales,[35] while Canada's share of the U.S. forest products market dropped from 69 per cent in 2000 to 62 per cent in 2004.

"They've gotten in and they aren't going to go away," says Binkley. "We don't have any exclusive access to the U.S. Wherever the wood is the cheapest, it's going to come in. And it's gotten more competitive."

In fact, Canadian industry is slowly waking up to the fact that what it thought was a lifetime warranty under NAFTA actually has an expiry date. Among the hardest hit has been the Canadian furniture sector, which had successfully transformed itself from a sluggish, domestically oriented industry before free trade into the number one exporter to the United States. After out-competing American furniture makers, its hard-won but short-lived leadership was quickly usurped by China, which now commands 50 per cent of the U.S. wood bedroom furniture sector, up from just 4.8 per cent in 1996.

Until now, Canadians have comforted themselves with the idea that somehow the Canadian and Chinese economies were "complementary": China was poor in natural resources, which Canada could happily supply. But while that assumption is true, it leaves out a crucial part of the equation, not to mention entire swaths of the economy. Not only are the Chinese manufacturing increasingly sophisticated products, from bicycles and barbecues to handsets and pharmaceuticals, that compete directly with Canadian goods, but foreign multinationals, Americans in particular, are moving to China to manufacture. "The U.S. companies are going to China big time, and we need to be there to support our U.S. clients, whether it's in the auto industry, banking, whatever. We need to be there because we are part of the North American fabric," explains Neil Tate, a special adviser to the Bank of Montreal on Asia. "We need to do that to protect ourselves, to survive, to increase our business not only in China, but in the U.S. and to increase our two-way trade between Canada and the U.S."

Yet we don't seem to be doing it. Canadian companies, large and small, have been slow to sign up for the new game in town: global supply chains. Canadians have lagged behind their peers in offshoring and out-sourcing, thus betraying a reluctance to tap into lower-cost markets as sources of cheap components or manufacturing bases. While the world's stock of foreign direct investment expanded a hundredfold between 1990 and 2002, Canada's increased just 4.4 times[36]—an indication that Canadian companies are neither creating their own global supply chains nor becoming part of someone else's.

According to a 2004 survey conducted by Canada's Automotive Parts Manufacturers' Association (APMA) of its members, Asian facilities accounted for a minuscule 0.29 per cent of their production and Asian suppliers repre-sented less than 5 per cent of inputs. Perhaps not surprisingly, 71 per cent of the respondents admitted that one or more of their major customers had threatened to switch to overseas suppliers in the previous three years.[37]

During APMA's 2005 annual convention in Hamilton, a GM vice-president warned that Canada's decades-long decision to rely on a sixty-five-cent dollar instead of increasing competitiveness was costing billions in new business. GM was expected to award just $200 million in new supply contracts to Canada in 2005, down from $2 billion in 2003, he said.[38] "China is nipping at our heels, and standing still is a recipe for disaster," says Gerry Fedchun, APMA's president. "A lot of companies in our industry say, 'I'm all right Jack.' But it'll catch up to them, and they will not be around. If you don't think you have to change, you're screwed." The proof is in the pudding: with a slew of auto parts makers in bankruptcy protection, Canada recorded a deficit in automotive trade in the second quarter of 2006—the first since 1991.

With some 60 per cent of all Chinese exports produced by foreign multinationals, putting the nation on track to become the world's largest exporter by 2010, billions of dollars' worth of foreign investment pouring into Brazilian steel capacity from China, South Korea and Europe, and more going into building India's back office to the world, opting out of the loop is akin to the "kiss of death," says Lorna Wright, associate professor of international business at York University's Schulich School of Business. "The world is getting more interconnected. If you are not careful, if you cut yourself out of the chain, you're dead."

Howard Balloch is willing to bet money on it. The former ambassador who now runs his own investment boutique headquartered in Beijing says it's only a matter of time before the Chinese are producing higher-quality parts more cheaply than they can be made in Canada. And those parts won't just be put into the cars coming off assembly lines in Shanghai—they'll be in the vehicles rolling out of Detroit and Oshawa.

"The auto parts companies that come to China establish themselves early, bring technology and, because they have a head start, end up owning the Chinese production facilities—they win," says Balloch. "Otherwise Chinese companies are going back to Canada and buying up what's left of our industry, and that's as inexorable as the tides."

THE ANTI-BRANDERS

An old Chinese parable explains Canada's place in the world, says David Fung, a Hong Kong–born self-made millionaire who now makes his home in Vancouver. It goes like this: A fox meets a tiger in the forest. The fox says to the tiger, "Don't eat me because I am really powerful. If you don't believe me, follow me around the forest and you'll find everyone bowing to me." Sure enough, everywhere the tiger and the fox went, all the animals bowed. "Well, of course, everybody was really bowing to the tiger," says Fung. "In Canada, we take the U.S. to be our tiger."

The problem is, as global supply chains weave their way around the planet, companies consolidate and free-trade agreements are thrown out like so many nets into the sea, the tiger may find better things to do than follow a fox around the forest. Shorn of its protector, the fox falls prey to the law of the jungle. And Canada, like the fox, has very little in the way of natural defences to shield it from the ferocity of global markets. In fact, on closer inspection, this fox, with its puffy tail and pointy ears, begins to resemble an overgrown squirrel.

The first telltale sign of Canada's vulnerability is in its companies. In an era where size matters, the country has precious few multinationals. Despite laying claim to the second-largest proven oil reserves in the world, Canada has no "super-majors" like Exxon Mobil or British Petroleum. Few countries are carpeted with such vast tracts of trees, yet there is not a single tier-one forestry company to rival those of the Scandinavians or the Americans. Canada's mining companies have traditionally been the most international, but only two—Barrick Gold and Teck Cominco—still have Canadian head offices and are pipsqueaks compared with behemoths like Anglo-American of the United Kingdom, Brazil's CVRD and Anglo-Australian miner BHP Billiton. Aluminum maker Alcan is perhaps the most global Canadian company, but with US$20 billion in sales it is considered small by international standards (the newly merged Arcelor Mittal steel giant has sales of US$77.5 billion) and is an increasingly likely takeover target.

As for Canada's blue chip banks, they are irrelevant internationally, dwarfed by multinational monoliths like Citigroup and Holland's ING Group and even outgunned by Australia, where poisonous animals outnumber the population.* According to the *Fortune 500* list of the world's biggest companies in 2004, Canada's leading entry was George Weston Ltd. at 240. But while Weston has grown fat plying Canadians with baked goods and President's Choice brand foods at its ubiquitous Loblaws and Superstore chains, French grocer Carrefour is in an entirely different weight class, with a global empire that includes more than two hundred stores in China alone.†

Canada's lack of global girth exposes an even softer underbelly. While Sweden has Ikea, Finland has Nokia and Italy has the fashion triumvirate of Armani, Gucci and Prada, Canada does not have, *nor has it ever had,* a single global brand. Even landlocked and impossibly mountainous Switzerland boasts

---

* Australia has three banks in the world's top fifty, according to the *Fortune 500* list of the world's biggest companies (2006), compared with *one* Canadian bank.
† Carrefour rings in at number twenty-one on the *Fortune 500* list, with an annual revenue of US$90.4 billion, compared with George Weston's US$23 billion.

a swath of high-altitude names, from banks and Rolex watches to Nestlé chocolate, Nescafé instant coffee and pharmaceutical giants Novartis and Roche.

In contrast, Canada is almost anti-brand. In a country without a lot of large companies, an inordinate number of them are generic manufacturers or outsourced contractors hired to make other companies' products. The no-name club includes Cott, which is now the largest private-label soft drink manufacturer in the world; Celestica, a contract electronics manufacturer; Apotex, a generic drug manufacturer; Patheon, a leading contract drug maker; and Peerless Clothing, which manufactures men's suits under licence for upscale brands like Calvin Klein and Ralph Lauren. Even Montreal-based Gildan Activewear, one of the largest T-shirt makers in the world, is no Fruit of the Loom.

Some say its because we're just too darn nice and middle-of-the-road to put our imprint on anything and duke it out for world domination. Finns, despite their socialist leanings, are definitely not soft and cuddly, say those who have dealt with them. The Australians, descended from convicts exiled to a distant island, are ballsy adventurers who travel the world over. And while Bern may rival Ottawa as the world's most boring capital city, the Swiss are "calculating, regimented and disciplined. They know what they want and are fantastic negotiators," says Jeff Swystun, the Toronto-based global director for the branding company Interbrand.

"It's a problem of our marketing aggressiveness. When has Canada ever conquered another country? We are a country that's never had a revolution, never had a civil war," says Swystun. "Unfortunately marketing is all about scrapping it out—for market share, for share of mind and share of wallet. That means being aggressive day in and day out. And that just doesn't appear to be in our character. It would mean taking a stand, and that's something we are loath to do."

So instead of being scrappers, we are skimmers. Whether it's the big banks that sit at home counting their billions, logging companies content to hew two-by-fours instead of manufacture tissue paper, or manufacturers churning out generic products rather than innovating, Canadian companies scoop the cream off the top rather than milk their products and services for all they are worth. Why go through the painful and risky process of building brands, expanding internationally and adding value when there is relatively easy money to be made carving up homegrown monopolies, cutting down trees and turning out component parts?

"The Americans phone us and say 'We need wood' and we sell it to them, and they sell it back to us as a cabinet," says Drury Mason, Alberta's assistant deputy minister of economic development. "And we're happy to do it because we made money on the wood."

That kind of inward-looking comfortable complacency has taken a toll on the country's entrepreneurial drive. The lag is reflected in a reluctance to invest in new technology, a reliance on cheap labour and a yawning productivity gap between us and the United States. Canada's investment per worker in machinery and equipment is about 60 per cent of U.S. levels, its companies spend less than half as much on research and development as the Americans do, and we are twenty years behind our neighbour in our stock of information technology.[39]

It's why, when I was in the Arctic, I was surprised to learn that all of Canada's fleet of Coast Guard icebreakers are powered by Finnish-made engines, and why Quebec, traditionally the largest source of aluminum for Alcan, doesn't have a single aluminum auto parts maker. It's also why, despite manufacturing cars for forty years as part of the Auto Pact, an automotive free-trade agreement between the United States and Canada, Canadians are essentially still assembly-line workers.

Not surprisingly, Canada continues to slip in the World Economic Forum's annual rankings of the world's most competitive countries. Its overall business competitiveness sank from sixth place in 1998 to fifteenth in 2006, largely due to a weak track record on innovation. According to the survey, Canada ranks thirty-second out of 125 countries in its propensity to compete based on unique products and processes. When it comes to the degree to which exporting companies go beyond the simple resource extraction and are involved in product design, marketing sales and logistics, it ranked a dismal forty-sixth. In contrast, Finland, Sweden and Denmark have topped the charts year after year, thanks to a private sector that according to the forum "shows a high proclivity for adopting new technology and nurturing a culture of innovation."

That's not to say that Canadians never come up with innovative technologies or ground-breaking inventions. They do. In fact, they do it quite often. The problem is that they seem to have a hard time making the leap from the laboratory to the marketplace. When a Canadian product does make it to the store shelves, it's usually because an American company made it happen. "What Americans are good at is taking a commercial venture and getting people excited about it," says Nizar Somji, owner of the Edmonton-based technology firm Matrikon. "We are not only unable to commercialize, but we are unable to get people excited." Adds Interbrand's Jeff Swystun: "We don't have a marketing mindset in this country at all. We're bad at making the finished product shine, and there's a real void in marketing talent, in aggression, in boldness of claim. It's truly a void in the business world."

The story of IMAX Corp., the iconic big-screen movie company, is the Canadian conundrum writ large. In the late 1960s, a group of Canadians developed a revolutionary technology for large-format film. The technique became a staple at science centres and museums, but eventually it stumbled on drab content and limited growth. Two Americans picked up the floundering company in 1994 and gave it a new lease on life. No longer merely a vehicle for documentary and educational films, IMAX now features Hollywood blockbusters using a technology it developed to convert conventional films to its format. The new owners, a pair of New York investment bankers, have signed licensing agreements with theatre operators around the world. There are now 366 big screens running in thirty-six countries, from Russia to Kuwait, while China is the company's biggest market outside the United States, with twenty-five theatres set to open by 2008.

John Mendlein, an American biophysicist and lawyer who spent four and a half years working in the Toronto biopharmaceutical sector, traces Canada's limp salesmanship back to another duo: Fredrick Banting and Charles Best. In 1921, the two Canadian doctors discovered insulin, the lifesaving secretion used to treat diabetes. The Nobel Prize–winning find is one of the greatest medical discoveries of the twentieth century, yet the two doctors never attempted to cash in on their work, considering it "culturally unacceptable," says Mendlein, to commercialize science.

A group of Danish scientists, however, were not bothered by similar concerns. On hearing of the Canadian breakthrough they immediately got to work producing insulin, and in 1923—just two years after the initial discovery—they launched a company and began treating patients. That company, Novo Nordisk, is today a world leader in diabetes treatment, employing twenty thousand people in seventy-eight countries.

Canada, in comparison, while having made world-leading advances in diabetes and stem cell research, is nowhere on the pharmaceutical industry map, according to Mendlein. It has been outmanoeuvred by everyone from Sweden and Denmark to India. "If you look at where you are on the level of research and biological science, you are probably in the G3," he says. "But Canada doesn't even make the G8 of pharmaceutical countries. It's tragic." While small towns like Indianapolis, Indiana, and Thousand Oaks, California, have spawned world leaders like Eli Lilly and Amgen, Toronto, which is home to Canada's largest cluster of biotech firms, has failed to produce a single stand-alone biotech company or blockbuster drug.

Canada doesn't even boast an insulin manufacturer; the original University of Toronto laboratory where diabetes was discovered was spun off into Connaught Laboratories, which busied itself with maintaining a domestic monopoly while handing out international licences to the likes of Eli Lilly and Novo Nordisk. It eventually lost its ability to even supply the Canadian market, and was taken over by the federal government in 1972 before being sold to a French pharmaceutical firm. Absorbed into the massive ranks of the world's number three drug company, Sonafi Aventis, the "Connaught campus" in north Toronto is the only remaining vestige of Canada's contribution to diabetes treatment.

"Canada has some software and electronics companies, a little aircraft, but no consumer goods, or cars, and it's not really happening for computers or pharmaceuticals," says Mendlein. "You could be the Norway in North America and rely on commodities, but you are not going to be Sweden, which is home to the top-selling drug in the world and probably the car you drive. The question is, where does Canada, which is a much bigger and much more powerful country, fit in?"

It's a good question. To answer it, I asked four related questions about the largest supposedly "Canadian" companies to the gauge the country's entrepreneurial drive and managerial capacity—the basic requirements for creating globally competitive companies:

1. How many companies were founded by immigrants?
2. How many had American or other foreign management?
3. How many were actually subsidiaries or spin-offs of foreign companies? (to be dealt with in Chapter 3)
4. How many, despite a listing on a Canadian stock exchange, had a CEO and/or a head office located south of the border?

The answers lead to an astonishing conclusion: an economy on cruise control, with foreigners and foreign-born Canadians at the wheel, while native-born Canadians snooze in the back seat. To begin with, almost every significant high-tech firm to come out of the Ottawa area, known in better times as Silicon Valley North, was started by a clutch of British entrepreneurs. The list includes Cognos, Corel, Zarlink Semiconductor, Mitel Networks, Tundra Semiconductor and Newbridge Networks. The exception—JDS Uniphase—was started by the beret-wearing Slovak, Josef Strauss.

Hungarian-born Peter Munk founded Barrick Gold, while compatriot Frank Hasenfratz heads up Linamar, Canada's second-largest auto parts company. Only Magna, the parts giant founded by Austrian-born Frank Stronach, is bigger. Two Germans, Klaus Woerner (now deceased) of ATS Automation Tooling Systems, a maker of manufacturing equipment, and Husky's Robert Schad, round out Canada's contribution to the tool and die industry. Says Schad of the preponderance of European immigrants: "We had a good technical education and then flourished in this country because there was no competition."

The field was equally unencumbered for brash and innovative entrepreneurs like Isidore Philosophe, who emigrated from Beirut, turning a basement business into Cinram, the world's largest manufacturer of CDs and DVDs; Aldo Bensadoun, the Moroccan-born owner of the Aldo shoe chain; Karl Kaiser, the Austrian co-founder of award-winning Inniskillin wines; Peter Nygärd, the high-flying Finn who launched a textile empire from Winnipeg; and Robert Friedland, the American hippie turned promoter behind the Ivanhoe energy and mining ventures. Moses Znaimer, the architect of the Toronto-based CITY TV media group, was born in Tajikistan, the son of holocaust survivors. Saul Feldberg also survived the war in Poland and went on to found the Global Group of Companies, one of the world's largest office-furniture manufacturers. German-born Stephen Jarislowsky, the flinty-edged octogenarian heading up the multi-billion-dollar investment boutique, Jarislowsky Fraser & Co., escaped from France just as the Nazis invaded in 1941. Even Galen Weston, the grocery scion, was born in Britain, whereas Mike Lazaridis, co-founder of the country's high-tech darling, Research in Motion, was born in Turkey. In perhaps the most telling example of all, Canada's most iconic brand, Roots, was started by two Americans from Detroit.

In the seemingly rare instances in which companies spring from Canadian-born loins, they are rarely managed by Canadians. Scratch beneath the surface of many a Canadian company and you will likely find an American. The elite fraternity oversees such national icons as Air Canada,* CN Rail, Saskatchewan Wheat Pool,† and, until 2006, Canadian Tire.‡ Other alumni include oil company Suncor Energy, electronics manufacturer Celestica, forestry firms Abitibi-Consolidated, Tembec and West Fraser Timber, Magna International and Nortel. Our southern cousins also oversee the mining interests of Cameco, Potash Corporation of

---

* American-born Robert Milton was chief executive of Air Canada before taking the helm of its parent company, ACE Aviation, and British-born Clive Beddoe heads up WestJet; now, both of Canada's major airlines are run by foreign imports.

† The Saskatchewan Wheat Pool was originally founded as an anti-corporatist co-operative by prairie farmers.

‡ *Canadian Business* magazine named Canadian Tire's Virginia-born Wayne Sales as Canada's top CEO in 2005. Sales stepped down in 2006.

Saskatchewan, and INCO, until it was acquired by the Brazilians. Even Stelco, since emerging from bankruptcy protection in March 2006, is run by the American-born former CEO of International Steel. British-born executives run McCain Foods and Talisman Energy, while an Australian headed up Ontario's Hydro One, the government-owned electrical utility, until resigning over a scandal involving expense accounts in December 2006.

Some companies are even double dippers. CN, Cott,* Lions Gate Entertainment, NOVA Chemicals, Brookfield Properties (which built the iconic Montreal Forum) and Thomson Financial are not only American-run, but their CEOs all live in the United States. ATI Technologies, one of the world's largest 3D-graphics-chip designers, has the distinction of being a triple dipper. Founded by Kwok Yuen Ho, the son of a wealthy Chinese family dispossessed by the communists, ATI's top management is American, including CEO David Orton, who commutes to work from California.† It seems only fitting, then, that the Canadian Council of Chief Executives, the country's leading corporate organization, is headed by American-born Chairman Rick George.‡

To foreigners this is striking. "Canadians don't have confidence in their own abilities. They often bring in Americans to run their companies," says Boris Rousseff, a European trade consultant to Canadian firms. "It's an issue of corporate culture. Canadians try to pretend they are not who they are."

And therein lies the root of the dilemma. Canadians are ensnared in a kind of Gordian knot: because their economy is essentially run by foreigners, they necessarily downplay or underestimate their own abilities, and by extension their own Canadian brand. And the fact that there are no Canadian brands reinforces Canadians' suspicions that they have no

---

* Cott's American CEO, John Sheppard, stepped down in May 2006 to be replaced by another American, Brent Willis.

† Orton may no longer need to commute, since Advanced Micro Devices (AMD), the California-based microprocessor manufacturer, announced in July 2006 that it would acquire ATI for US$5.4 billion.

‡ George moved to Calgary in 1991 to head up Suncor, and in 1996 he proudly took up Canadian citizenship.

value. Why is it, asks Andrew Stodart, vice-president of marketing and business development for Diamond Estates Wines and Spirits, that uniquely Canadian brands like Coffee Crisp candy bars and Molson Canadian beer were never marketed around the world? "Canadians abdicate brand building," he says. "It comes back to the great Canadian inferiority complex."

Sadly, it becomes a self-fulfilling prophecy. Without the premium and protection that brands afford—not to mention the estimated 30 per cent boost they bring to a company's stock market price—the only other option is to be a commodity. "You are condemned to be second rate," says Stodart, competing on price instead of market position. And in today's global market, "there's always somebody cheaper."

Even the Chinese realize it's a losing proposition. Their national champions have begun acquiring internationally recognized brands like RCA televisions and IBM's personal computer division. China's leading car maker, Nanjing Automobile Group, has bought the design rights to the United Kingdom's bankrupt MG Rover Group and plans to make its own high-end brand sedan, which it will sell in Europe and the United States. In 2006, a Chinese brand (telecom giant China Mobile) ranked, for the first time, among the world's most valuable brands,* coming in fourth after Microsoft, GE and Coca-Cola. Its estimated value: US$39 billion. Beijing-based Longfa Decoration Corp., in an attempt to copy the American franchise model, launched its own furniture retailer, Mermax, in the United States. "We want to provide a full service and create a brand," said Yan Shihong, the enthusiastic Chinese store manager of its first Chicago location. "It's the American way, right?"[40]

Canada, in contrast, seems to have turned the normal evolution from low-cost manufacturer to value-added brander on its head. "We are a component nation," says Jeff Swystun. "We are a bit like China in the last century going into this century. We've flipped it on its head. But China is sick of playing that game. And we need to get real sick of playing that

---

* According to a ranking by BRANDZ, a list compiled by London-based market research firm Millward Brown.

game real fast." While the no-name, behind-the-scenes nuance may be part of the Canadian character, says Swystun, "it's not going to allow us to win on the global business playing field." Instead, it will brand us as "the economy that stands for nothing," a squirrel in a menagerie of tigers, dragons and elephants.

CALL CENTRE NATION

It's hard to get your knickers in a knot when the economy is firing on all cylinders. For most of this decade, Canadians have basked in the glow of the best economic conditions of the past fifty years, with unemployment at historic lows, companies posting record profits and skyrocketing oil and commodity prices bringing a new sheen of respectability to the loonie. So what if we don't have brands or that we suck as salespeople? So what if we're not the Americans' number one trade partner or that our companies are decidedly domestic? Our GDP per capita is higher than that of Finland, a nation that is supposedly more innovative and competitive than we are, and a shot of vodka will only cost you five dollars here, compared with fifteen dollars in Sweden.

"Who cares," asks Andrew Sharp, Canada's resident productivity guru, if Canada does not have a single bank among the world's top thirty, or that Scandinavian pulp and paper mills are "five times" more productive than Canadian ones? Pointing to a United Nations survey of world values, the economist noted that Canadians are among the "happiest" people on earth. And who wouldn't be? Thanks to a combination of sheer luck and relatively little effort, Canadians are among the wealthiest people on the planet. But while most blithely shrug their shoulders and go about their business, some have glimpsed the future; and they are scared.

"Unfortunately, today I'm nervous," says Deszö Horváth, dean of York University's Schulich School of Business. "Canada, by default, not by design, again became raw-materials-oriented as China's demand for raw materials and energy has created a total dislocation in the world. We can live on raw materials and oil and gas, but it's going to go down one day, and unless we develop an alternate corporate structure here, we're not going to be a very successful nation in the future." Alvin Segal, the chairman of Montreal's Peerless Clothing, was less sanguine. "We're a make-believe country, and our make-believe country is falling apart. We can't compete with the world—we have nothing to offer," he says. "We're going on American coat-tails. We have space galore, we're too liberal and we're spoiled."

The telltale signs of the country's stealthy slide, say observers, are all around us. Despite years of respectable, at times enviable, economic growth, foreign investment into Canada has virtually dried up. Dubbed the "canary in the mineshaft" by the Conference Board, Canada's share of world FDI has more than halved over the past twenty-five years to 3 per cent in 2003—levels not seen since the Great Depression of the 1930s.[41] "No one seems to care (about Canada)," admits a puzzled John Klassen, assistant deputy minister of International Trade Canada's investment branch. In contrast, the United States remains atop the global charts, second only to the United Kingdom. Its share of NAFTA-bound investment, along with Mexico's, has grown at the expense of Canada, which has watched its continental take decline by 30 per cent over a decade.[42]

For Chris Lindal, executive vice-president of Ontario homebuilder Viceroy Homes, the most damning proof of Canada's waning allure is China, where a torrent of foreign money has glossed over rampant corruption and political oppression to build gleaming, modern cities that would put Toronto to shame. "This is hugely serious," he says. "Resource-wise and freedom-wise, we are one of the best countries in the world. So why aren't we attracting mammoth amounts of capital investment? We are not. Shanghai is. The rest of the world is passing us by in leaps and bounds, and we don't even realize it."

What many Canadians don't realize is that the dearth of new investment is having a direct effect on their wallets, says Lindal, by helping to hold down wages and sucking the life out of what should be steadily rising living standards. While wages have recently been creeping up on the back of Alberta's oil boom, Canadians' take-home pay has been "stagnating" for years under the twin weights of high taxes and low salaries. Personal disposable income has dropped from 80.5 per cent of U.S. levels in 1985 to 67.7 per cent in 2003, according to the C.D. Howe Institute.[43] "The economic well-being of the average Canadian," concluded the TD Bank in 2005, "has barely advanced in 15 years."[44] Not surprisingly, Canada has gone from having the fifth-highest GDP per capita in the world in 1990 to tenth spot today, surpassed along the way by Ireland, Denmark, Norway, Australia and Austria. Of course, it hasn't been all downhill—to keep up appearances, Canadians have racked up the highest level of personal indebtedness in their history.

The relative decline in prosperity is a harbinger for the country's other major Achilles heel: productivity, or output per worker. A synonym for competitiveness and a driver of living standards, productivity hinges on investment in things like technology, machinery and equipment, research and development, and human capital. Without it, output per worker drops, and so do wages.

Canada's productivity has fallen off dramatically over the past half century, sliding from its third-place ranking among developed countries in 1960 to seventeenth in 2004.* Between 2000 and 2005 it grew just 6.7 per cent (and actually contracted in 2006), while in the United States output per worker expanded by a phenomenal 21.7 per cent. The cumulative effect is a Canadian business sector only 74 per cent as productive as that of the United States—its poorest showing since the mid-1950s and a dramatic drop from 1999, when it registered a comparative productivity of 82 per cent.[45] The lacklustre performance can be measured in dollar bills. The Institute for Competitiveness and Prosperity calculates Canada's growing income gap with the United States at $8,700 per person or an additional $12,100 in after-tax disposable income per family.[46] In 1981 the gap was less than half that, and at the current rate of decline Canadians are expected to earn 50 per cent as much as Americans within twenty-five years.[47]

---

* Between 2000 and 2004, Canada's productivity performance ranked twenty-fourth out of twenty-nine OECD countries.

Some argue that the U.S. "productivity miracle" is a chimera that obscures the cost of competitiveness. In its bid to innovate, offshore and outsource, the United States cut 3.3 million manufacturing jobs between 1998 and 2003, while Canada's employment swelled as business substituted capital with cheap labour to bolster output. But what was thought to be the triumph of a kinder, gentler alternative is turning out to be a pyrrhic victory.

The combination of China's ascendancy and the sudden rise in the Canadian dollar after two decades as a bottom feeder effectively pulled the rug out from under the well-trodden path of least resistance. Between 2003 and 2006, some 300,000 manufacturing jobs were lost as the forestry, furniture and automotive industries hemorrhaged jobs. The number could reach 400,000 by 2007, as close to seven hundred manufacturers went bankrupt in 2005 alone, squeezed by a high dollar, skyrocketing energy prices and shrinking shipments to the United States. The sudden decline had economists busy slashing optimistic growth forecasts for 2007 as Ontario, hit with the bulk of the job losses, flirted with a recession.

With the sector teetering dangerously on the brink, many manufacturers see little choice but to move south of the border to remain competitive. Celestica, Gildan Activewear, Distinctive Designs Furniture, Grant Forest Products, Exco Technologies and E.H. Price, among others, are shifting production south of the border. "If we don't get the productivity, then we'll just switch our production to the U.S.," warns Jim Pattison, whose vast holdings include timber, fisheries and food packaging.[48] As Gerry Price, CEO of Winnipeg-based E.H. Price, explains: "All our plants are highly productive. However, the reality is that all of the niche products we build in Winnipeg could be made even more profitably in Phoenix. There's no economic reason to continue operating in Winnipeg, other than it's my home."[49]

This is not to say that jobs aren't being created. In 2006, new jobs, particularly in the higher-paying professional and managerial ranks, were springing up like weeds on the back of the Alberta oil boom. But for the most part, Canada has largely been churning out temporary

McJobs while relying on self-employment and government to pick up the slack. Between 2000 and 2004, job growth was driven by restaurant work and new security personnel, clerical and retail sales jobs, which both grew by 15 per cent.[50]

One of the big winners has been the telemarketing industry. According to Site Selection Canada, a company that helps American outsourcers set up in Canada, six thousand call centres have been established here over the past decade, creating 400,000 jobs. The jobs pay on average $12.45 an hour and have been portrayed as the magic bullet for towns from Sault Ste. Marie to Red Deer, all struggling with shuttered industries and declining populations. And it's not just small towns that are jumping on the call centre bandwagon. In Ottawa, considered to be Canada's high-tech hub, research-intensive jobs at companies like Corel and JDS Uniphase have quietly migrated south, replaced by the call centre operations of the likes of U.S. computer giant, Dell.[51]

In one magazine article, an American telemarketing company sang the praises of a cheap workforce in which 67 per cent of employees have a post-secondary degree. "You could still pay a Canadian less money [than an American] and have a college graduate, for God's sake, doing the work for you," enthused the company's general manager. "You're dealing with a far more intelligent person here in Canada that will do the job, versus the type of people that they will attract in the States."[52]

Wayne Marston, the Hamilton labour activist, just shakes his head in wonder when he thinks of the country's newest answer to foreign investment—a combination of cheap labour and low capital expenditure reminiscent of Mexico's low-wage, assembly-for-export sector: "It's minimum-wage jobs, transient workers and high turnover. To say call centres are a symbol of the future is idiotic."

Add that to the tens of thousands of skilled immigrants forced to work as cleaners and cab drivers, the software engineer who makes $57,000 compared with an American making $125,000,[53] while the Canadian cities with the highest family income—Oshawa, Ottawa and Windsor—are propped up either by American car makers or the government. Sweeten the pot with a number of important industries teetering on the brink, and the concept of an economy operating at full capacity becomes, well, relative.

Canada's performance is even more questionable when one considers all the Canadians who have been forced to leave the country because the high-quality jobs they seek simply don't exist. The lack of globally oriented firms means that the career path for many is confined to the domestic market while foreign multinationals are increasingly relocating their higher-end jobs abroad, limiting their Canadian presence to sales positions. Schulich Business School launched its international MBA program in 1988 with the aim of supplying Canadian companies with internationally minded graduates, but as Dean Horváth quickly learned, there were no jobs waiting for them when they got out. "So many ended up going abroad and they are still abroad, and it's not getting any better," he says. David Pecaut, senior partner with the Boston Consulting Group in Toronto, can attest to the problem. "I can't tell you the number of people I can think of right now who say they would come back to Canada if they could work in a company that's truly global," he says. "They can't find the opportunities."

Which is why Eamon Hoey, a Toronto businessman, is making sure his daughter doesn't hit her head on the Canadian glass ceiling. "My recommendation to my daughter is to find another country. She'll go to grad school in the U.S. or the U.K., and hopefully that's where she'll end up," he says. "You can't be proud of a country that truncates its youth, prevents it from accomplishing and sets up barriers and systems that create winners and losers."

Glen Hodgson, chief economist with the Conference Board of Canada, admits he's also concerned about his kids' future: "The realist in me is worried. Are we going to go down as a country? Because if you look at the data and use China as a litmus test, we're not succeeding; we're actually seeing our presence in the world shrinking." Canada's long-term economic potential, he says, is "clearly fading." According to a study by Global Insight released in 2006, Canada's growth is forecast to lag behind almost every other major economy within the next twenty years, slipping to below 2 per cent and a far cry from the 3.25 per cent of the 1980s.[54]

So, will Canadians be spurred to action? Husky's Robert Schad doesn't think so. "The Romans didn't wake up until Hannibal was right at the front gates, and the reports came in every day. He was getting closer and closer, and nothing changed until he was there." Schad figures Canada's embarrassment of riches can keep a Hannibal-like incursion by global markets at bay for some time to come. "If things get tough, we will just sell everything off to keep the status quo—just like when you sell your last jewels for a piece of bread," he shrugs. "We can sell off the future for a long time. We can sit on the sidelines for quite a while."

Maybe. Who knew that diamonds were buried beneath the Canadian tundra, or that Alberta's tar-laden oil sands would pump out so many millionaires almost overnight? But while some have hit pay dirt, others are watching as their wells run dry. Just ask the residents of Kitimat, B.C. Founded more than fifty years ago, the picturesque town of ten thousand was supposed to be a model for the province's industrial future. Neat housing subdivisions were carved out of the forest and rock along the northern coast, and industry was lured with the promise of government subsidies. Alcan built a massive aluminum smelter as well as a hydro plant. It was followed by a pulp and paper mill and a petrochemical complex operated by Methanex, the world's largest producer of methanol.

Yet there is growing unease in Kitimat as the population continues to decline and property values plummet. The town is slated to become the port terminus for an ambitious pipeline project that would transport crude oil from Alberta's oil sands to the B.C. coast before being shipped to Asia. But a lack of Chinese buyers for the oil has forced pipeline builder Enbridge to put the project on hold until 2014.* In the meantime, the community has been locked in a decade-long struggle with Alcan to upgrade its aging smelter. In 2006, Alcan finally agreed to go ahead with a US$1.8 billion modernization project on the condition that it be allowed to sell excess electricity from its nearby hydro dam—to the tune of

---

* In contrast, Australia has signed 20- to-30-year energy supply deals with China worth some $30 billion.

$97 million a year—to B.C. Hydro. It's a bitter pill for Kitimat, which argues that the aluminum maker was given privileged access to cheap electricity in return for providing smelter jobs. Instead, new efficiencies at the upgraded smelter would cut the workforce by 30 per cent.* But according to the company, Kitimat, with its high labour and construction costs compared with places like Cameroon and Brazil, is lucky to be getting any new investment at all. As Michel Jacques, head of Alcan's primary metal group, noted, without a deal to sell its surplus electricity, "[i]t makes no economic sense for us to build a new smelter in B.C."[55]

Methanex, the community's other economic anchor, has already cut town. Too fed up to fight with municipal officials over high property taxes and increasingly gouged by the high cost of natural gas (a key ingredient of methanol), the company closed its two plants in November 2005. It is now embarking on plans to build a US$500 million complex in Egypt. "Our experience in Kitimat has been pretty sorry," says Bruce Aitken, Methanex CEO. "Globally we are doing very nicely, thank you very much. But if we were dependent just on our plants in Kitimat, the company wouldn't exist anymore.

"I don't think the government goes out of its way to understand the dynamics of what it is doing to industry in the province," he adds. "Our companies will put up with it for a while, but eventually we will shut the plant down, and that's it."

Sadly, the writing has been on the wall for Kitimat—and Canada—for quite some time. Michael Porter, the Harvard University professor and competitiveness guru, warned of the country's "gentle drift downward" in a 2001 report he co-authored with Roger Martin, dean of University of Toronto's Rotman School of Management.[56] The conclusion followed Porter's watershed assessment of the Canadian economy a decade earlier, entitled "Canada at the Crossroads." At the time, Canada had two options:

---

* In December 2006, the British Columbia Utilities Commission rejected Alcan's electricity agreement with British Columbia Hydro and Power, arguing it was not in the public interest. As a result, Alcan threatened to scrap the project.

either blaze a new trail based on innovative and globally competitive companies, or continue along the path of least resistance. "Canada," Porter and Martin wrote ten years later, "took the lesser path."

As a result, Canadian companies that show potential will continue to be cherry-picked by Americans, depriving Canada of all-important head offices and the means to acquire global management skills.* When it comes to Canadian biopharma companies, says John Mendlein, "they are just going to get acquired by U.S. companies. Full stop." Either that, or they will be overlooked altogether. According to a 2004 Conference Board of Canada survey, three quarters of foreign executives who responded felt that Canada's business environment was "not favourable" for investing, citing, among other things, the slowness of companies to adopt technology and the poor quality of employees.[57] "They see Canadian workers in general as too often undereducated and lagging behind other workers in productivity," wrote board president Anne Golden.[58]

Even China, which is scouring the planet for new investments, seems a bit circumspect. Despite initial panic that China's Minmetals Corp. would acquire Canadian miner Noranda, negotiations trailed off in 2005. Not long after, the Chinese sealed a US$2 billion deal with Chilean copper giant Codelco, and they have invested billions more in Russian housing projects and Australian mining. More than six hundred Chinese-funded companies have set up in Africa over the last decade, investing in Angolan oil, Zambian copper and tropical timber from Congo—all "at the cost of Canada," says BMO's Neil Tate. In 1995, Canada was the leading destination for Chinese outward investment. Today, it doesn't rank among the top ten.

"Canada will just become a nice, pleasant country to visit," says Fred Lazar, of the Schulich School of Business. "We'll have resources and some large companies coddled by government. More and more, foreigners will wonder why they even bother, and the relative standard of living will continue to decline."

---

* Interestingly, the only two major miners still headquartered in Canada, Barrick Gold and Teck Cominco, are both run by Canadian CEOs.

THE TIES THAT BIND

The thing about Gordian knots is they are virtually impossible to unravel. When King Gordius of Phrygia tied the first one, in homage to the god Zeus for making him monarch, the mass of woven bark did not reveal a single exposed end. The intricacy of the knot became a thing of wonder and eventually prompted an oracle to prophesy that the first to untie it would be the next ruler of Asia. The knot remained intact until the arrival of Alexander the Great, who promptly unsheathed his sword and sliced through the bundled fibre. The rest, as they say, is history.

The answer to Canada's own conundrum could be just as deceptively simple. It's not about coming up with convoluted "innovation agendas," productivity perks or even tax-relief schemes tied to the next election. It's about breaking the ties that bind and getting out of our Canadian comfort zone. "What's missing is a bit of moxie," says Interbrand's Jeff Swystun. "The biggest question facing Canada is, do we want to be a player?" Adds federal trade commissioner Bill Johnston, "At the root there has to be ambition, and it comes from having a passion in the first place. The question is whether as a people we have that passion."

If the answer is yes, then the surest way to enter the big leagues is, well, to join them. Trade and foreign investment, in particular, are crucial to being globally competitive. By outsourcing, offshoring and manufacturing abroad, companies can lower costs and boost productivity, resulting in higher profit margins and higher wages. Foreign exposure not only allows companies to access new markets and new technologies, but it hones competitive skills, driving innovation and nurturing managerial know-how.

According to Stephen Poloz, senior vice-president and chief economist at state-run Export Development Canada, "foreign investment by Canadian companies is the biggest factor pointing to productivity gains."[59] A study by TD Bank shows that trade-oriented Canadian firms increased their productivity from 5 to 12 per cent between 2001 and 2004, whereas firms geared solely to the domestic market suffered a decline of 0.4 to 10 per cent.[60] Outward-oriented companies, as numerous studies have shown, are not only more productive, but enjoy higher growth and a better return on capital.

Canadian Manufacturers and Exporters, as part of an action plan to confront what it describes as a "crisis" in Canadian manufacturing, is recommending that Canada not only dramatically increase the share of exports directed outside the United States, but also double the annual growth of outward investment to 16 per cent by 2020. The two goals are highly complementary. Every dollar spent on foreign investment generates on average two dollars in future trade. For fast-growing developing countries, the return is even higher—between three and six times the initial investment.[61] Foreign investment creates "trade bridges," says Poloz, "and once they are built you can't help driving on them."

The economy as a whole also benefits from repatriated profits and the redeployment of the domestic labour force to more sustainable high-value-added jobs. "There is always this agonizing debate about those people who lose their jobs, and nobody talks about the fact the whole growth curve moves outward and makes everything better," says Poloz. "Everyone is better off in this thing, and we know it."

Just look at the United States. Over the past fifty years, U.S. manufacturing output has increased by a factor of six while its share of the workforce dropped from 31 per cent to 11 per cent, says Poloz. And while millions of manufacturing jobs were lost between 1998 and 2003, close to six million new service-sector jobs, mostly professional and high-paying, were created. (A further 5 million non-manufacturing jobs were added from 2003 to July 2006.) Many of the job losses and much of the concomitant surge in productivity, he says, can be traced to investment abroad, with U.S. offshore subsidiaries representing 37 per cent of all U.S. imports and generating $3 trillion in annual sales.

If Canadian companies want to compete in the United States they will need to follow suit—and not only to service their American customers. The real competition is coming from the South Koreans, Taiwanese, Japanese and others who are harnessing China's cheap manufacturing might, says David Fung. A single Taiwanese facility, Shenzhen Foxconn, a subsidiary of

Hon Hai Precision Industry, shipped us$8.3 billion in exports from China in 2004. "Everyone is using the competitive Chinese manufacturing infrastructure to take over our American market. By the time we figure it out, it will be a bit late," says Fung. "If we are willing to fight with one arm tied behind our back, it's our choice. The Asian train is coming down the track. We can stay on the track and get rolled over, or we can steer the train."

The difference between being in the driver's seat and becoming a casualty of the commodity aisle is the ability to source people, materials and technologies internationally, says Michael Novak, executive vice-president of snc–Lavalin. It allows companies to keep their head offices in Canada and to focus on value-added components, such as design, branding, intellectual property and managerial knowledge, that keep them one step ahead of the competition. "We have to see ourselves as managers of a global supply chain, and we have to keep moving up that chain," says Novak.

For Fung, who has made his fortune stitching together international projects that might, for example, marry European technologies and Chinese venture capitalists with Canadian resources, the next rung in the ladder for Canada should be as a global go-between in the tradition of Switzerland or Hong Kong. Neither location has much in the way of natural resources, yet both are international arbitrageurs par excellence, parlaying financial and managerial expertise into global might.

"The Swiss are smarter then we are. They manage to use our resources to make money for themselves," says Fung. "Fortunately or unfortunately, we are spoiled by our own wealth. The hope is, more people will realize we don't need to hack trees down to make a living. We can use our brain power."

According to Amos Michelson, we already do. Former ceo of the Vancouver-based digital printing company Creo, Michelson argues that Canadians have superb technical skills and are relatively *more productive* than their American counterparts. He notes that while Canadians work 75 per cent of the hours of someone in, say, Silicon Valley, they are paid half as much. The upshot is a "cost performance that is much better in Canada than in North America overall," he says. "And you get great people."

The country's real weakness, he says, lies elsewhere. Unfortunately it is the key to unravelling our own Gordian knot. Michelson, who navigated Creo's ballsy breakout from $20 million in sales in 1995 to becoming an $800 million challenger to global leaders like Agfa and Fuji before being bought out by Kodak in 2005, doesn't believe Canada has the raw material necessary to produce high-tech successes like, for example, his native Israel does.

The war-torn, desert-parched spit of land of 6.3 million people is a hotbed of technological innovation, with more high-tech listings on New York's NASDAQ exchange than any other country except the United States. While Canada is flush with all kinds of advantages that other countries might only dream about, it lacks the one thing Israel has in abundance: drive. "Israelis are enormously aggressive in their desire to achieve something. The U.S. is somewhere in the middle, and Canadians are at the other end of the spectrum," says Michelson. "We're nice. But business and nice don't work. Some people do whatever it takes to win, and other people just stop. That's why there are not a lot of important companies in Canada—people are not willing to walk the distance because it's not important to win."

THE ROAD LESS TRAVELLED

Newton, Ontario, is just two hours northwest of Toronto, but it might as well be five centuries away. Horse-drawn buggies kick up dust on the shoulder of quiet country roads while boys in overalls and girls in floppy bonnets and flower-print dresses wait patiently for the school bus to pass. If Hamilton seems a Dickensian relic of the Industrial Revolution, then this small Mennonite community is a portal to a time before the steam engine or the spinning jenny were invented.

Yet the town, which has largely eschewed the trappings of industrial modernity, is a testament to the newest global revolution. Just past the smattering of buildings that line the main street sits the nondescript, aluminum-sided headquarters of Mitchell Mill Systems. A shiny new silver

Cadillac is parked outside, a sure sign that company owner Paul Mitchell is in town from Beijing for one of his shotgun visits home.

An affable fifty-six-year-old with greying hair and ruddy cheeks, Mitchell got his first taste of China in 1989. His company, which manufacturers and installs grain and animal feed–handling equipment, was asked to participate in a project in northern China. Mitchell was immediately struck by the inferior quality of Chinese equipment and thought he could scoop up a share of the market with his superior product while helping to improve China's grain-handling system at the same time.

It was the beginning of a fifteen-year odyssey that Mitchell admits would test his belief in himself and come at great personal cost. He moved to China in 1994 but, unable to afford the astronomical rent that most foreign companies paid to keep their employees in comfort, moved into a rundown flat with bad heating that cost just one hundred dollars a month. "I lived pretty rough for a long, long time," says Mitchell, who also taught himself Mandarin. "I wouldn't do it again if I knew how tough it was. But I was pretty stubborn—I wasn't going to give up now."

But, he acknowledges, he almost did. Not long after he first ventured into China, he sat on his bed in a hotel room, his bags packed, resolved never to return. He had "hit the wall," his nascent joint venture with a Chinese partner had dissolved in acrimony, and he was exhausted by the relentless price gouging and unenforceable contracts. That night, three employees came to visit him and begged him to stay, offering to pick up their families and follow him wherever he went.

Mitchell took them up on their offer and built his own factory outside Beijing. In the end, despite all the hardship, it has paid off. Mitchell estimates that manufacturing component parts in China has made the company 30 per cent more competitive while its presence there has opened up vast new business opportunities. Multinational giants are now knocking on his door to build dozens of feed mills in China, while in Canada, says Mitchell, you are lucky if one mill gets built.

"We never would have gotten these connections just being in Canada," he says. "Being in China has been so beneficial to the company.

So many people have contacted us because we are there. We're recognized more as an international company."

The company, in turn, has grown by leaps and bounds, with more business than Mitchell knows what to do with. In the past decade, the workforce has expanded from thirty to eighty people and sales have increased tenfold. And like a stream that flows downhill, it all trickles back to Canada. "All the profit comes right back here," he says. "The business is growing, so I hire more people, I buy more equipment from here [for the Chinese operations] and I can hire more salespeople here. Everybody is benefiting from us being in China."

Yet despite finally reaping the rewards after years of struggle, Mitchell sold the Chinese subsidiary in 2006. His two sons, who both work at the Newton factory, live on sprawling acreages outside of town. They saw what expanding into China cost their father, and they are not willing to make the same sacrifices. Nor do they have to. Mitchell, a farmer's son, immigrated to Canada at the age of nine from England. His family lived hand-to-mouth, eating a lot of vegetable soup and crackers and maybe, if they were lucky, meat on Sundays. He remembers, at fourteen, vowing he would never be poor.

That conviction, and "a pioneering spirit," is what he believes compelled him twice in his life to take the road less travelled. The first time was when, at the age of just sixteen, he signed up for the navy. The second was when he was twenty-nine, with three kids and two mortgages, and he decided to forfeit a steady paycheque and strike out on his own.

In both cases he started out with a Canadian-born companion, and both times he was abandoned at the last minute, left to make the risky journey alone. Just as he was about to board the train for Halifax, the high school friend who had enlisted in the navy with him backed out. When it came time to start his own business, his would-be partner changed his mind, opting to keep his job at their old place of work. Mitchell eventually went on to hire his former co-worker. "He used to tell me," says Mitchell with a smile, "that it was the biggest mistake he ever made."

3 | TARIFFS AND TRAINS: HISTORY'S LAST SPIKE

> "Canadian businessmen, in their cautiousness, have carried
> their slowness to decide upon a matter too far for their own
> good, and have in their desire to be absolutely safe let pass
> many a good opportunity."
>
> FRANCIS HECTOR CLERGUE, FOUNDER OF ALGOMA STEEL, 1901

SIR JOHN A. MACDONALD, Canada's first prime minister, spent much of his long and colourful career haunted by demons, real and perceived. In the mid-1870s, the threat was particularly ominous for the country's number one nation builder and unabashed power broker. The fledging confederation of thinly populated and disparate territories that Macdonald cobbled together in 1867 seemed in danger of dying on the vine. The world was grappling with the first-ever global depression, as advances in transportation and technology had sent commodity prices tumbling. Trade in Canadian cod and logs had fallen flat while a quarter of the country's four million inhabitants had headed south to work in the textile mills of New England and the blast furnaces of Pittsburgh.

America's newfound industrial might and the threat of annexation loomed large over the newly minted country, adding to the dark clouds already swirling over Macdonald's uncertain political future. Forced to resign in 1873 after being caught offering railroad entrepreneurs lucrative concessions in return for handsome campaign contributions, Macdonald was anxious to rehabilitate his tarnished reputation and reclaim his hold on power. The question was, how?

Cheap, American-made products were flooding the Canadian market, prompting wide-scale layoffs and factory closures. It was becoming increasingly clear that "marauding Americans" and high U.S. tariffs, imposed after the Americans abrogated the reciprocity agreement with the provinces in 1866, were to blame.* Was there not a way to harness the growing disaffection in the streets and its strong anti-American undertones, in such a manner as to rehabilitate Sir John's sagging fortunes while securing Canada's fragile nationhood?

In the latter half of the 1870s, the Ontario Manufacturers' Association,† riding a wave of protectionist sentiment, provided Macdonald with just such an opportunity. The group proposed raising a tariff wall around domestic industry. By keeping foreign manufacturers out, local producers could expand their market with unhampered and mutually beneficial trade within the Dominion. Ontario could ship her breadstuffs to the Maritimes in exchange for Nova Scotia steel, all the while providing desperately needed jobs for the nation. The tariff would not only earn Macdonald the loyalty of the manufacturing interests but, if presented in the proper light, that of the working class as well, while appealing to the nascent tugs of nationhood.

The close alliance forged between Macdonald's Tories and the Ontario manufacturers struck a highly effective chord, and in 1879 Sir John, successfully reinstalled in the prime minister's office, unveiled the now-famous National Policy. The plan, which aimed to foster nascent industries through a high protective tariff, evolved into an ambitious

---

* The United States abrogated reciprocity for two principal reasons: to protest British involvement in the American civil war by pressuring Canadians to drop their allegiance to the British, and as a reprisal for Canada's Cayley–Galt Tariff of 1858, which imposed a 20 per cent tariff on imported manufactured goods.

† The Ontario Manufacturers' Association became the Canadian Manufacturers' Association in 1877.

blueprint for national development that included the building of a trans-continental railway and the settlement of the West. Each prong of the policy would be to the benefit of the others and would be financed through the revenue-generating tariff.

The natural outgrowth of a colonial mindset that had long been geared to favouring corporate elites and heavy-handed government intervention, the tariff also appealed to an already deeply rooted belief that Canada's "infant industries" needed to be nurtured if they were to grow and eventually compete in international markets. Before the tariff was erected, Ottawa was flooded with petitions for protection, notes Ben Forster, a Canadian business historian, in his book *A Conjunction of Interests*: "A bemused Lord Lorne reported to England that 'everyone who has ever raised a pig or caught a smelt wants protection for his industry.'"[62]

But what made the National Policy so different and ultimately seared it into the Canadian consciousness was its ability to equate the protection of vested interests with a nationalistic endeavour to protect the Canadian identity. As Sir John ably explained, the country needed to foster industry "to bring out the national mind and the national strength and to form a national character."[63] For a country whose half-hearted move from colony to British dependency had been a dry act of legislative calculation, it was the closest thing to a popular call to arms. "It was a brilliant political play by the manufacturing class," says Duncan McDowall, professor of Canadian business history at Carleton University. "It combined protectionism, national policy and the identity of the country."

The emotional link between trade and nationalism would colour Canadian policy decisions for the next century, inextricably melding patriotism and protectionism. The National Policy, under the guise of serving the public good, would encourage the creation of coddled state-sanctioned monopolies while entrenching a clique of well-connected businessmen trained to seek government favour. Perhaps most damaging of all, the high tariff walls and obsession with making "Canadian goods for Canadian people" would blind Canadians to selling to the rest of the world.

Originally presented as a temporary measure aimed at pressuring the Americans into reciprocity, the tariff became indelibly etched into the Canadian business model. Protecting national turf and shutting out foreign competition became part of the "genetic code" of the business community, says McDowall. According to Roger Martin, dean of the Rotman School of Management, "The National Policy was the most damaging thing to happen to Canadian business. There should have been a sunset clause, like parenting."

At the time, however, it appeared to work, at least in the beginning. The economic depression seemed to end as agricultural prices rose and as factories, refineries and mills sprang up across the country. Quebec and the Maritimes, hoping to repeat the success of New England, built textile mills. Sugar refineries went up in Halifax, Montreal and British Columbia, while tariffs on coal and iron fuelled ambitious iron and steel works—the symbol of industrial success in the nineteenth century—in Nova Scotia.

But as miners in Cape Breton dug for coal to feed the forges and blast furnaces, it quickly became clear that tariffs on primary steel and iron also hurt a number of industries that relied on the primary material, including foundries, sewing machine manufacturers, agricultural implement makers and engine works. As Sir Richard Cartwright, the former Liberal finance minister and free-trade supporter, pointed out at the time: "A great many manufacturers are suffering seriously from the National Policy, and that fact can hardly be brought out too prominently."[64] Hamstrung by highly taxed inputs, manufacturers were effectively condemned to the Canadian market, their products too costly to compete abroad.

But there was an even more insidious and, in the long run, arguably more damaging side effect of the National Policy. Despite their ostensible goal of erecting walls to keep out unscrupulous Americans, the tariffs had the opposite effect. While later Canadian "nationalists" would argue that American firms had somehow managed to circumvent the tariffs, the barriers expressly or indirectly encouraged the wholesale relocation of American subsidiaries to Canadian soil.

The combined effect of the National Policy and of the 1872 Patent Act, which allowed non-residents to hold Canadian patents on the condition that they manufacture domestically within two years, was to graft American industrial might onto its weaker northern neighbour. The result was the immediate transfer of American technology and the growth of Canadian manufacturing, and, most importantly, jobs. By that measure, it was a resounding success. The trickle of American investment widened into a torrent as U.S. transnationals set up branch plants to serve the Canadian domestic market or to re-export to the British Empire using Canada's imperial trade preferences.

The Americans were often lured by municipalities, anxious for industrial development, that vied with each other to offer cash bonuses, tax exemptions, free land, interest-free loans and even wage subsidies. Hamilton offered a free seventy-five-acre site and $100,000 for American investors to erect an iron and steel mill in the city. Similar enticements were dangled in front of Westinghouse and International Harvester. By the early 1900s, many of the biggest U.S. companies had jumped the wall, including Singer Sewing Machine, American Tobacco, Gillette and Coca-Cola. By 1914, Canada was home to 450 branch plants and subsidiaries. Fifteen years later, more than 40 per cent of the nation's machinery, 68 per cent of its chemical products and 83 per cent of its automobiles were manufactured in American-owned factories.[65]

As Americans piled into Canada, scant few Canadians were attempting to scale the high walls they had erected around themselves. There were some exceptions. A year after Samuel Moore launched his business-forms printing company in 1882, he opened a factory in Niagara Falls, New York, to manufacture sales books. He expanded into Australia and Britain, and in 1929 moved into Latin America, eventually turning his Moore Corp. into the world's largest business-forms company.

For many years, however, Ontario farm-equipment manufacturer Massey Harris was Canada's first and only true multinational. By 1888, buoyed by its strong marketing and innovative designs, the company was exporting to Australia, Africa, Germany, Russia, South America and

Jamaica. Not surprisingly, Massey Harris opposed the tariff policy, arguing that duties on steel and metal parts made it impossible to compete against American rivals in foreign markets. In 1894 the company threatened to shift production to the United States if the government didn't refund the onerous levies.

Massey Harris's contrarian stance was indicative of pattern that would quickly emerge in Canadian business: Daniel Massey, the company's founder, was an American who had moved to Northumberland county in the early 1800s. (The Harris family, who merged their farm-machinery company with Massey, were also American émigrés.) According to Glen Williams, author of *Not for Export*, Massey's opposition to the tariff was symptomatic of "many aggressive expatriate Americans who did not fear world competition and who, in fact, had not given up their dreams of access to the larger U.S. market."[66]

The other significant international foray was by a coterie of businessmen in Montreal and Toronto who had grown rich on the railways and had branched out into streetcar franchises and electric utilities. In 1898, a Canadian syndicate led by Fred Stark Pearson bought a concession to build an electric streetcar in São Paulo, Brazil. The group went on to build the trolley system in neighbouring Rio de Janeiro as well as the power plants for both cities. Eventually incorporated as Brazilian Traction, Light and Power Co.—better known until recently as Brascan*—the company's reach was so extensive that it became known as the "Canadian octopus" and until the 1950s was Canada's largest overseas investment. "There is no denying Rio and São Paulo are the cities they are today because of the access to cheap energy [that Brascan provided]," says McDowall.

Pearson, a brilliant engineer and indefatigable adventurer, followed up on the Brazilian success by branching out into Mexico and later Spain. One of his main backers was Sir William Van Horne, the fabled president and general manager of the Canadian Pacific Railway, who had built Cuba's railway and backed another in Guatemala, along with utilities in

---

* In 2005, Brascan changed its name to Brookfield Asset Management.

Jamaica. The two men had at least two things in common: they were both at the forefront Canada's newly forged engineering prowess and they were both American.

Perhaps as a sign of things to come, the Ontario energy utilities were nationalized in 1906. The move was once again backed by the Canadian Manufacturers' Association, which, unhappy with high electricity prices, had lobbied for public ownership of the utility. Sadly, despite the impressive engineering ability and experience in power generation, Canada would never again venture into international markets on such a scale, limiting itself to obscure forays by bureaucratic and ill-equipped provincially run corporations.

For the vast majority of Canadians, however, the domestic market was the only one that mattered. Perhaps chafing from the high U.S. tariffs, domestic producers defended what they saw as their rightful claim with an almost siege-like ferocity: "In these days of overproduction, when nation is fighting against nation for possession of markets, and when commercial war is hotter the civilized world over than ever it was before—what seems the most sensible course for us?" asked an editorial by the Canadian Manufacturers' Association during the return of economic turmoil in 1885. "Clearly this, we should say to hold our own—to keep a fast grip of the home market, the only one that we can hold, if we choose, against all comers."[67]

Not only was the international success of companies like Massey Harris "inconceivable" to most, according to historian Michael Bliss, but Canadian manufacturers displayed an "almost neurotic abhorrence of exporting."[68] As one frustrated trade commissioner, based in Argentina, wrote in a 1912 dispatch to Ottawa: "It is an inexplicable thing but many manufacturers appear to fear the very thought of the export trade; they apparently harbour the delusion that it is full of pitfalls for the unwary, full of unknown risks, and that once embarked upon it there can be no return to domestic trade."[69]

As Glen Williams assiduously documents in *Not for Export*, Canadian companies rarely even responded to queries from overseas buyers. When they did export, it was usually sloppy, with the sole aim of dumping surplus stock. Manufacturers routinely failed to fill orders on time, exporting substandard and obsolete product, in some cases not even taking the time to properly package the goods for the long overseas journey.

The shoddy performance, Williams and others argue, can in large part be blamed on Canada's reliance on American technology and branch plants. Instead of replacing imports with domestic production, subsidiaries acted as a conduit for American parts, machinery and brand names while Canadian licensees of U.S. patents had no incentive to develop an indigenous technological base. The result was the creation of a backward and un-innovative industrial structure that was highly dependent on Americans for technology, capital and managerial expertise. "Canadian manufacturing from its point of origin," Williams writes, "was never in a position to become a competitive force in the world economy."[70]

It would be in direct contrast to Sweden, a country that faced many of the same challenges as Canada—a sparse population and forbidding geography—and until the early 1900s had lagged behind Canada in industrial development. Although Sweden relied on similar resources such as forestry, farming and mining, and had a smaller home market than Canada, it exhibited a penchant for developing engineering innovations. More importantly, it saw international markets as a natural extension of its domestic economy.

In 1907, the Swedish firm SKF invented the modern ball bearing, and within five years it was the world's leading exporter. In 1876, Lars Magnus Ericsson adapted Alexander Graham Bell's invention to create the first table telephone. Within twenty years Ericsson's company set up its first foreign plant and was exporting 80 per cent of its production. When the country's forest reserves began to run low, the Swedes looked for value-added alternatives, first inventing and exporting matches and then establishing the first chemical pulp factory in 1872. By 1914, Sweden was the world's leading pulp exporter.[71]

Academics point to the fact that Sweden blocked foreign investment and had a powerful military, which fostered technological development.

But they acknowledge that the underlying determinant and what ultimately differentiated Sweden from Canada had more to do with "inventiveness, entrepreneurial ability" and most importantly a "sense of national identity."[72] By 1914, Canada was the only "late developing" industrial country—a list that included Japan, Sweden and Italy—that had not developed an independent manufacturing economy. The National Policy's central purpose of creating an indigenous industrial base had, instead, produced the opposite effect.

Perhaps that is why Prime Minister Wilfrid Laurier, who had presided over an unprecedented era of economic growth and prosperity, decided to change tack and campaign on a bold bid for unrestricted reciprocity with the United States. His subsequent humiliating defeat in the 1911 election would leave a lasting psychic mark on government policy-makers and perpetuate the belief for the next eighty years that Canadians couldn't compete in the world.

Everything that came after would in some way reinforce or expand upon the original National Policy tariff. During World War I, when Canadian exports surged, it was the government that procured the foreign contracts to supply bullets and uniforms, secured the financing for overseas buyers and often oversaw production in Canada's factories. As the war wound down, leading members of the Canadian Manufacturers' Association called for the creation of a government agency that would drum up business for Canadian factories in foreign markets and divvy up the sales orders among local manufacturers. If Canadian product was not competitively priced, argued F. H. Whitton, president of the Steel Co. of Canada, "our manufacturers should have the right to call on the government to make up the difference."[73] He also demanded that the government furnish the boats to ship the goods overseas. Amazingly, the government acquiesced, supplying a sixty-three vessel merchant marine fleet. But by 1923, almost half of the vessels were decommissioned due to their high cost and lack of use.

Not surprisingly, Canada failed to capitalize on European post-war reconstruction efforts, only to be hit by the Great Depression and a reinforced wall of U.S. tariffs. Prime Minister R.B. Bennett, a Conservative, responded by upping the tariff to its highest level yet and introducing industrial cartels, otherwise known as marketing boards, which allowed trade associations to effectively price fix—a legacy Canada still wrestles with today.

By the time World War II rolled around, everyone agreed the government had to "protect" Canadians from the brutalities of the free market. That guiding hand would come in the form of C.D. Howe, whose twenty-two-year reign as "minister of everything" left the most lasting imprint on the modern Canadian economy of any politician or businessman in the nation's history. A businessman at heart, Howe was nevertheless far from laissez-faire. He believed the Canadian economy was best served by private, regulated monopolies or Crown corporations, establishing the CBC and sponsoring the country's nuclear ambitions while subsidizing everything from steel to airplane manufacture. In 1935, as minister of transport, he quashed a private airline initiative and organized Trans-Canada Air Lines, a subsidiary of another Crown corporation, Canadian National Railways, and hand-picked its senior managers.*

After the war, the steady flow of foreign investment seemed to reach a kind of apex when Howe unveiled plans to build the first transcontinental gas pipeline. The mega-project would mirror in many ways the country's first transcontinental nation-building exercise, the CPR. Like the railway, the government-subsidized monopoly would largely be the work of Americans. Not only was TransCanada PipeLines, the company behind the project, American, but so was Howe.

This fact was increasingly starting to grate on Canadians' evolving sense of national identity. Rich and confident in their post-war prosperity, they became convinced that the American money that had often been actively enticed across the border was now holding them back. Canadians weren't exporting, many argued, because U.S. companies

---

* For a fascinating account of this episode see Shirley Render, *Double Cross: The Inside Story of James A. Richardson and Canadian Airways* (Vancouver: Douglas & McIntyre, 1999).

were barring their Canadian subsidiaries from developing markets. How that stopped Canadian entrepreneurs from going abroad—despite a myriad of government subsidies and regional development programs—nobody seemed to ask.

To wean the country off its reliance on the Americans, Prime Minister John Diefenbaker promised to divert 15 per cent of Canadian trade to England from the United States. Not long after Pierre Trudeau came to power in 1968, a sustained attack against foreign ownership was launched. In what seems now like a kind of Orwellian paranoia more suited to the likes of Venezuelan generals, the Trudeau government set up the Foreign Investment Review Agency in 1975 to determine whether foreign acquisitions of Canadian assets were of "significant benefit to the Canadian economy."

The iron curtain also came down on cultural industries. In what Michael Bliss describes as "an elaborate extension of the old tariff based on the economic nationalism of the National Policy,"[74] foreign ownership was banned in key strategic industries that somehow became intimately identified—as manufacturing had been a century before—with the Canadian identity. The protection of fragile cultural industries like broadcasting, the press, financial services, publishing and motion picture distribution became the new National Policy.

The National Energy Policy of 1980 was the icing on the cake. Trudeau, like John A. Macdonald, thought he could protect Canadians from the global oil crisis by *legislating* the price of oil, independent of world markets. Through a combination of expropriation and massive subsidies, the federal government also attempted to wrest control of the oil industry from foreign operators in an effort to create Canadian and government-owned oil giants. A dangerous mix of naïveté and hubris, the grand scheme ended in a spectacular flame-out when the price of oil, which the government had forecast to reach $80 per barrel, plunged, and it was forced to bail out bankrupted oil companies to the tune of hundreds of millions of dollars.*

---

* By 1987 the spot price for oil tanked to $10 a barrel.

The ensuing economic crisis finally forced the government's hand. After having exhausted its National Policy treasure chest, it seemed the only other option was to acknowledge the 800-pound gorilla the country had tried to ignore since the time of John A. Macdonald: reciprocity. It would take more than a century and generate spectacular waste and massive deficits, but the National Policy was finally laid to rest with the 1989 Canada–U.S. Free Trade Agreement. But, as Professor McDowall notes, its legacy lives on.

Vestiges of the policy remain, from the government support for Bombardier to the decision by the Ontario government to bail out Stelco. It is there in the painful absence of Canadian multinationals and the plethora of "pridefully dozing"[75] oligopolies that continue to eschew competition in favour of divvying up the domestic market. It is there in the flagging technological innovation, over-reliance on natural-resource exports and the corporate strategies that Michael Porter describes as "distinctively incompatible with global competitiveness."[76]

It can even be found in the woefully few women who lead the country's corporations. The vested interests that the National Policy helped to entrench are still evident in the amazingly resilient old boys' network that continues to control the top echelons of corporate power. In a listing of the top five hundred Canadian companies in 2004, there were only two women CEOs, and both were daughters of the owners. Likewise, in a 2005 survey of Canadian corporate boards by the *Globe and Mail*, 44 per cent did not have a single woman member.[77]

Most of all, it is in the mindset—one in which lobbying government is often the first point of sale and decisions are taken in isolation from the broader global context, as if the rest of the world were static and somehow secondary. Like a snail that retracts when prodded, Canadians tend to react defensively to foreign stimuli rather than aggressively seek out opportunity. The problem is, hiding in one's shell is about the most dangerous thing one can do these days.

"We're genetically geared to Ottawa and the national market and we've got it into our minds that international markets are threatening," says McDowall. "The old mindset has been instilled in us since Confederation, and it will take a long, long time to get rid of, especially in today's precarious, dog-eat-dog world. At home it's comfortable, we know the market, the levers to pull. The international market is not that simple and therefore not that comfortable.

"We've still got a long way to go to transition to the international economy," adds the historian. "We're babes in the woods."

THE REAL PIONEERS

So if the Dominion, as the Canadian Manufacturers' Association counselled in 1890, could enjoy "the acme of prosperity, although it has never a ship upon the ocean and has no foreign trade whatever,"[78] how did Canadians get where they are today? With their eyes trained on the vast territory they had inherited, were they scouring the glacier-scarred bedrock and wind-whipped plains in a breathless bid to unlock the country's hidden riches? Did they take high-stakes risks to harness the power of Quebec's roiling rivers or, defying the odds, sink shafts deep into the rust-flecked granite of northern Manitoba? Was it their wit, pluck and dauntless ambition that breathed life into the untamed hinterland, laying the foundations for what would become bastions of Canadian natural-resource and industrial might?

There were, without doubt, some amazingly resourceful and entrepreneurial Canadians, from the rush of hardscrabble mining prospectors out to stake their claim, to Fred McMahon, the indomitable wheeler-dealer whose company, Westcoast Transmission, carved the first pipeline through the Canadian Rockies to Vancouver. But if we dig below the surface, to the roots of not only many of the country's mining and lumber towns but also its most important companies, we invariably find American money, management and ingenuity. Whether it was Nova Scotia steel, Saskatchewan potash, B.C. logging, Alberta oil, Quebec aluminum or Ontario uranium and copper, "Yankee promoters," as they used to be called, were behind them all.

Our story begins with Samuel J. Ritchie, an irrepressible entrepreneur always on the lookout for the next great windfall. A school teacher by trade, he dabbled in the lumber industry and owned a carriage manufacturer before a fire destroyed his sewer-pipe factory in 1878. He turned his attention north, buying a stake in a railroad and fifteen thousand acres of a mining property in central Ontario that soon proved worthless. By 1885, he was on the verge of bankruptcy when a sample of copper-rich rock from Sudbury, on display at an Ottawa museum, caught his eye.*

Ever the itinerant salesman, Ritchie lost no time convincing his Ohio business partners to purchase a number of mining properties in Sudbury, forming the Canadian Copper Co. in 1886 with headquarters in Cleveland. He begged, borrowed and bought second-hand mining equipment, only to discover his supposed copper mines had a significant percentage of nickel, at the time a minor metal of very limited use. After spending months in Washington lobbying the American government to lower the tariffs on the import of unrefined nickel, he set about cajoling the U.S. military to investigate potential military applications for the resilient metal.

Despite Ritchie's doggedness, the "father of Sudbury" was beset by financial woes, and his backers ousted him from the company in 1891. He spent the next decade fighting them in the courts. In 1902, when a settlement was finally reached, the company was sold and amalgamated with a series of other mining American-controlled ventures to become the International Nickel Co. (INCO), headquartered in New Jersey. Ritchie was compensated and built himself a sprawling mansion back home, but he would never reap the rewards of INCO's new majority owner, Charles Schwab,† president of U.S. Steel, and the American managers who would transform it into the world's largest nickel company.

---

* As Matt Bray, a retired professor from Laurentian University and INCO historian, notes, Ritchie first spied a Sudbury rock sample in a Montreal railway office. He had it tested but did nothing about it until seeing a second sample in Ottawa.

† Schwab was assumed to be acting on the behalf of U.S. Steel and its controlling shareholder, American financier J.P. Morgan, although this was never proven.

A New York banker, Ambrose Monell, was the president of INCO for its first fifteen years, before handing the reins over to Robert C. Stanley, an American engineer and inventor of a pioneering rust-resistant nickel alloy, who presided over the company for a quarter of a century. His successor, John Fairfield Thompson, after whom the northern Manitoba mining town Thompson is named, was a scientist from Maine and an early developer of the stainless steel sink. INCO's American tradition continued right up until 2006, when current chief executive Scott Hand, a former New York City lawyer and U.S. Peace Corps officer, sold the company to Brazil's CVRD.

Both Monell and Stanley were also involved in another major mining development just north of Sudbury, in Timmins. In the summer of 1909, prospector Jack Wilson discovered a vein of gold dubbed the Golden Stairway in an area known as the Porcupine. Wilson was financed by a Chicago businessman, W.S. "Pop" Edwards, who later recruited other American backers, including Monell, to launch what would become Dome Mines. In 1915, Dome was listed on the New York Stock Exchange, and under the tutelage of Jules Bache, a New York investment banker who headed the company until 1942, Dome developed mines in Val-d'Or, Quebec, and branched out into oil and gas exploration, spearheading the ill-fated Trudeau-era push into the Arctic that bankrupted the company.

A few years after the Porcupine discovery, Harry Oakes, a flamboyant gold digger who had travelled the world in search of his fortune, finally hit the jackpot at Kirkland Lake in 1918. Born in the sleepy town of Sangerville, Maine, Oakes joined the Klondike gold rush, was shipwrecked off the Alaskan coast and taken prisoner by the Russian czar, eventually making his way from Australia to the Belgian Congo before ending up in northeastern Ontario. His Lake Shore mine was, for a time, the largest gold producer in the western hemisphere. Oakes became a Canadian citizen in 1924, but after hefty campaign contributions to the Liberal Party failed to win him a Senate appointment and massive new taxes were levied on his property, he moved to Nassau, Bahamas. He was later found brutally murdered in his bed, his body doused with gasoline and burned.

Just across the Quebec border from Kirkland Lake, another mine was developed a few years later, this time a copper-gold interest in the township of Rouyn.

In 1922, a syndicate of American investors looking for mining opportunities bought the options to a claim that would form the cornerstone of one of Canada's leading companies. The syndicate, led by Humphrey Chadbourne, a mining engineer, included former U.S. ambassadors, New York lawyers and former executives from U.S. Steel and the chemical company DuPont. A secretary in the syndicate's New York office suggested a name for the new mine—since it was in northern Canada, why not call it Noranda?

Around the time the Noranda mine was coming on stream, another American had made his way up to Sudbury to found that city's other major mine. Thayer Lindsley was born in Japan to an American father working as an executive for the Canadian Pacific Railway. Endowed with the ability to "see into rocks," Lindsley, together with a handful of colleagues, bought a group of claims from famed U.S. inventor Thomas Edison, in the Falconbridge Township. Edison thought the deposits could be a source of nickel for a storage battery he had designed, but he was discouraged by the difficult terrain. Lindsley kept drilling, however, and Falconbridge Nickel Mines was born.

Considered one of the fathers of Canadian mining, Lindsley was a driving force in the development of a half dozen major mines in Canada, including the Giant mine in Yellowknife and the Yukon's United Keno Hill. He was also behind the development of an ore body staked in the harsh Canadian Shield of northern Manitoba by a young American-born trapper and prospector, Carlton Sherritt. Just five years after striking it rich, Sherritt died when he fell out of his brand-new plane shortly after taking off from The Pas. His name, however, would live on in Sherritt Gordon Mines and the town of Sherridon, where he made his fortuitous strike.

About 150 kilometres southwest of the newly sunk Sherridon mine, another copper deposit was coming on stream under the aegis of Cornelius Vanderbilt Whitney. The rough-and-tumble town of Flin Flon was as incongruous a place as any for the scion of American wealth and aristocracy. Cornelius was the son of Gertrude Vanderbilt Whitney, heiress to the Vanderbilt railroad and shipping fortune and founder of the Whitney Museum of American Art in New York. Cornelius's paternal family were fabulously wealthy thoroughbred horse racers whose ancestors included Eli Whitney, the inventor of the cotton gin.

A prodigious talent in his own right, Whitney was co-founder and chairman of Pan American Airways, wrote several books, produced the Hollywood blockbusters *Gone with the Wind* and *A Star Is Born* and served as U.S. assistant secretary of the air force and undersecretary of commerce. Perhaps it is not surprising then, when, in 1928, a group of American engineers approached him with the idea of developing a vast, low-grade ore body, far from railway links or hydroelectric power, he took them up on it. The property had languished for more than a decade, but within three years of incorporating Hudson's Bay Mining & Smelting, Whitney had an operating mine, smelter, hydroelectric dam and railway link.

One of the other great mining landmarks of the 1920s was the creation of Placer Development. Unlike the other mining companies being built at the time, its founders were not American, nor were its mines, at first, in Canada. Charles Banks was a British-educated mining engineer from New Zealand, whereas Addison Freeman was an Australian with American business connections. The two entrepreneurs incorporated the company in Vancouver to take advantage of favourable tax laws and immediately set out on a risky venture to dredge alluvial gold on the other side of the world, in New Guinea. From the South Pacific the company moved to South America, only entering British Columbia in a significant way much later. In 1987, it merged with Dome Mines to form Placer Dome.

So whether it is INCO, Noranda, Falconbridge, Sherritt Gordon or Placer Dome, just about every major Canadian mining company is the product of foreign, mostly American, investment. And it's the same story with steel. The great blast furnaces that became the hallmark of Sydney, Nova Scotia, and the countless coal mines tunnelled below Cape Breton were the domain of H.M. Whitney, a Boston industrialist who had made his fortune building streetcars. In 1899, Whitney, with government aid, built the first modern blast furnace and open hearth in Canada. In 1921, Nova Scotia's various steel and coal properties as well as its shipyards were merged and modernized under a British-backed syndicate headed up by Roy Wolvin, an American-born shipping expert whose brutal clampdown on striking steelworkers earned him the dubious moniker "Roy the Wolf."

While Wolvin would go down in Nova Scotia history as a rapacious capitalist, another American steel promoter would be hailed as one of Canada's greatest captains of industry. Francis Hector Clergue, a charismatic entrepreneur from Maine, had tried his hand at streetcars, mountain-top resorts and a railway across Persia, with varying degrees of success. In 1894, on hearing of an opportunity to buy a hydroelectric company at Sault Ste. Marie, the intrepid promoter, backed by a group of Philadelphia investors, made his way into the backwoods of Ontario.

The utility became the basis of an entire complex of industrial ventures. Clergue used the power to fuel a large pulp mill, machine shop and foundry, and then set his mind to exploring for minerals. His iron ore mine became the largest in Canada, and he not only built a railroad and lake freighters to move the ore, but a huge iron and steelworks at Sault Ste. Marie. In 1902 Algoma Steel rolled out the first steel rail ever made in Canada. Clergue had taken on the steel supremacy of Pittsburgh and Birmingham, accomplishing what no Canadian steel producer had ever dared. As historian Michael Bliss noted, "The irony of course was that Clergue, an American, had had more faith in Canada than the Canadians themselves."[79]

Clergue's steely tenacity would be matched by another American, Clifton W. Sherman, a foundry manager and son of a Pittsburgh blast furnace superintendent who moved to Hamilton from Buffalo. In 1912, Sherman was in his forties and had no business experience, but it did not stop him from launching the Dominion Steel Casting Co.—better known today as Dofasco.

Hamilton's other major steelworks, Stelco, was the product of an amalgamation in 1910 of five separate companies, orchestrated by New Brunswick–born Max Aitken, whose brilliant financial machinations later earned him the title of Lord Beaverbrook. Needless to say, several of the companies had American underpinnings. Stelco's main Hilton Works foundry was originally developed by a group of New York industrialists and bankers attracted to Hamilton by the promise of free land and a two-dollar-per-ton bonus on pig iron.

Canadians would take an equally complacent, almost expectant, attitude to the development of other resources, from lumber to aluminum, although when it came to oil they were simply overwhelmed, at least at first. The tariff protection offered to Ontario's small independent oil producers was no match for John D. Rockefeller, the billionaire oil tycoon. His Standard Oil flooded the Ontario market and in 1898 bought Imperial Oil of Canada, the last redoubt of domestic producers.

Imperial opened Canada's first service station in 1907, built the nation's first pipeline and for years enjoyed a virtual monopoly over oil refining. In 1947 it struck oil at Leduc, Alberta, marking a watershed in the province's development. The discovery sparked an influx of foreign oil giants in the 1950s and 1960s, and by the early 1970s, 90 per cent of the oil and gas industry was foreign controlled. In fact, most major independent Canadian oil producers operating today—Nexen, Talisman and Suncor—are spin-offs of foreign multinationals.

Although oil had not yet been discovered in neighbouring British Columbia, its lush forests also drew foreign corporations and fortune seekers. The once-mighty lumber giant Crown Zellerbach, based in San Francisco, moved north in the early 1900s, eventually building pulp and paper mills in Campbell River and Ocean Falls. Columbia Cellulose of New York built the Prince Rupert pulp mill, while Bloedel, Stewart & Welch, a family company operating out of Washington state, developed the Port Alberni mill.

Walter, Leon, Otto and Theodor Koerner, Czechoslovakian Jews who rebuilt their family lumber empire on Vancouver Island, were among a wave of Europeans to escape to the B.C. coast in the wake of World War II. John Prentice and L.L. "Poldi" Bentley founded Canadian Forest Products soon after arriving from Austria. The company, better known today as

Canfor, is Canada's largest softwood producer. Prentice and Bentley were followed by three brothers, Samuel, Henry and William Ketchum, who made their way up to Vancouver from Washington state in 1955 in search of a new source of lumber for their family-owned wholesale business. Their West Fraser Timber is now the third-largest lumber producer in North America.

Of course, the history of British Columbia's forestry industry would not be complete without mentioning Harvey Reginald MacMillan, the hard-driving lumber baron who built the largest integrated forest-products company Canada had ever seen. Unlike so many of the country's industrial leaders, MacMillan was Canadian, born on a farm outside of Toronto, poor and fatherless from the age of two. But what really made him different, especially from his own countrymen, was that he travelled.

The B.C. industry was heavily reliant on U.S. brokers to sell its wood, and with the outbreak of World War I there was concern that it would become particularly vulnerable to a wartime disruption in trade. The provincial government decided to send out its chief forester—MacMillan—to gain firsthand knowledge of world markets. He toured the globe, visiting Britain, South Africa, India and Australia, and quickly saw the money to be made by coordinating the sale of lumber on international markets. In 1921, he founded his own shipping company, and by 1928 H.R. MacMillan Exports controlled a quarter of British Columbia's lumber exports. When the company merged with Bloedel, Stewart & Welch Ltd. in 1951 to form MacMillan & Bloedel Ltd. (later MacMillan Bloedel), it was one of the largest forestry firms in the world.

MacMillan's iconoclasm, compared with the predominant Canadian tollbooth mentality of collecting fees on foreigner investors, is underscored by the long-obscured origins of Alcan, the country's multinational poster child. With operations in thirty-eight countries dating as far back as the 1920s, the world's number two aluminum producer is Canada's most global company—except for the fact that it was never really Canadian.

Much like Nortel, which started out as a manufacturing subsidiary of AT&T, the U.S. telecommunications giant, Alcan traces its roots to the

Aluminum Company of America, Alcoa, the world's largest aluminum producer. In 1900, Alcoa built its first Canadian aluminum smelter at Shawinigan Falls, Quebec, followed by a massive aluminum and hydroelectric complex at Arvida on the Saguenay River in 1925. Three years later, Alcoa spun off its Canadian and other non-U.S. operations into a separate unit, which remained firmly in the control of Alcoa shareholders.

Alcan's first president until 1947, Edward K. Davis, was the brother of Alcoa's founder and chairman.* He and his key corporate lieutenants were Americans who not only managed the company from New York and Boston, but were behind its expansion into the United Kingdom, Germany, China and Australia. Nathaniel Davis, who succeeded his father Edward, serving as president for thirty-two years until 1979 and chairman to 1986, is credited with spearheading Alcan's most ambitious international expansion and steering the company into an era of unparalleled growth.

In 1950, an anti-trust suit in the United States forced the largest shareholders of Alcoa and Alcan to dispose of their stock interests in either one or the other company. However, the control and management of Alcan remained heavily influenced by Americans, and it does so to this day. Until stepping down in October 2005, Alcan CEO and president Travis Engen, an American, regularly flew into Alcan's Montreal headquarters from his home in Connecticut. He was replaced by Richard Evans, who was born in Oregon.†

Of course, the question that begs to be asked is, why were so many of this country's greatest industrial achievements, from Alcan's immense aluminum smelters to hardrock mining towns in northern Manitoba, built by Americans? Many Canadians, fed on a steady diet of veiled envy masquerading as derision, would say: greed. It surely played a part, but it doesn't explain why more Canadians did not exploit the many opportunities Canada had to offer.

---

* Alcoa's founder was Arthur Vining Davis, after whom Arvida, Quebec, was named.
† In its eighty-year history, Alcan has had two Canadian-born CEOs: Jacques Bougie and David Culver.

Part of the answer may be found in the story of Joseph H. Hirshhorn, whose rags-to-riches saga serves as a cautionary tale for Canada's future ambitions. A Latvian Jew, Hirshhorn immigrated to the United States as a boy, selling newspapers on the streets of Brooklyn to support his impoverished family. He became a messenger boy on Wall Street and, before long, had made his first million. But it was in Canada where his immense fortune was truly made.

In 1933, Hirshhorn trumpeted his arrival in Canada by taking out a full-page ad in the *Northern Miner* newspaper, proclaiming: "My Name is Opportunity and I am Paging Canada." It was money well spent. He went on to finance the discovery and development of the Blind River uranium fields north of Lake Huron, Ontario, as well as uranium and gold and copper mines in northern Saskatchewan.

Hirshhorn used his vast wealth, literally dug out of the Canadian Shield, to assemble one of the world's largest private collections of modern art. In 1966, he donated the entire collection, some six thousand works, to the U.S. federal government, which agreed to build a museum to house the stunning array of Rodins, Picassos, Matisses, Gaugins and Pollacks on the National Mall in Washington, D.C.

In a speech marking the 1974 inauguration of the internationally renowned Hirshhorn Museum, the aging tycoon told an audience, "It is an honour to have given my art collection to the people of the United States as a small repayment for what this nation has done for me and others like me who arrived here as immigrants. What I accomplished in the United States I could not have accomplished anywhere else in the world."

In an ironic twist, Hirshhorn appeared to have forgotten to what nation he owed his good fortune. But the truth is, he had not. Hirshhorn had tried to donate at least part of his collection to the Canadian government, but was politely rebuffed. The Canadians, he later told an archivist with the Smithsonian Institution, were unwilling to build even an additional wing, never mind an entire museum, to house the sculptures and paintings. Sadly, his contribution to the National Gallery of Canada in

Ottawa is a single work by Albrecht Dürer, entitled *Nude Woman with Staff*.*
As Hirshhorn explained about Canadians, "They're not spenders."[80]

THE OUTSIDERS

Amid the jumble of crumbling tenements, richly ornate colonial cathedrals and grimy art deco buildings, the sleek glass and mirror contours of Latin America's highest office tower pierce the heart of downtown Mexico City like an obsidian sword hilt embedded in its ancient foundations. On the opposite bank of Paseo de la Reforma, the capital's wide imperial avenue, the tower's naked ambition is juxtaposed with the discreet sophistication of the Four Seasons Hotel, its inner courtyards of burbling fountains and bougainvillea a sanctuary to visiting Wall Street bankers and London fund managers.

While dramatically different in tone and tenor, the two landmarks share more than the same city block. They are both the work of Canadian entrepreneurs who have left their mark in the annals of international business. The fifty-five-storey Torre Mayor is the construct of Paul Reichmann, the indomitable real estate developer whose Olympia & York was at one time the largest real estate company in the world. The Four Seasons is the magnum opus of Isadore Sharp, dubbed "Razzle Dazzle Issy" for launching the world's leading luxury hotel chain.

With buildings and iconic brand names recognized the world over, both men eschewed the Canadian ethic of "domesticity by default," earning them a spot among the country's small but impressive pantheon of multinational pioneers. While many blame the Americans, the conservative banking system and stifling government paternalism for quashing the country's entrepreneurial spirit, the pair are part of a group of brash visionaries who overcame the obstacles to embrace the world's wider possibilities.

---

* The piece was actually an "assisted purchase" in which Hirshhorn and a group of his Toronto business partners raised funds for the gallery to acquire the painting.

What made them different? Well, for one thing, they were, without exception, not part of the "Canadian Establishment." Despite their immense wealth, the members of the Anglo-Scots commercial class of Toronto and Montreal were strangely absent from risky international ventures, moving instead among the intermingled boards of various banks, life insurers and railroads, their entrepreneurial energy employed in a complex machination of government favours, American money and tariffs. It was those left out of the cozy club who would conquer the world. I call them The Outsiders.

A few, like Roy Thomson and Laurent Beaudoin, emerged from the obscurity of small-town Canada to launch global companies. The $30 billion Thomson Corp., whose modest beginnings can be traced to a radio station in North Bay, Ontario, and a local newspaper in neighbouring Timmins, is now the third-largest provider of financial data after Reuters and Bloomberg, reaching twenty million people in 130 countries. Beaudoin took his father-in-law's snowmobile invention and turned Bombardier, based in Valcourt, Quebec, into one of the world's top manufacturers of planes and trains.

But overwhelmingly, Canada's first internationalists were immigrants and Jews, or what Milton Parissis, a Toronto-based international turnaround specialist, refers to as "ethnics." "International trade in Canada was spearheaded by the ethnics. They knew what the rest of the world had to offer and they were willing to pay the price," says the Greek-born Parissis. "The biggest teacher in life is pain. It makes you learn a lot faster. I don't advocate it, but it sure as hell works."

Life certainly was not easy for Samuel Bronfman, born at sea, on a ship bound for Canada, after his parents were forced to flee the pogroms of czarist Russia in 1889. The pugnacious overlord of the Seagram liquor empire, Bronfman was surely driven to succeed by his family's struggle to survive in the foreign and unforgiving cold of the Prairies. Arriving as homesteaders in Wapella, Saskatchewan, the family's efforts to grow tobacco and wheat failed, and they were forced to move to Brandon, Manitoba. They lived in a shed while Sam's father, Ekiel, worked in a sawmill, peddled firewood and whitefish and even rustled wild horses to feed his eight children.

Eventually, the Bronfmans bought a string of modest hotels in Manitoba and Saskatchewan, catering to the new settlers and railway workers who were opening the West. But as the temperance movement began to take hold, the family turned their attention to whisky. Sam opened a liquor store in Quebec, where alcohol was still legal, launching a booming mail-order trade. When Ottawa banned interprovincial trade in liquor two years later in 1918, Sam and his brothers jumped on a loophole in the law that allowed pharmacies to dispense alcohol for medicinal use. They immediately set up a pharmacy in Yorkton, Saskatchewan.

By the time the United States ushered in Prohibition, the Bronfman (a name that literally means "liquorman" in Yiddish) family had a string of liquor warehouses, known as "boozoriums," skirting the U.S. border. Sam and his brothers made a fortune reputedly selling whisky to American bootleggers and crime bosses, and by the time Prohibition ended in 1933 they boasted the largest reserve of aged whisky in the world. "Mr. Sam," who emerged as the head of the family business, never looked back, buying distilleries in the United States and the West Indies and international brands like Mumm's Champagne and Chivas Regal scotch while cultivating a stable of high-end Seagram label liquors, including V.O. and Crown Royal. Under Sam's command, Seagram sold 1.5 million bottles of liquor a day in 175 countries.

Sixty-nine years after his family arrived in Canada as struggling Jewish immigrants, Bronfman was at the helm of the world's largest distiller, a fact he unabashedly celebrated with the construction of the Seagram Building on Manhattan's swanky Park Avenue in 1958. The thirty-eight-storey, bronze-tinted skyscraper designed by renowned architect Ludwig Mies van der Rohe would become not only a New York City landmark, but a testament to what could be achieved in a supposedly cold, harsh hinterland like Canada.

The first inductee into Canada's "global hall of fame," Bronfman was followed by Thomas Bata, another hard-driving and exacting taskmaster. Born in the Czech town of Zlín, where his family had been cobblers for more than three hundred years, Bata's father revolutionized shoemaking by replacing artisanal leatherworking with the conveyor belts and mass production he'd seen while working on the assembly line of a shoe factory in the United States. The Bata Shoe Co. was already the world's largest footwear exporter when young Thomas, in a dramatic bid to save the company, immigrated to Canada two weeks before the Nazis marched into Czechoslovakia. He brought a hundred key Bata employees and their families—as well as more than a thousand machines—with him and relocated to a settlement north of Trenton, Ontario, which he named Batawa. After the war, Czechoslovakia's incoming communists national-ized the Zlín operations, which had employed forty thousand workers, and Bata's temporary home became permanent.

Despite the company's strapped finances and its exiled outpost, Bata and his coterie of devoted employees "were determined to rebuild the com-pany bigger than it was before," recalls his wife Sonja. "They were absolutely fanatic about it." They immediately turned to the still-undeveloped African market and, in a story that has become part of company lore, dispatched two salesmen, one to traverse the continent's east coast in search of poten-tial shoe markets, the other to traverse the west. The salesman sent to investigate the east wrote back saying it would be virtually impossible to establish a market, as no one wore shoes, says Sonja. His colleague on the west coast reported that the "opportunities were unlimited" because "nobody wore shoes."

In order to be able to furnish consumers in developing countries with shoes they could afford, Bata employed a unique "multi-domestic" approach to international markets in which inputs were sourced locally, manufactured in the country and sold to a local Bata retail store. In nations with no infrastructure or history of manufacturing, it was a chal-lenging task, and Bata even established tanneries and hide workshops. "In many places there were no spare parts, no equipment, no nothing," says Sonja. "But they refused to give up. The word 'impossible' was not in the vocabulary." At its zenith, Bata was the world's largest footwear com-pany, selling one million pairs of shoes a day in practically every country outside the former Soviet bloc. As one business colleague put it: "Bata considered the world a very small thing, and very accessible."*

Franz Strohsack was another victim of the war that roiled through Europe. By the age of twenty-two he was anxious to escape the economic depression that hovered over his hometown of Weiz, in the Austrian Alps, and see the world. Canada was the first country to offer him a visa, and in 1954 he arrived in Montreal with a single suitcase and, the story goes, forty dollars in his pocket. A trained tool-and-die maker, he worked at odd jobs, cleaning dishes and picking up golf balls at a driving range before taking out a thousand-dollar bank overdraft and opening his own small machine shop in Toronto in 1957.

Frank Stronach, as he now called himself, slept on a cot by his lathe, and in 1960 won his first job making auto parts for General Motors in Oshawa. His big break came with the 1965 Auto Pact agreement between the United States and Canada. While most Canadians worked the assembly line for the Big Three automakers, Stronach and other European immigrants saw an opportunity to supply parts. Today Stronach's Magna International, with US$23 billion in annual sales, eighty thousand employees and three hundred facilities worldwide, is one of the world's largest auto parts manufacturers. The former dishwasher is unapologetic about his annual pay packet of some $50 million, maintaining that "Canada would be better off with more Frank Stronachs."

Harrison and Wallace McCain weren't immigrants or ethnics, but as third-generation Irish-Canadian farmers from rural New Brunswick, they were definitely outsiders. When, in 1957, they decided to use their family inheritance to build a frozen french-fry plant in their hometown of Florenceville, no one believed they could compete against the big agrifood manufacturers across the border in Maine. But instead of using a

---

* After the fall of Czechoslovakia's communist regime in 1989, the Batas relaunched operations in the Czech Republic and closed the company's Ontario headquarters. Run by Bata's son, the company is now based in Switzerland. Still a powerful force today, Bata boasts 4,600 shops worldwide.

government grant and a 17.5 per cent tariff on American processed pota-toes to barricade themselves behind the Canadian border, the McCains went global.

Within a decade they were selling the frozen spuds to the United Kingdom, Australia and the United States. As the fast-food craze gained momentum, they hooked their fortunes to food chain giants like McDonald's, becoming the world's largest french-fry manufacturer. With fifty-five factories on six continents and $5.7 billion in sales, McCain Foods accounts for a third of the world market. Harrison, in an effort to manage his ever-expanding empire, once said he spent 140 nights a year sleeping on the corporate jet. Speaking at his funeral in 2004, former New Brunswick premier Frank McKenna told a packed church: "Harrison McCain was a globalist before the word was even invented."

While Bronfman, Bata, Stronach and the McCains are known for their domineering, larger-than-life personalities, Issy Sharp is said to be the most unassuming of tycoons. His father Max was born in Oswiecim (Auschwitz), Poland, before moving to Palestine in 1920 as a pioneer set-tler on Israel's first kibbutz. In 1925, Max immigrated to Canada, working as a plasterer before he eventually began building his own homes. To get by, the family would move into each newly built home, decorate it and sell it. As a child, Sharp recalls living in fifteen different houses.

Perhaps it was that nomadic lifestyle that first gave Sharp the taste for hotel life. In 1961, he opened his first motor hotel in Toronto's seedy east end. A decade later his ambitions had moved decidedly upmarket, and he built the Inn on the Park overlooking the leafy grounds of London's famed Hyde Park. As of 2006, Sharp's cautious, thought-out expansion had grown to include seventy properties and landmark hotels in thirty-one countries. But instead of being an owner and developer, Sharp focused on hotel management, turning his Four Seasons hotels into a global brand. In 1994, the Jewish businessman struck an unlikely part-nership with Saudi Prince Alwaleed bin Talal al Saud, whose Kingdom Holdings is one of the largest hotel developers in the world. His next conquest: the Middle East.

Where Sharp was a careful gradualist, Paul Reichmann was a monumental gambler. The last of the founding members of Canada's small international pantheon, the former rabbinical student built the largest real-estate development company the world had yet seen, only to see it collapse in the biggest corporate failure of its time. But while his family fortune, at one time estimated at us$10 billion, may no longer rank among the world's richest, Reichmann's signature buildings live on as a tribute to his tenacity and perseverance.

Born in Vienna in 1930, Paul and his family fled Nazi-occupied Austria in 1938, briefly residing in Paris before renting a flatbed truck and making their way to Tangier, Morocco, in the wake of encroaching German forces. Paul's father flourished as a currency trader, but the family was forced to move again as the rise of Islamic nationalism and the creation of Israel in 1948 prompted the mass exodus and expulsion of Jews throughout the Arab world.

After immigrating to Montreal and Toronto in the mid-1950s, the Reichmann brothers set up a business importing Spanish tiles before moving into real estate. By 1973, Paul had won a hotly contested bidding war for a property in the heart of Toronto's financial district and was planning to build the highest office tower in the Commonwealth. With the watershed First Canadian Place barely completed, Paul moved on to Manhattan, where, in the biggest property gamble in New York history, he turned a sandbar on the city's abandoned lower west side into the glittering World Financial Center.

The sprawling complex of soaring palm-treed atriums would be dwarfed, however, by his ambitious bid to develop Canary Wharf, a us$6 billion, twenty-four-building mini-city in the wastelands of London's east end. The high-stakes gambit would be his Waterloo. An economic downturn unlashed the moorings of his highly leveraged Olympia & York, and in 1992 creditors took over the company. But as the business world was still breathlessly composing his epitaph, Reichmann was already mounting a comeback, cobbling together a group of investors to buy back and develop Canary Wharf.

At the same time, with his empire freshly in ruins, he embarked on another daring venture, becoming one of the first international developers to move into the highly risky and still untapped Mexican market. His timing couldn't have been worse. A devastating currency crisis in 1994 paralyzed Mexico, putting Reichmann's ambitious development schemes on hold. A year later, investment partner George Soros, the billionaire currency speculator, pulled out of the venture. Reichmann refused to give up. As he once explained, "The only question that enters our minds is: Will success happen immediately or later?"

For Canadians there is another question: will others pick up where Reichmann and Bronfman left off? Some are trying. But invariably, if you pull back the Canadian veneer, you find many—in fact, a disproportionately large number—of the country's globally minded entrepreneurs continue to come from the same historical stock of Americans, immigrants and "ethnics" responsible for so many of Canada's achievements, both inside the country and out. As Carleton University's Professor McDowall sums up: "The good thing about Canada is it didn't stop people from being entrepreneurs. It just didn't encourage it. We have some shining examples of people who come equipped with another genetic code, ready to embrace the rest of the world."

4 | THE MILK MAFIA AND OTHER STORIES

"We're used to having such an incredibly wealthy resource, we could burden it with just about anything and it would be prosperous. But it won't prosper anymore."

RUSSELL HORNER, CEO, CATALYST PAPER CORP.

MICHAEL HALL EMITS that sturdy, slightly salt-of-the earth quality that most city folk assume to be naturally occurring in farmers. Don't be mistaken—there's no overalls or telltale dirt under his well-kept fingernails. Dressed in a casually sophisticated suit and open-necked dress shirt, Hall is thoroughly modern and urbane, just as comfortable in the bustle of Toronto as he is on his farm outside Ottawa, where he runs a successful dairy operation. Since buying out his dad's small, sixteen-cow herd, he has steadily built up the business and, in a joint venture with another farmer, now milks 130 cattle.

He's effusive about Canada's top-notch dairy industry: unparalleled quality, the highest standards, excellent marketing and research. "The Canadian dairy industry is one of the most efficient in the world," says Hall. "Our cows are sought after and we are as competitive as any country out there." Yet the cosmopolitan farmer and his competitive cows prefer to stick close to home. "We have chosen to stay out of the international market," he affirms.

In fact, Hall and his fellow dairy farmers are doing everything they can to ensure they never have to compete in global markets. That may seem oddly incongruous, given the industry's evident success, but from Hall's perspective it makes perfect sense. Why? Because like so many industries in which Canada could be flourishing on the international stage, farmers are discouraged by dysfunctional government policies that not only dissuade them from even thinking globally, but actively prevent them from being able to operate and compete in foreign markets.

A direct descendant of the National Policy, Canada's supply-managed dairy industry is one of the many hostages of the Byzantine regulations and self-defeating market structures that continue to infiltrate and order almost every corner of the Canadian economy, from banking and tele-communications to fishing and forestry. Like Pavlov with his dogs, these policies train Canadians to eschew global aspirations in favour of domes-tic reward and are the reason why, despite the country's natural strengths and leadership in a number of areas, going as far back as the 1800s, so many economic sectors remain stunted and internationally irrelevant.

Canada is the world's second-largest wheat exporter, yet it does not have a single multinational grain handler, grain trader or processor akin to Cargill of the United States, Europe's Louis Dreyfus or Argentina's Bunge. A Dutch–Norwegian conglomerate controls much of Canada's once-formidable fishing prowess, while its unparalleled forestry resources are hopelessly outgunned by the global firepower of tiny Finland. At the turn of the last century, Canadian banks, thanks to their steely Scottish overlords, were North American powerhouses. No longer. In every case, a direct line can be drawn to a government policy that stymied potential and, like a plant that will contort itself to seek out the sun's rays, directed industry's gaze inward.

It may be too late for many of them. That's why the story of the Canadian dairy industry is so poignant. It has the potential to be a world leader—if it were ever given a curd of a chance.

CHRIS BIRCH BUILT tires at a factory in Barrie, Ontario, but his real dream was to own his own dairy farm. Unfortunately, milking cows wasn't as easy as it was when he was a boy and his family raised hogs and grew sweet corn back on the farm in Phelpston. To run a dairy operation, Birch would first have to buy quota, which is the right to produce and sell milk under the supply-management system. With quota priced at upwards of twenty thousand dollars per cow, he didn't have the several million dollars in investment he'd need to make a living as a full-time dairy farmer.

So Birch kept his job and borrowed money to buy a little bit of quota and a handful of cows, expanding the herd whenever he got a chance. But then the tire factory closed in 1992, and Birch couldn't make ends meet. By 2000, unable to hang on any longer, he sold his quota to pay off the debt he'd incurred to buy it. Birch still had the cows, though, and he started looking for other ways to sell his milk. He got a permit to export to the United States and soon had a thriving business. Birch formed a co-operative with twenty-nine other local producers, and together they sold more than one million litres of a milk a month across the border. "There are tremendous opportunities in the U.S.," he says. "It's a huge, huge market."

But while Birch thought he'd finally found an answer to his problems, he was soon confronted with new, even more difficult challenges. He was quickly overwhelmed with court challenges, cease-and-desist orders and random diktats from government officials. By 2005, the beleaguered farmer had spent nearly $1 million in legal fees trying to defend his right to export to the United States. Who was he defending himself against? Well, not the Americans. It's farmers like Michael Hall.

The Dairy Farmers of Ontario, and the complex web of provincial marketing boards and federal councils created to service and support them, have gone to extraordinary lengths to shut down what many would consider an export success story. That's because in the world of supply management, farmers are not rewarded for conquering new markets. Their payoff comes from guarding their government-ceded monopoly over the domestic dairy market. Anything that might chip away at that assumed right to supply Canadian consumers—including exports—therefore has to go.

The farmers need the monopoly and the high prices it ensures, because without it the entire supply-managed system would collapse. Under the system, prohibitive tariffs of 200 to 300 per cent effectively bar imported dairy products. At the same time, farmers, through provincial marketing boards, are allowed to fix domestic milk prices, which, according to the Organization for Economic Co-operation and Development (OECD), are more than double world prices. It's an elaborate balancing act, scrupulously managed and vehemently defended, all to one end: protecting the quota.

Dubbed dairy's "dirty little secret," quota is both the monkey on farmers' backs and a cash cow. Originally given out for free by the government in the 1960s, it is now a highly sought after commodity, traded on special exchanges. A fifty-cow herd is worth $1.45 million in quota, representing half the assets of an average farm, including land, equipment and animals. With farmers either forced to take out loans to buy quota or using it as collateral against other debt, quota is at once a tremendous financial burden and the price of entry into an exclusive club. But however you see it, the results are the same: it jacks up the cost of producing milk and means that the price for milk and, by extension, quota stay high.

"The Canadian dairy industry is really no longer about milk," says Jim McIlroy, a Toronto-based trade lawyer and long-time critic of supply management. "It's about quotas, and the number one objective is to protect the value of that asset."

Which is why dairy farmers would rather lose the ability to export than give up even a single dollop of their domestic monopoly. They were faced with that very choice in 2002, when the United States and New Zealand successfully challenged Canada at the World Trade Organization (WTO), proving that its high milk prices were used to subsidize cheaper cheese exports. Rather than tamper with the system, the farmers voluntarily forfeit their right to export. "Okay, so we can't export," says Hall matter-of-factly. "We chose to live with it because we chose to focus on the domestic market."

For Hall, who owns sixty-five cows and probably close to $2 million in quota, it only makes sense. But his decision—to, in effect, stake his entire future on a small, captive Canadian market—not only flies in the face of sweeping global trends, but threatens the viability of Canada's agrifood

industry, to the long-term detriment of Hall himself. He and other sup-
porters of supply management argue that Canada's ability to supply its own
market is a question of sovereignty. But just as Hamilton's industrial might
quickly crumbled once the walls supporting its artificially enhanced muscle were knocked down, so too will the dairy industry evaporate.

It's already happening. Since the farmers opted out of export markets,
multinational processors like Nestlé and Parmalat, which turn milk into
cheese and yogourt, have been steadily closing their Canadian operations.
Limited to the Canadian market, the processors are running their plants
below capacity, with no way of offsetting the high cost of milk with increased
production. "Every month, one or two dairy plants close. They are getting
out of here," says McIlroy. "We've already lost a tremendous amount of the
future of the industry. It's gone and it's never coming back."

Montreal-based Saputo is among those seeking greener pastures.
Founded by Sicilian-born Lino Saputo, who immigrated to Canada in
1950, the company is the world's number two mozzarella maker, with 40
per cent of the Canadian cheese market and 6 per cent of the U.S. market.
Since 2002, Saputo has closed seven cheese processing plants across
Canada. Within months of the WTO ruling effectively barring Canadian
dairy exports, Saputo spent US$51 million to buy Argentina's third-largest
dairy processor. From Argentina, Saputo exports to over thirty countries.
In November 2005, company chief executive Lino Jr., citing high milk
prices in Canada, said he was looking to invest in Australia and New
Zealand, which boast the world's most competitively priced milk since
dismantling their supply-managed systems.[81]

In a bid to stem the flow, dairy farmers are encouraging the processors to import cheaper milk products from abroad, which can be used for
re-exporting processed cheese and yogourt. The imports, part of a government quota program referred to as "the shortage" that processors must
make up for in order "to compete," has more than doubled since the WTO
ruling to 49 million kilograms in 2005–2006.[82] The dairy farmers have
already made similar leaps of logic to keep food manufacturers like
McCain and Kraft from going stateside. The food companies pay 30 per

cent less for the cheese they use on their frozen pizzas; otherwise, they say, they wouldn't be able to compete with U.S. manufacturers. Altogether, the dairy farmers have had to create eighteen separate categories of milk prices to remain competitive with the U.S. and other markets.

But like a dike that constantly springs leaks in the wake of a rushing river, as soon as the system plugs one hole, another bursts open. The cheaper prices paid by the frozen-pizza makers put restaurants like Pizza Pizza at a competitive disadvantage, forcing the chain to use less cheese and hampering its ability to innovate and come up with new product offerings. "We are completely hamstrung by the system," says Ron Reaman, vice-president of food supply for the Canadian Restaurant and Foodservices Association. "We're stuck in an outdated mode that has left us behind in terms of innovation and production development."

It's the same story for ice cream makers, who import "butter–oil" blends that get around the high tariffs rather than use Canadian milk products. For Reaman, it's no coincidence that per capita milk consumption in Canada has declined 15 per cent in the last twenty years. But while so many are hurt by what he describes as an "archaic and Byzantine" system, the farmers are largely immune to the fallout. By shorting the system—issuing negligible amounts of new quota, which invariably stifles farmers' own ability to grow, expand and be more productive, they ensure that demand outstrips supply.

Safely ensconced behind the quota, tariffs and high milk prices, farmers have very little incentive to be more efficient and innovative. According to the OECD, over 60 per cent of the value of production is subsidized by the Canadian government through higher milk prices. Birch, who travels frequently between the United States and Canada, notes the difference between dairy operations on either side on the border. "The U.S. farms are lean and mean, and they're expanding to compete globally. The Canadian farms are neat, tidy, forty- or fifty-cow operations, just like in the U.S. back in the 1960s," he says. "They are caught in a time warp—and they like it that way. Why would you want to milk two hundred cows when you can continue to make a living with sixty? It's just a big hose job."

Some might argue that running a fifty-cow dairy farm is a nice alternative to the mass monoculture factory farming that now pervades the agricultural sector and robs it of its human side. But if that's something Canada would like to encourage, the best way to protect it is to make it self-sustaining, which it is not. If it were, anyone who had a hankering to be a dairy farmer would be one, and those who produced the best, most-sought-after milk at the best price would succeed. Instead, the system is "a little like agriculture in the Soviet Union. And we all know how that ended," says Valentin Petkantchin, the Bulgarian-born director of research at the Institut économique de Montréal. Which is why it needs the government to pass laws and institute favourable legislation that will keep the creaking system intact. What's not as clear, though, is, who exactly is running the show? With 16,300 dairy farmers owning an estimated $20 billion in quota, each one is technically a millionaire. Together they represent a powerful lobby group that has politicians "running scared," say critics. Birch likens them to a "mob," their political clout comparable to that of a Colombian drug cartel. How else to explain the government's willingness to sacrifice long-term national interests in favour of a few thousand farmers?

But there are things that not even Ottawa and the provincial governments can protect them from. The sheer force of globalization will continue to draw multinational manufacturers to the most competitive markets while moves towards freer global trade are steadily chipping away at the kind of prohibitive tariffs essential to sustaining supply management. New Zealand, which used to produce 25 per cent less milk than Canada, now produces 80 per cent more and is leading the charge into the huge, untapped Chinese market.

Meanwhile Canada, the world's tenth-largest milk producer in 1969, is now ranked twentieth.

"There's something much bigger than the farmers out there. It's bigger than Ottawa and it's bigger than Queen's Park [the Ontario legislature]. It's called globalization," says McIlroy. "When trade barriers inevitably come down, we'll be buying products made by Saputo, but they won't be produced in Canada. They'll be made in Argentina. And we'll have to ask ourselves how on earth we let it happen—how we drove the future of the industry out of this country to protect a few thousand millionaire farmers. It just doesn't make sense."

Of course, the story doesn't have to end this way. Chris Birch successfully competes in the U.S. market, making a tidy profit selling his milk for forty to forty-five cents a litre, transportation costs included. In contrast, dairy farmers under supply management say they need to charge sixty-five to seventy cents a litre. The 30 per cent price differential is a direct result of the quota. "The only reason the industry can't compete is because it's hobbled with a tremendous burden that people have to work under whether they want to or not," says Birch. "It's called quota."

Experts like Mike Gifford, Canada's lead agricultural negotiator during the WTO's Uruguay Round of trade liberalization, say it's about time the government started thinking about buying the farmers out of their quota. Once unshackled, their high-quality breeding stock, combined with the relative proximity of Quebec and Ontario farmers to the fluid milk sheds of the northeastern United States, would give them a distinct advantage over dairy farmers in Wisconsin. And when it comes to cheese, Canada has plenty of potential; a century ago cheese was the country's second-largest export after wood, with thousands of small factories stretching from Ontario to Prince Edward Island.

For the moment, however, the high-end cheese industry, which is enjoying a resurgence in the United States and the United Kingdom, remains stifled by the same intrusive regulation. Dairy farmers who want to make cheese must first sell their milk to the provincial marketing board and then buy it back, paying the board a transportation fee to move the milk from the barn to their cheese house. If a producer wants to use someone else's milk, it has no choice in what milk it gets. In either case, the would-be producer must still be lucky enough to get its hands on some cheese-making quota already in circulation. The only other option is to convince the government that your cheese won't compete with an already-existing cheese. To get this "innovation quota," regulators actually taste the cheese and decide whether it tastes different enough from other products already on the market.

Despite the impressive obstacles, Quebec manages to produce close to four hundred varieties of artisanal cheese. Only a very minute amount, however, is actually exported. Ron Reaman doesn't understand it. "Why wouldn't you want to be exporting around the world? Why wouldn't you want to be a global leader?" J.L. Kraft may very well have asked himself the same question in 1903 when, in order to get around stiflingly high tariffs, he decided to move from Stevensville, Ontario, to Chicago, where he founded what would become the world's largest cheese company.

Laurent Pellerin, head of the powerful Union des producteurs agricole, the Quebec farmers' union that represents almost half of all Canadian dairy farmers, doesn't see it quite that way. "There's not a lot of people in North America who lack food—there's plenty of food everywhere," says Pellerin. "This whole idea that we could be market winners, it's the American dream. But it's not my dream."

Is it any wonder?

GLOBALLY STUMPED

As far back as anyone can remember, Cornwall, Ontario, has brimmed with potential. The city of 45,000 near the Quebec border is smack in the middle of the densely populated Quebec City–Windsor corridor, an hour's drive from Ottawa and almost within spitting distance of northern New York state. Its central location on the banks of the St. Lawrence River is what first drew Loyalist settlers here two hundred years ago along with the silk factories and paper mills that followed. By the 1970s, Cornwall was a thriving industrial town in which anyone out of high school was able to walk into a well-paying mill job.

But then the factories started closing. First it was the cotton mills, then the chemical plant and the massive rayon complex, which is now just an empty field on the edge of town. In 2005, Montreal-based Gildan shuttered its yarn-spinning operations and the Swiss multinational Nestlé closed a dairy plant, bringing to 2,100 the number of layoffs over an eighteen-month period. "Everyone always talked about Cornwall's potential," says

Claude Macintosh, a Cornwall native and associate editor at the local *Standard-Freeholder* newspaper. "But it never really happened. Instead, we've watched factories close one after another."

Still, no one, not in their wildest dreams, imaged that the towering, fume-belching stacks of the Domtar pulp and paper mill could ever be snuffed out. In November 2005, the Montreal-based company closed the one-hundred-year-old icon, laying off nine hundred workers and setting adrift the community that had grown up around the sprawling mill. "Nobody ever believed Domtar could close," says Macintosh. "It was such an institution. Domtar and Cornwall were all one thing. We were a pulp and paper town."

While Canada has almost gotten used to the slow dismantling of its branch-plant economy, the forestry industry is as old as cod and beaver pelts, its deep roots and vast canopy providing sustenance and well-paying jobs to hundreds of communities. Which is perhaps why its long-heralded collapse has been routinely ignored and discounted for more than a decade. But there is no ignoring it any longer. As Cornwall reels in disbelief, towns from Miramichi, New Brunswick, to Squamish, British Columbia, are being felled by an industry-wide crisis that is cutting a swath through the country's rural backbone.

"It has never been this bad," says Jamie Lim, president of the Ontario Forest Industries Association. In 2004 and 2005, close to twelve thousand sawmill workers and pulp and paper machine operators lost their jobs in forty-six communities. Half the cuts came in Ontario. "It's different this time," she says. "The valley is deeper than anyone has ever been in before, and when we climb out, the industry is not going to be the same."

Whether it emerges pruned back but sturdy, or shrunken and withered, will depend on whether the industry is able to address the roots of the crisis. In 2005, Ottawa and the provincial governments coughed up more than $2 billion in emergency aid to stanch the damage caused by a costly softwood lumber dispute with the United States, a sharp rise in the loonie and surging energy prices in Ontario. The conjunction of events, some argue, combined to form the perfect storm at a time when the global forestry industry is being revolutionized by new technologies and the emergence of low-cost competitors in South America and Asia.

What is not as easy to explain away is why Canadian companies failed to anticipate the looming changes and remain the least prepared of their global peers to survive the inevitable restructuring.

It shouldn't be this way. Canada is home to 10 per cent of the world's forestry resources and is the leading exporter of wood products; it is responsible for 21 per cent of the global trade. Yet its companies are light-weights by international standards, with not one among the world's top twenty. Not only are these companies among the least global of their peers—they are even confined to regions within Canada—but their mills and machines are among the most antiquated and unproductive on the planet. They churn out commodity goods like two-by-fours, pulp and newsprint instead of producing high-value-added products like tissue paper and engineered wood products. As for Canadian manufacturers of printing presses and paper machines, well, there aren't any.

It's a stark contrast to Finland, which in 1949 received the World Bank's first-ever forestry loan to rebuild its industry, which had been left decimated after World War II. Sixty years later, the country of five million still has a fraction of Canada's resources, but three of its companies are among the world's ten largest. Helsinki-based Stora Enso, with sales of US$15 billion, is three times the size of Canada's leading forestry-products company, Abitibi-Consolidated. Stora Enso is also the most globalized for-ester, with far-flung operations in Russia and China and a US$1.2 billion pulp mill joint venture in Brazil. In neighbouring Uruguay, a trio of Finnish firms, together with the Spanish, are investing US$2 billion to build the world's largest pulp complex.

The Finns have gone global on the back of a dynamic domestic indus-try. They harvest 65 per cent more lumber per hectare than do operators on New Brunswick Crown land, and their labour costs are less than a third of those of coastal British Columbia, thanks to massive investments in research and technology. Their mills are not only three times as large as the average mill in Quebec, but state-of-the-art, with equipment furnished by homegrown companies like Metso, the world's largest supplier of paper-making machinery.

So why is it that tiny Finland is a forestry giant, while Canada, with its towering Douglas-firs and lumberjack legacy, watches as communities from Cornwall to Kenora are left to scramble for twelve-dollar-an-hour call-centre jobs? According to forestry experts, the slow decline that has culminated in the current crisis can be traced back to the public owner-ship of Canada's timberlands and the onerous government regulations that have at the same time bred complacency and handcuffed companies' ability to compete.

Unlike Finland (and in fact most other major forestry producing nations), where timberland is privately owned, Canadian companies are given provincial licences to harvest an annual "allowable cut" for a period ranging from five to twenty-five years. In some cases, the area to be har-vested can change from year to year and is shared by several companies at once, while the amount to be cut is calculated on the basis of forestry yields rather than market conditions. At times, companies must harvest trees even when it's unprofitable, or risk losing their licence, resulting in both a drag on efficiency and a subsidy at the same time. In return, com-panies pay a government-set stumpage fee and are subject to a web of regulation, the most important of which ties cutting rights in a specific area to a local mill.*

Designed more as social policy than as industrial strategy, the tenure system is essentially a pact between government and industry that affords companies cheap access to wood in return for providing forestry jobs that average a comfortable $68,000 a year. The arrangement worked as long as Canada was the world's pre-eminent forest-products supplier. But as new sources of cheap logs are being tapped in Russia and fast-growing trees in Brazil can be turned into pulp at half the North American cost, the hair-line cracks in Canada's forestry industry are now gaping wounds.

---

* British Columbia finally removed its appurtenance clause, which links cutting rights to mills, in 2003.

In 2005, Quebec announced a dramatic 20 per cent reduction in its allowable cut following decades of overharvesting and meagre reforestation efforts. Other provinces are facing similar challenges, as companies that have no real attachment to the land they harvest have no incentive to replant more than they have to by law. And why would they? When trees take fifty years to grow, twenty-five-year licences reduce operators to renters in someone else's home, explains Clark Binkley, managing director of Massachusetts-based International Forestry Investment Advisors and the former dean of UBC's Faculty of Forestry.

With no guarantee that they will ever harvest the trees they plant, loggers don't invest in genetic research to improve seed resistance, while site preparation, planting and fertilizer regimes are much less intensive than those in the United States. "Under those kind of weak tenure arrangements, spending money on silviculture is like walking over to the boardroom window, tearing up dollar bills and throwing them out," says Binkley. "It comes back to incentives—why do you never wash a rental car?"

But while companies cut corners on R&D, they pay the price by being forced to maintain so many remote and inefficient mills. Consolidation is actively discouraged by provincial governments that either swoop in with bailouts or threaten to confiscate timber rights in the case of a mill closure. As a result, century-old clunkers long destined for the scrap heap are kept alive with retrofitting and costly maintenance, leaving companies unable to redeploy capital and invest in new technology.

The government's overwhelming, not to mention compromised presence, as both tree salesman and industry regulator, means companies focus an inordinate amount of their creative energy on managing "government issues." Even the softwood lumber dispute, which has absorbed the industry for two decades, is a direct consequence of the fact that Canadian timberland is owned by the Crown. This situation leaves companies little time to notice what's happening in the rest of the world and keeps them from honing the skills required for competing globally.

"The overwhelming focus on government issues means management spends a huge amount of time dealing with the government instead of concentrating on how to create wealth, how to improve production or how to expand the value of the company by moving to China," says Binkley. "These are not exportable skills. It's not going to help you deal with the Chinese government or give you a competitive advantage elsewhere."

The problem is exacerbated by competing provincial jurisdictions that discourage movement within Canada while a reluctance to allow mergers stops companies from acquiring the scale and scope needed to compete internationally. According to Russell Horner, chief executive of Vancouver-based Catalyst Paper, unless the industry is allowed to retrench, the cost to Canada will be far greater than the recent round of job losses. "If we don't do the necessary restructuring, it is going to be much more painful and much more damaging," he says. "We need players that are going to come out of this as robust companies. Otherwise, we'll just be picked off by offshore players."

It's already happening. Just look at what remains of the once-mighty MacMillan Bloedel. The forestry giant founded in the 1920s by H.R. MacMillan had all the makings of an industry leader. At its apex in the 1960s and 1970s, MacBlo marketed one third of B.C.'s lumber exports and had operations worldwide. One of the originators of oriented strandboard (OSB), the now-ubiquitous plywood substitute, MacBlo opened the world's first waferboard plant and invented a reconstituted lumber product called Parallam. But despite its innovation and rich resource base, MacBlo was never able to capitalize on its leadership.

While many of the world's most profitable forestry firms owe their success to the flourishing OSB business, MacBlo failed to market and develop its inventions. And although it was a large forestry company in British Columbia, it was relatively small in the global scheme of things. That didn't stop the provincial government and the public from alternately attacking MacBlo for its size and blocking local acquisitions while accusing it of exporting jobs when it expanded abroad.

By 1999, MacBlo had been adrift for over a decade when Weyerhaeuser, from neighbouring Washington state, bought it. In 2005 Weyerhaeuser dismantled the company, selling off its coastal B.C. timber assets to

Toronto-based Brookfield Asset Management. "We have ourselves to blame," says Richard Haskayne, MacBlo's former chairman. "We had a base to work with, but we didn't capitalize on it."

The same could be said about Domtar. Less than a year after closing its Cornwall plant, the century-old company was acquired by Weyerhaeuser, which took a 55 per cent stake in the struggling firm and reincorporated it south of the border (where the majority of its mills are located).

Forestry watchers like Clark Binkley, however, aren't ready to give up just yet. Canada has a lot going for it, including its location so close to the U.S. market, more than a third of the world's installed capacity and two centuries of know-how. The B.C. interior, where operators are racking up record profits despite the costly softwood lumber dispute, is an instructive case in point. Forced to cut costs in the wake of 27 per cent U.S. duties, companies began merging and building some of the biggest, most technologically advanced mills in the business. "Canada has got the core ingredients," says Binkley. "If we can't figure it out, shame on us."

Back in Cornwall, Claude Macintosh is less optimistic. Most people here only have a high school education, and the biggest employers are the hospital and the municipality. As for the private sector, well, Wal-Mart, the U.S. retailer, opened a massive distribution centre with nine hundred employees. The other big money maker is smuggling. The city, complacent in its ephemeral potential and confident that well-placed members of Parliament would win it government contracts, never really worried about its future.

"It's like World War II, when the Nazis invaded Poland," says Macintosh. "All the signs were there. When you look back you say, 'How did we miss it?' I guess we just didn't want to see."

BANKING ON PROTECTION

In 1982, Citigroup was teetering on the brink of bankruptcy. The American behemoth and world's ninth-largest bank by assets had overextended itself with big loans to shaky Third World countries that suddenly became worthless in the wake of huge debt default and currency devaluations. The timing was ripe for a takeover and some of the Canadian banks, well endowed with cash and assets, even flirted with the idea of taking a run at the distressed institution.

The Bay Street Boys never took the bait, but miraculously had a second chance less than a decade later when Citigroup once again got itself into hot water over risky overseas investments. The bank went around the world seeking potential investors to provide it with a life-saving capital injection. The Canadians were sitting right there, but never answered the call. Instead Saudi Prince Alwaleed bin Talal al Saud stepped forward, taking a leap of faith that would transform Citigroup and global financial markets forever. With operations in over 100 countries and $1.7 trillion in assets, Citigroup is now the world's largest company, according to *Forbes* magazine, and a prime mover in the dramatic consolidation that has resulted in a clutch of global banks increasingly dominating the financial sector worldwide.

Sadly, the Canadian banks are no longer members of that elite club. After taking a pass at arguably their best chance to enter the global big leagues, the Big Five are small potatoes on the world stage. The venerable Royal Bank of Canada, the country's second-largest company by market capitalization, was ranked forty-ninth among world banks in 2005,[83] with assets of $457 billion. At one time bigger than Chase Manhattan, Credit Suisse and JP Morgan, Royal's assets add up to just one quarter of Japan's Mitsubishi UFJ and Switzerland's UBS. In the past two decades, the major Canadian banks have sat back and watched as they've been surpassed by Holland's ING Group, London-based HSBC and even the Spanish and the Belgians.

While the Spaniards reconquered Latin America, Citigroup scooped up insurers and brokerage firms and HSBC circled the globe, Canadian banks, despite their enviable financial strength, could barely bring themselves to cross the border. In 1984, Bank of Montreal bought Chicago's Harris Bank and has not made a major acquisition since. The others bided their time until as late as 2004, when TD finally took the plunge with the US$3.8 billion purchase of a bank headquartered in Maine. It can now proudly lay claim to being the ninth-largest bank in New Jersey. Yet despite their cautious entry into the United States, the banks have been roundly criticized for buying "third-rate" assets that often produced disastrous results. The Royal Bank of Canada, for example, has little to show for the $8.4 billion it has spent for Minneapolis brokerage firm Dain Rauscher and the problem-plagued Centura Bank of South Carolina.

CIBC, however, has borne the brunt of the U.S. missteps, first selling its newly acquired investment bank, Oppenheimer & Co., and then shuttering electronic bank Amicus on losses of $700 million. It became ensnarled in a string of scandals, paying out US$2.4 billion to defrauded Enron investors—the largest settlement of any bank—while in 2004 a CIBC manager in New York was led away in handcuffs over improper mutual fund trading. The shell-shocked bank retreated to the safety of Canada, reflecting a general global retreat begun in the late 1980s, when a wave of Third World debt crises prompted many Canadian banks to close representative offices around the globe.

The one exception to the rule has been Scotiabank, with its string of acquisitions in Latin America. But even there, its strategy has been cautious and largely peripheral to blockbuster deals by the Spanish, Citicorp and HSBC. The banks can afford to be extraordinarily careful, even incurious, when it comes to branching out abroad; they have a monopoly on one of the most profitable markets in the world. The Big Five banks control more than 80 per cent of the Canadian market—the highest market concentration among developed countries outside Sweden and the Netherlands. It's an almost guaranteed licence to print money, and they don't have to worry about sharing the spoils.

Canadian banks don't have to compete on their home turf because of government restrictions that effectively ban foreign banks from entering the market. Although foreigners are no longer technically barred from buying big Canadian banks, in practice they are, due to ownership restrictions that prevent a single shareholder from controlling more than 20 per cent of a bank's voting stock and 30 per cent of its non-voting float. At the same time, foreign financial institutions have been discouraged from opening retail bank branches in Canada, thanks to onerous rules requiring them to establish a separate Canadian incorporated subsidiary. As one Australian banker observed, "The Canadian banking market is probably the most protected in the developed world."

The upshot is what some observers describe as "a gentlemen's agreement" to carve up the market, in essence an oligopoly that allows the banks to earn above-average returns. The Big Five consistently rank among the world's top ten in profitability, and as BMO's chief financial officer noted in 2006, they "are sitting on more excess capital than any other banks in the world."[84] It's a striking achievement, considering that Canadian banks are less efficient than their international peers. They not only lack the economies of scale of the big global players, but invest a third less in technology on a per worker basis than do their U.S. counterparts—a gaping differential that is considered to be at the heart of Canada's lagging productivity.[85] Labour productivity in the Canadian financial-services sector is not only 60 per cent that of the U.S., but has grown by less than half the rate of Canadian manufacturing over the last decade. "We've never exposed the banks to full competition. It's no wonder they are not as productive as the rest of the world; they don't have to be," says Glen Hodgson, chief economist at the Conference Board of Canada. "The market is carved up, so their principal concern is domestic market share."

It's a great deal if you can get it, but it has come at an incalculable cost. The banks' sheltered existence has made them exceedingly risk-averse and psychologically ill-equipped to operate in less reliable financial markets (that is, every country outside of Canada, with the exception of maybe Sweden). "It's not easy to work in foreign markets. You have to have staying power and be able to stick it out through thick and thin," says Troy Wright, managing director of capital markets for Scotiabank Inverlat. "The Canadian market is protected, so when things don't go well it's natural for banks to pull back to a safe haven. It's the easiest thing to do."

The banks were quick to high-tail it out of Latin America during the debt crises of the late 1980s, and even Scotia distinguished itself as the first foreign bank to pull up stakes in Argentina, preferring to take a $540 million writedown rather than soldier through the spectacular debt default and banking crisis of 2002. But while banks are overly cautious abroad, their predilection for taking the easy way out is equally apparent at home. They are overwhelmingly focused on retail banking, a steady and reliable source of income, but essentially a commodity compared with the more sophisticated and riskier investment banking sector.

In Canada, the absence of a single major Canadian investment bank along the lines of a Merrill Lynch or a Goldman Sachs means that huge swaths of the national economy are either ignored or are increasingly being serviced by more aggressive foreign banks. A case in point is the growing popularity of joint "public–private" partnerships to fund sorely needed infrastructure projects. The Canadian banks, used to cherry-picking safe, short-term financing deals, weren't interested in offering the riskier, long-term financing needed to underwrite big projects. The Europeans and Australians swooped in and now account for most of the market, financing projects like British Columbia's Sea-to-Sky Highway and Ontario's 407 toll road.

Ironically, once the Canadian banks realized they were losing out on all the business, their reaction was not to try to compete, says one foreign banker. Rather, they tried to lobby government to either block the structured deals or modify them to better suit their way of doing business. "They tried to lobby against public–private partnerships and almost get special treatment," says the banker. "It says something about the mindset. Rather than acting commercially, their first port of call is to phone their political lobbyist instead of their financial analyst. They see it as a problem they would rather make go away than as an opportunity to make money."

To be fair, they've been taught to think that way—by overweening government minders that see fit to decide on the wisdom of their business decisions. Why? Because, as Queen's University economics professor Thomas Courchene explains, the government ultimately views them as "social institutions" rather than inherently economic ones. That was the trade-off, after all. Like the logging companies that are forced to operate sawmills where the government gives them cutting rights, the banks are expected to provide retail services to every corner of the country in return for their monopoly. Regulations make it almost impossible for banks to close branches, even though Canada has more ATM machines per capita than any other country on the planet.

The formidable branch system is arguably an even greater barrier to foreign entry than are the ownership restrictions initially introduced in 1967 to block Citibank's attempts to buy a Canadian bank. But while few foreigners can afford to build a branch network from scratch—each outlet costs an estimated $1 million—the system has also shackled the banks to Canada. "For the banks, the branches were a perfect barrier to competition," says David Bond, a leading industry expert. "Now it's a millstone around their necks."

When Canadian banks attempted to lighten the load with a proposed merger involving four of the five major banks in 1998, they were slapped down by the federal government. The banks argued they needed to join forces so that they would have the bulk to buy into foreign markets without betting the company. Ottawa, in vetoing the move, maintained the banks would first have to prove the mergers met the requirements of the "public interest," code words for cheap and accessible retail banking services.

Stanley Hartt, chairman of Citigroup Global Markets Canada, calls the decision "bad policy." A former deputy finance minister under Brian Mulroney, he recalls former prime minister Jean Chrétien sitting in his Bay Street office declaring that he would never let mergers happen. Instead, as the US$58 billion tie-up between J.P. Morgan Chase and Bank One in the United States created industry giants, Ottawa equivocated through task forces, policy white papers, Senate reports, a House of Commons study and public consultations without ever issuing merger guidelines. "The long-term policy implications are enormous," says Hartt. "The attitude towards bank mergers is a symptom of the absence of policy, and as a result they are condemned to be small players in a very small pond."

That might be okay for the dairy industry or even forestry, but an inward-looking and hamstrung financial sector has massive implications for the country's long-term prosperity. When Rick Waugh headed up

Scotiabank's corporate banking operations in New York from 1985 to 1993, the Canadians could go head-to-head with any of the big Wall Street bankers. Back then, Scotiabank ranked among the top ten in syndicated lending in the United States. Now it's dwarfed by the likes of Merrill Lynch and J.P. Morgan. "When I was down there we could compete with Chase, Manny Hanny [Manufacturers Hanover Trust] on anything," says Waugh, now Scotiabank's CEO. "We were on a more equal footing with the American banks. We are no longer. We lost that one... because the other guys have gotten bigger."

For Scotia and its confrères, it's not just about missing out on lucrative advisory fees and underwriting commissions in New York. The big U.S. banks are now moving in on corporate Canada, as the Big Five, limited by their scale and lacking the expertise of a bulge-bracket investment bank, are less able to handle major mergers and acquisitions or take Canadian companies global. In 2003, for example, foreign banks accounted for 43.4 per cent of investment banking fees paid in Canada, taking leading roles in the country's biggest corporate transactions, from the overhaul of Air Canada and Stelco's restructuring to Alcan's US$4.6 billion purchase of France's Pechiney.

In perhaps the most telling example, the Canadian government hired Merrill Lynch, together with RBC and CIBC, to sell its remaining 19 per cent stake in oil company Petro-Canada to the stock market. "Here is a Canadian asset, sold by the Canadian government, and it went to Merrill Lynch to get it done. It was sold in Canada to Canadians," says Waugh. "It's mind-boggling. It has implications for international competitiveness, for head offices and for talent."

Faced with the banks' limited scope, the CEOs of Canadian companies opt to live close to U.S. financial centres, says Hartt. He reels off the names of Canadian companies now headquartered in the United States: IPSCO, Moore-Wallace, Laidlaw, NOVA Chemicals and Thomson Corp. The American-born heads of CN and Cott also reside stateside, making periodic trips to their Canadian offices. "Why are they there? Because they want to be near where the deal flow is and where the decisions are made," says Hartt. "When Bombardier, JDS Uniphase, Manulife, Alcan and CN go abroad and buy foreign companies and become world leaders, they all turn to international financial institutions because Canadians are not there to help. When foreigners target Canadian companies, with their international bankers and advisers, it eventually leads to the hollowing out of corporate head offices."

Not everyone agrees that the banks need to join forces to be competitive. In 1984 the Australian government deregulated its banking industry by allowing foreign banks to compete domestically (although the foreign ownership of local banks remained restricted). The decision triggered a radical makeover, with local banks slashing costs, expanding abroad and specializing in high-end niche sectors.*

Macquarie Bank, Australia's principal investment bank, began acquiring real estate, energy and infrastructure projects around the globe as part of a unique business model it developed that bundles assets into funds that clients can invest in. Its US$110 billion in assets (including debt) under management include Korean toll roads, Italian airports and Taiwanese cable operators. Its Canadian holdings include the Ontario elder-care centre Leisureworld, container terminals in Halifax, the Edmonton Ring Road and mortage lender Cervus Financial. Macquarie even made a US$2.6 billion hostile bid for the London Stock Exchange, which it was later forced to abandon. The bank, which makes money not only on the assets themselves but also on fees from underwriting related IPOs and managing the funds, enjoyed fourteen successive years of record profits as of 2005. "We had to be innovative in order to survive," says Nicholas Hann, managing director of Macquarie's North American division, based in Vancouver. "The foreign competition made the Australian banking market much more competitive and innovative than the Canadian banking market."

---

* A government decision banning Australia's big four banks from merging is still being vigorously challenged by the banks. Unlike Canadian banks, however, they are allowed to buy insurance companies.

When HSBC decided to embark on a global expansion in the 1980s, it had only US$47 million in deposits and was the world's twenty-fourth-largest bank. RBC, in contrast, boasted US$65 million in deposits and was number twelve globally. Instead of mega-mergers, HSBC opted for a "string of pearls" strategy and between 1998 and 2003 acquired eighty-six companies valued at US$43.4 billion. One of its earliest forays was into the Canadian market, where it had established a local subsidiary and in 1986 was allowed to buy the failing Bank of British Columbia after every other Canadian bank refused to buy it. In 2004 it pioneered foreign investment into Chinese banking by taking a 19.9 per cent stake in the country's fifth-largest lender. With US$1.5 trillion in assets and ten thousand branches in seventy-seven countries, HSBC is now the world's fourth-largest bank by assets. As outgoing chairman Sir John Bond was quoted as saying in 2005, "HSBC is resolutely international, and 'international' is a mindset."[86]

It seems to be a mindset that eludes Canadian banks. "HSBC woke up and saw the writing on the wall," says business consultant John Gruetzner of HSBC's decision to buy the Midland Marine Bank of Buffalo in 1980. "If none of the five major Canadian banks can drive to Buffalo and buy a bank, then what hope is there to amalgamate and be competitive?" Says Alan Middleton, an executive director with York University's Schulich School of Business: "They basically played with themselves behind the 49th parallel. Not one of them saw themselves as a significant player outside Canada, and for all the wrong reasons."

It wasn't always this way. The Bank of Montreal had a spectacularly successful merchant banking operation in New York in the second half of the nineteenth century and was at one time the largest incorporated bank in North America. The precursor to CIBC financed the bulk of U.S. cotton exports and was the principal banker to the U.S. government during its occupation of the Philippines in the early 1900s. The Bank of Nova Scotia followed the British rum trade to the Caribbean, while the Royal Bank went into Havana after the 1898 American victory over the Spanish in Cuba, eventually controlling 94 per cent of U.S.–Cuban trade and opening 121 branches worldwide.

The banks were, along with the nation's life insurers, Canada's most international institutions. During the late 1890s and early 1900s intrepid Canadian life insurance salesmen roamed the world; two thirds of Sun Life Financial's policy holders were outside Canada, and the company was the largest foreign insurer in Japan. Manufacturers Life (now Manulife Financial) sold insurance from Chile to Sumatra. As historian Michael Bliss noted in *Northern Enterprise,* "the sun did not set on either the British empire or Canadian life insurance salesmen."[87]

The insurers retrenched after the world wars, and in 1958 Prime Minister John Diefenbaker backed a move to mutualization—the private ownership of insurers by their policy holders—in a bid to protect them from foreign takeover. In 1999 Ottawa approved the first in a wave of demutualizations, as insurers went public in search of fresh sources of investment capital. Though still protected from foreign takeover, they have since expanded aggressively into Asia, with Sun Life rebuilding its historic presence in India and Manulife moving into China, Indonesia and Japan. In 2004 Manulife bought Boston-based John Hancock for $14.1 billion, the largest cross-border acquisition in Canadian history. It is now the second-largest insurer in North America and fourth in the world, based on market capitalization. Interestingly, neither Manulife CEO Dominic D'Alessandro nor Sun Life's Duncan Stewart was born in Canada.

Meanwhile, Canadian banks are still waiting to see whether they will be able to merge. In 2002, a Senate banking committee recommended that mergers be allowed, noting that "[i]n seeking to determine the 'public interest'... the paramount consideration should be the prosperity and competitiveness of the national economy."[88] Paul Martin's short-lived Liberal government, however, seemed to have no interest in explaining that to Canadians. John McKay, parliamentary secretary to Finance Minister Ralph Goodale, was quoted as saying, "It's up to the banks to convince Canadians that the public interest will be protected in any bank merger proposal."[89]

But while Ottawa may have abdicated what is arguably its *real* job—to provide Canadians with leadership in the quest to maintain and enhance the standard of living—global economic realities may soon trump any options that Canadians may have had. That Canadian banks can buy into the United States and Mexico, whereas banks from those countries cannot make acquisitions in Canada, is strikingly inconsistent—and Ottawa will eventually have no choice but to lift the ownership restrictions, says Waugh. "Why can TD buy Banknorth, why can we buy Inverlat, and Citigroup can't come up here and buy? Eventually it's going to happen because they are going to want reciprocity... and then we're all gone."

Canadian banks will have little defence against global giants like HSBC that have the firepower to buy the entire domestic banking system if they wanted. For Citibank, it will be like adding another state to their network, says Waugh. Head offices, with all their costly overhead and six-figure salaries, would be closed. For David Bond, a former chief economist at HSBC, it's already too late. "The train has left the station and it's not coming back. Within ten years Toronto will be as important as Des Moines, Iowa."

TO MILK OR TO BILK

Or Winnipeg. At one time touted as "the Chicago of the North," the modest prairie mid-cap town is a monument to arrested development, cut down in its prime and slowly left to moulder under the stifling weight of government paternalism. Winnipeg's short-lived reign as a thriving metropolis and gateway to the West is an ode to what might have been. Its wide avenues that famously intersect at the corner of Portage and Main are now pockmarked with derelict buildings and strewn with garbage, its stunted skyscrapers forever denied from reaching greater heights.

Relics of the city's former glory can still be found in the crumbling warehouses and abandoned bank offices that litter its historic downtown core, known as the Exchange District. Once covering forty city blocks, the area is named for the Winnipeg Grain Exchange, an impressive ten-storey Italian palazzo-style office building that was at one time the largest in the Dominion. Built in 1906, it was the foundation of the city's prodigious wealth and burgeoning commercial class, drawing merchants and traders from around the world to buy, sell and speculate on the future of "prairie gold."

Second only to Chicago for commodity trading in North America during its heyday, the Winnipeg Grain Exchange's first setback came with the 1914 opening of the Panama Canal, which made it easier to transport grain from Vancouver than through Winnipeg, the hub of Canada's transcontinental railway traffic. But it continued to grow, surviving two world wars, the Great Depression and no less than six government-sponsored royal commissions, called on the urgings of farmers' groups suspicious that speculators on the exchange were manipulating the price of wheat.* The Tory federal government of R.B. Bennett eventually capitulated to popular pressure, forming the Canadian Wheat Board, a state trading agency, and gave it a monopoly in 1943 to market wheat and other grains. It was, as Peter C. Newman has observed, the "decisive blow" for the exchange.[90]

In his book *The Acquisitors,* Newman wrote: "With the federal government intrusion into the business through the Canadian Wheat Board... many of the great grain families of Winnipeg dropped from prominence." With a few exceptions, he noted, "these family grain businesses have all vanished as if they never existed."[91] The Richardson family, the most prominent of the scattered survivors, controls the country's largest privately owned network of grain facilities, but its operations remain limited to Canada. George Richardson, the family patriarch, recalled the early effects of the board on the industry in an interview in the 1980s: "One regulator after another became stifling on the grain trade and there appeared to be a very limited future. There were mergers, people became discouraged and eventually went out of business."[92]

The Canadian Wheat Board and the tattered ruins of the Atlantic fishery are perhaps the greatest testaments to the destructiveness of ill-conceived government policy and regulation. But, as we have seen, there is barely a corner of the Canadian economy that is not in some way hobbled by interventionist policies that stifle entrepreneurism and condemn

---

* No evidence of wrongdoing was ever found.

Canadians to being inward-looking commodity producers. The proof is all around us, from the lag in adopting technology and the lack of globally relevant companies to, in some cases, entrenched poverty. Most disturbing of all is the almost wilful blindness to the systemic failures and the refusal to acknowledge the real source of the problems. Canada continues to cleave to policies and institutions rooted in a different economic and technological era in the name of some misguided nationalism that has only served to weaken its economic sovereignty.

Beer is a case in point. Unlike some things, Canada's reputation for brewing superior beer is not unfounded. The Prairie provinces boast ideal growing conditions for barley, beer's main ingredient, and are home to over two thirds of North American acreages. Yet as of 2006 the last three malting mills were built in the United States, even though it costs up to 50 per cent less to manufacture malt in Canada. But while Western Canada is arguably a more cost-effective location, what's even more imperative to maltsters, and ultimately brewers, is the ability to tailor the barley to their own specifications. They prefer to contract directly with farmers to get the protein content they want and to have the ability to trace crops for the purposes of food safety. In Canada, they can't do that—they have to buy directly from the Wheat Board. As a result, an industry study for the Alberta government concluded, the Canadian malting industry lost an estimated US$400 million in new investment as well as some US$30 million in annual operating expenditures that the new capacity would have generated.[93]

But that's not all they lost. Canada exports roughly 70 per cent of its malt, half of which goes to the United States—an export market that will be increasingly eroded by the new U.S. capacity. And since most Canadian-based maltsters are owned by U.S. multinationals anyway, they risk being phased out of the United States entirely by their freedom-loving parent companies, banished to Canada and any offshore business they can drum up. However, their biggest customers, the Canadian brewers, may just decide to relocate their processing facilities south of the border. The brewers, rather than having a competitive advantage in barley, actually pay higher malt prices than their U.S. rivals because of the Wheat Board monopoly and quotas on imported barley that ensure a captive market. Now that the two major brewers are foreign owned, they may not feel the same inclination to pay higher prices in the name of patriotism.

Sadly, it's the farmers who are the big losers. A shrunken Canadian malting industry means less demand for barley, while increased U.S. reliance on its own farmers means fewer exports to the United States at a time when barley-producing giants like Russian and Ukraine are increasingly competing in international markets. At the same time, because U.S. malt producers can't buy directly from Canadian farmers, there is no price competition, so the barley often ends up as lower-priced feed. "The Prairies should be the malting barley and beer capital of North America," says Rolf Penner, a Manitoba barley farmer. "We have this great opportunity, but we can't capitalize on it."

It's the same story with flour milling and the pasta industry. Leading Italian pasta makers actually advertise the fact they use Canadian durum wheat right on the box. So where are the Canadian manufacturers? From pasta brands Catelli and Lancia to flour miller Robin Hood, it's all American-owned. The Wheat Board has argued that it is precisely because of the American hegemony that farmers need it to defend them against massive U.S. conglomerates. In reality, the board has helped ensure that there would never be a Canadian industry to rival the Americans.

It's not as if Canadians haven't tried; in the late 1990s a group of some two hundred farmers from all three Prairie provinces got together in the hopes of starting up their own pasta-milling enterprise. Calling themselves the Prairie Pasta Producers (PPP), they were hoping to join forces with a farmers' co-operative in neighbouring North Dakota, which had become the third-largest pasta producer in the United States. The PPP planned to supply the North Dakotans with specialized wheat varieties in exchange for becoming members and owners in the multi-million-dollar endeavour.

The deal never happened. According to Wheat Board rules, farmers must first sell their wheat to the agency, which in turn will sell it back to farmers at its pooled price. The price was so high that it didn't pay to resell the wheat. The farmers tried negotiating with the board for years, but after continuous stonewalling they finally gave up in 2005. "We are not allowed to innovate," says Wally Mieli, a farmer from Moose Jaw, Saskatchewan, and the PPP's grimly resigned chairman.

Innovation has also proved strangely elusive for corporate giants like Bell Canada Enterprises (BCE) and an industry that is supposed to be on the leading edge of technological innovation. According to some accounts, Alexander Graham Bell invented the telephone in an Ontario farmhouse, yet when it comes to taking advantage of the latest gadgetry, Canada trails most of the developed world. It lags in the introduction of third-generation mobile phone systems, which combine high-speed mobile services with Internet access, as well as in rolling out cellular digital networks, coming in twenty-eighth out of thirty countries in cellular subscriptions per person, according to the OECD. Among industrialized nations, Canada ranks twenty-sixth in the modernization of its telecommunications industry.

BCE and others have been slow to invest in new applications, and consumers have been slow to buy them, because of a deeply flawed regulatory regime that has mistaken carving up the market between coddled oligopolies for true competition, says Eamon Hoey, a Toronto-based telecommunications consultant. With ownership restrictions keeping foreigners at bay,* government regulators handed the domestic wireline monopolies, BCE and Telus, cellular licences. Unlike an independent cellular company, which would have no choice but to grow, the carriers, buoyed by their perennially profitable wireline business, have little incentive to invest in the much more capital intensive cellular market. "The only way to be profitable is by not spending," explains Hoey. "They don't want to grow too fast, because then they would have to invest more."

In an ostensible bid to foment competition, the Canadian Radio-television and Telecommunications Commission (CRTC) has compensated by tying down the carriers with regressive regulations. BCE has been loaded

---

* Canada has the ignominious bragging rights to the most restrictive barriers to foreign investment in the telecommunications sector of any OECD country.

down with all manner of price caps, price floors and bizarre decrees that limit the discounts it can offer and bar it from calling back clients it has lost to rival carriers. In 2005, the CRTC imposed a price floor for what BCE could charge for VoIP (Voice over Internet Protocol), which uses the Internet to make long-distance calls, making Canada the only country except for Singapore to regulate the newly emerging technology.*

Under such stultifying circumstances, the one-time national champion, turned shrinking violet, has pursued two parallel strategies, neither of which contributes much in the way of economic wealth or ensures that the company remains globally competitive. On the one hand, BCE burned through millions of dollars investing in companies from TransCanada Pipelines to Quebecor in a bid to avoid the CRTC yoke. On the other hand, it employs an army of lawyers and lobbyists in Ottawa to deflect further controls and ensure that its cozy cut of the market remains intact.

Both approaches have ended up being a big waste of time; while other telecommunications carriers have extended their reach around the globe, Bell is no further ahead than it was a decade ago. If anything, it has fallen hopelessly behind—forced to cut thousands of jobs and sell off assets to counter declining profits and a shrinking share of the domestic market. In arguably the clearest sign of defeat, Bell parked its local phone lines and Internet accounts in parts of Ontario and Quebec into a regional income trust in 2006.

But Bell is not unique; Canadian companies in general waste an inordinate amount of time either cozying up to bureaucrats, tied up in trade disputes or fighting what they see as an autocratic and unfair system. And that's all in addition to the gauntlet of red tape and interprovincial trade barriers that cost the economy an estimated $8 billion annually. In a sad caricature of the old National Policy, each province has erected its own mini-barriers in a bid to protect its turf. Until recently, Ontario construc-

---

* In November 2006, Stephen Harper's Conservative government took the unusual step of reversing the CRTC's decision. In December, Industry Minister Maxime Bernier unveiled plans to free the big telcos from the most prohibitive regulations by as early as mid-2007.

tion workers couldn't work in Quebec, and B.C. logs couldn't be exported to Alberta, while a truck can't carry a load from one end of the country to the other without stopping to repack according to local provincial regulations. Each province insists on its own milk marketing board and even its own securities commission. According to the Royal Bank of Canada, the bank is subject to oversight from more than fifty financial services regulators across fourteen jurisdictions.

Companies and individuals that want to succeed must learn to either milk or bilk the system, with dairy farmers trading in government freebies and media companies manufacturing schlocky Canadian-content productions so they can skim a cut of the U.S. advertising revenue that's blocked at the border. It's often hard to tell the difference between government and industry in the telecommunications sector, with former BCE employees heading up the CRTC's telco division and the federal Competition Bureau—the former head of which now runs BCE's government-relations department.

Those who can't be bothered to court Ottawa either move their business to the United States or, at least until recently, sought tax-free status by converting their publicly traded companies into trusts, which avoid income tax by paying out all taxable income to their shareholders. The loophole triggered such a feeding frenzy, with just about every big-name company from Telus and Bell Canada to oil company Encana ready to sell their soul for a tax break, that Ottawa felt forced to finally intervene in late 2006 and throw away the loot bag before corporate Canada did itself some permanent damage. In a highly controversial move, Stephen Harper's Conservative government, fearing Canada was "moving to an income trust economy,"[94] held its nose and slapped a new tax on the trusts.

The industry's prolific popularity, however, left unchecked for so long, attests to the country's state-sanctioned proclivity to trade in ambitious global dreams for a quick, easy buck. While other countries actively discouraged trusts, they were allowed to flourish as a made-in-Canada alternative to putting up a "for sale" sign when companies got too big for their Canadian crib. Their decidedly domestic structure discourages foreign takeovers, helping to ensure more Canadian offices than there might otherwise have been. But instead of overseeing dynamic, internationally competitive firms, these corporate headquarters often serve as a last redoubt for Canadian globophobes.

Calgary-based Precision Drilling is a case in point. Previously one of the world's leading contract drilling companies, in 2005 it sold its international division to an American rival for US$2.3 billion in order to qualify for trust status. Precision founder Frank Swartout argued that he had no choice if the company's stock was to compete against other trusts' richer shareholder returns. Eric Reguly, a columnist with the *Globe and Mail* and a harsh critic of the trust stampede, lamented the loss of "one of Canada's few global champions" and the epidemic of navel-gazing it provoked throughout corporate Canada. "Months and months have been spent devoted to the pursuit of gaming the tax system, not building the company, hiring top talent, making strategic decisions and all other ingredients of competitiveness," he wrote. "The cost is impossible to measure, but it's there."[95]

Thomas Courchene has calculated the cost, at least to taxpayers, for the myriad of failed policies and development schemes aimed at propping up Atlantic Canada's sagging fortunes: $1 trillion. But this was not enough to save Newfoundland or the fishery, still mired in a petri dish of poverty and missed chances. At the height of the have-not province's bloated make-work bonanza, it boasted more than two hundred mostly government-funded fish-processing plants, dispersed among its tiny population of 500,000. Many of these plants were no more than plywood sheds operating two months a year—just enough time for workers to qualify for year-long unemployment insurance.

Each community was given a quota of fish to process, and any attempts to close unproductive operations or introduce new labour-saving technology were vigorously opposed. While Iceland was building state-of-the art trawlers that could flash freeze whole fillets on-board, Newfoundlanders insisted on using pitchforks to unload their catch, destroying the value of the fish and ensuring they could only be sold in chunks to fast-food outlets. "Atlantic Canada was perfectly positioned, like Iceland, to export to the world, but because of incredibly stupid government policies, we couldn't produce the quality fish the world demanded," says Fred McMahon, a director at the Fraser Institute. "Iceland went into high-quality fish processing. We tried to preserve every traditional job that ever existed."

These days, Iceland has to import labour from Europe to work at its booming processing plants, which operate year-round and pay out annual salaries of $40,000 to $50,000. Its large processing companies are now expanding into China. As for Newfoundland, the cod moratorium has largely destroyed the fishery, yet there are still 139 plants and an estimated twelve thousand fishers, many eking out a living between a few months of fishing and their welfare cheques. "You can't build an economy when half the population is off work half or two thirds of the time," says Peter Fenwick, an industry commentator and mayor of the hamlet of Cape St. George. "We've been poisoned by a social policy so badly designed it's just destroyed us."

And therein lies at least part of the problem. Whether it's the fishery, forestry or financial services, resources in Canada are viewed as a public utility whose prime purpose is to dole out jobs and insulate Canadians from the harsh realities of the marketplace. By buying up and selling the wheat produced by every Canadian farmer, guaranteeing the price of milk and handing out timber licences, the government has attempted to remove the risk from doing business while, whenever possible, retreating into the safety of make-work projects rather than facing the uncertainty of entrepreneurism.

That same search for security and stability is reflected among Canada's corporate class, which all too often is a willing accomplice in the government's ambitious safety net. "Canadian CEOs much prefer getting restricted entry into a restricted market rather than having to really compete," says Eamon Hoey. The consultant attributes the trait to Canadians' "fundamental belief that competition is destructive." But rather than issuing from some kinder, gentler wellspring, the belief is a byproduct of a less appetizing trio of idiosyncrasies, a deep distrust of change, laziness and fear—fear of failure, fear of success and fear of not making the grade.

That fear is manifestly obvious in the other defining characteristic of most government policies: their flagrant anti-Americanism. More than keeping Canadian companies in Canadian hands, ownership restrictions on everything from cable companies to bookstores are an attempt to keep Americans out. According to a representative of the Canadian Wheat Board, a repository of anti-American rhetoric, without the state trading agency, "Americans would take over the grain industry and we'd have no say as Canadian farmers, no say as the Canadian government. It's a sovereignty issue."

More than an indictment of American economic imperialism, the board's rationale is a telling admission of just how little Canadians think of their own abilities. For some reason, we need all these protections and supports, because without them our ability to fend for ourselves is so fragile that it would crumble like a house of cards. If we were allowed to strike out on our own and fail—even once, the reasoning goes—we risk losing everything. More importantly, wouldn't it prove something we've suspected all along? That somehow we're just not good enough to compete on an equal footing with the Americans?

In 1948, C.D. Howe thought the best way to cure Canada of a balance-of-payments crisis was by way of a reciprocity deal with the United States. The confident, U.S.-born cabinet minister assumed that Canadian manufactured goods would succeed if they had access to the vast American market. His boss, Prime Minister William Lyon Mackenzie King, flirted with the idea, but eventually balked. As King wrote in his memoirs, the idea of a Canadian selling manufactures to an American was "absurd."[96]

The same lack of confidence spurred the government of Pierre Trudeau to nationalize large swaths of the Canadian economy and introduce the Foreign Investment Review Agency to monitor foreign takeovers of domestic companies. In an interview, Donald MacDonald, finance minister under Trudeau, explained that the policies at the time were motivated by an inferiority complex. "We felt we couldn't take on the big boys south of the border—the notion of opening the market as a whole seemed inconceivable."

It's a fear that still haunts us today and is embodied in the prevalence of quasi-monopolies, from BCE to RBC, trapped in their gilded cages, too big for Canada, too small for the world. It's why so many Canadians feel most comfortable being employed by someone else, rather than striking out on their own, and why so few are prepared to step outside the safe confines of Canada to compete internationally. "They underestimate us," said one Saskatchewan farmer of the Canadian Wheat Board. "And in turn, we underestimate ourselves."

Luckily, not everyone believes that as Canadians they have to settle for second best. Increasingly, farmers like Chris Birch are challenging supply management, in some cases all the way to the Supreme Court of Canada. In the West, they are willing to go to jail for their right to sell their wheat to whomever they choose. The Prairie Pasta Producers aren't giving up either; they are looking to harvest a new variety of wheat that is not patented in Canada and therefore doesn't fall under the Canadian Wheat Board's monopoly. It's a move reminiscent of the Winnipeg Grain Exchange (now known as the Winnipeg Commodity Exchange), whose members, in an effort to find new niches outside the Wheat Board's control, were instrumental in developing a crop that has become synonymous with Canada: canola.

Despite the Exchange's best efforts to diversify into beef and even gold, it remains a shadow of its former self and now operates from the fourth floor of one of the city's colourless mid-rises. As of 2001, the exchange even gave up selling seats on the bourse, which used to go for $30,000 in the 1930s. In contrast, Chicago, building on its beginnings as a commodity trader, is home to one of the world's largest financial markets, with seats on its Chicago Board Options Exchange auctioning in 2006 for a record US$1.5 million. As for wheat, the acreages continue to shrink and prairie gold now makes up less than 40 per cent of farmers' incomes, compared with 78 per cent in 1950.

A century ago, when the exchange unveiled its stately new headquarters, the *Winnipeg Free Press* described it as "a lasting monument to that produce that has made Winnipeg famous throughout the world."[97]

It echoed the confident pronouncements of the visionary railway builder William Van Horne, who, during an 1892 visit to the new Gateway to the West, declared: "I regard the great future of Winnipeg as certain as sunrise, and I do not know any place on this continent with such magnificent prospects ahead of it."[98]

Sadly, the sun is setting, and the once-grand Winnipeg Grain Exchange is only a faded monument to what might have been.

5 | WHY MEXICANS DON'T DRINK MOLSON

> "Canadian business is very naïve. They think they are very
> self-sufficient; they have this 'We know what to do' attitude.
> Then they get into big trouble."
>
> **JAMES MOHR-BELL, EXECUTIVE DIRECTOR OF**
> **THE BRAZIL–CANADA CHAMBER OF COMMERCE**

DAN O'NEILL NEVER tired of warning his staff at Molson breweries about the perils of doing business in Brazil. "We are dealing with very tough people—they are tigers," he'd repeat ad nauseam. The former brewery chief came by his opinions honestly; unlike most Canadian executives, O'Neill had international experience, having spent four years in Rio de Janeiro working for consumer-products company S.C. Johnson. He was even fluent in Portuguese. "You guys in Canada think you have something to teach the Brazilians; you think that they are not as developed, not as sophisticated as you are," he'd admonish. "You can't imagine how much you have to learn from them."

Unfortunately, Molson had more to learn than even O'Neill realized. It would be a lesson the brewer would never forget.

Like the deceptively lethal Venus flytrap, the exotic promise of the Brazilian market had lured more than one Canadian company to its death. In the 1990s, Bell Canada International (BCI), enticed by the state sell-off of phone and cable licences, spent millions before going belly-up, effectively putting an end to its global ambitions. Telesystem International Wireless (TIW), the brainchild of Quebec entrepreneur Charles Sirois, quickly followed suit in a spectacular misadventure replete with thuggery and backroom machinations that all but decimated the company. That Molson would so quickly join its luckless compatriots in the growing graveyard of failed Canadian ventures in Brazil continues to confound analysts and shareholders alike.

Less than four years after buying Brazil's number two brewery, Cervejarias Kaiser, for US$765 million, Molson's Brazilian illusions crumpled like an aluminum beer can. Despite O'Neill's warnings, the venture imploded, almost on impact, as Molson helplessly watched Kaiser's market share tumble from nearly 17 per cent in 2002 to 7 per cent when it sold the venture for a meagre US$8 million and US$60 million in debt. Along the way, North America's oldest brewery seemed to commit glaring sins of omission that left it incapable of getting a handle on its marketing and distribution, two ingredients as basic to beer as barley and hops. The question is, who's really to blame? The murky Brazilian market or Molson?

The trail of Canadian corporate blood would seem to point to the market's man-eating tendencies. In 2003, for example, the owner of Brazil's third-largest brewery, Schincariol, was shot dead as he drove out of his garage. Five members of the Schincariol family were arrested in 2005 on charges of defrauding the government of some US$254 million in annual taxes. The Canadian beer market is positively collegial in comparison. "Let's face it, Brazil is pretty corrupt. You have to know who to bribe," says Michael Palmer, president of Veritas Investment Research in Toronto. "Molson was way out of its depth. It's like a bunch of little kids playing with sharks. They knew dick about Brazil and they didn't have a fucking clue what they were doing."

But to believe that Molson was unprepared for the complexities of Brazil is obviously not the whole story. The fact that three substantial Canadian companies would all fail so spectacularly speaks to fundamental flaws in the way Canadians approach foreign markets. More to the point, it underscores how the internal corporate structures and mindset indigenous to many of them are anathema to global expansion. In each case, the companies not only underestimated the sophistication of the market they were in, but over-estimated their own abilities. They were arrogant. Operationally, their goals were usually short term, opportunistic and focused on making a quick buck. And in the words of one Molson executive, when it came to making the necessary investment, they were "cheap, cheap, cheap."

"They come with the wrong attitude and the wrong strategy, and they make bad business decisions. And then they leave, blaming Brazil as a difficult market to do business in," explains James Mohr-Bell, executive director of the Brazil–Canada Chamber of Commerce. "It has nothing to do with Brazil and being corrupt. It's just mismanagement and poor strategy. Canadians don't have a very professional approach to doing inter-national business." In Molson's case, the company blithely ignored repeated warnings that the key to selling beer successfully in Brazil was a strong distribution system. Says Mohr-Bell: "You cannot be so naïve."

Molson was naïve, stunningly naïve; just not in the way you'd expect. O'Neill and company knew Kaiser was a lousy brand, and they knew the sixteen Coca-Cola bottlers who were looking to sell it had artificially boosted the beer's market share with cut-rate prices. Most importantly, they knew they couldn't rely on those bottlers, whose first allegiance was to Coke, to distribute the beer to the country's more than one million points of sale. Molson needed its own dedicated sales team if it was to have any hope of breaking into a foreign market where the competition was fierce, yet it opted to rely on the cola bottlers, who gleaned only minimal revenue from Kaiser. "Everybody knew it was a mistake. We knew it in advance," says a Molson executive familiar with the Brazilian venture. "If you give your distribution to someone else, you can just forget it."

With that realization, even before the acquisition was complete, the seeds of the company's swift downfall were sown. Subsequent missteps only sealed Molson's fate that much quicker. To begin with, of its three thousand employees, the company dedicated fewer than ten people to overseeing the acquisition and management of Kaiser, a company that pro-duced the same volume of beer as Molson. An investment banker wasn't hired to execute the purchase because it would have cost too much. "It sounds a bit cartoonish, but Molson really made decisions like that," said an observer familiar with the acquisition.

More attention would have been paid to buying a brewery in New Brunswick, an executive acknowledges; yet despite the meagre resources, Brazil was a constant source of tension and jealousy within the company. While Dan O'Neill heartily embraced the venture, doubling as Kaiser's de facto CEO, the Molson rank-and-file rebelled against the foreign foray that seemed to consume executive management's limited time and resources. "It was a day-to-day war within the organization. It was terrible," admits an executive. "We felt like the forgotten second child." Many were convinced that the effort was fruitless, given Molson's failure to even penetrate the U.S. market. "The employees didn't understand Brazil. The feeling was if we can't do this in the U.S., how can we do it in Brazil?"

O'Neill helped realize their fears when he committed the company's second major strategic error. When it came time to put someone in charge of the Brazilian operations, he called on Robert Coallier, Molson's chief financial officer and O'Neill's second in command. Not only did Coallier have no operational experience, but he'd never lived outside of Quebec. To make matters worse, Coallier, who spoke no Portuguese, was sent *alone*, without any Molson managers to back him up—the sole representative of the majority shareholder in a market already known to be notoriously difficult for Canadian companies.

In making his decision, O'Neill argued that he didn't want to influence the much savvier Brazilians at Kaiser with Molson's plodding ways. Coallier was simply there to make sure the business plan was executed. It was also a convenient way to save money. The move nevertheless baffled Molson management and market analysts alike. "Everybody was surprised. It was the icing on the cake," says one observer. "How do you send a guy from finance, who has spent his whole life in Quebec, to be an operator, not somewhere in Canada, his country, but to do a career shift in *another* country where the company made an acquisition that has to be integrated?"

Once in Brazil, Coallier had to make decisions in a vacuum, without being able to bounce ideas off fellow Canadian colleagues from Molson. Instead, he had to rely on advice from the Brazilians, whose cultural context he did not understand and whose interests and motivations may or may not have coincided with those of Molson. "He had to deal with two challenges at once. He had to deal with corporate issues, and he had to try and understand the people, how they think and how to decode their recommendations to understand what's good for the company. Some things might be good for Kaiser, but not for Molson," explains a person close to the company. "When they tell you, you have to do something, is it really the case? What experience does he have to decode what they are telling him?"

At the same time, Coallier was constantly in a tug-of-war with head office for more resources. It was a losing battle. "You could feel in talking with him that it was really tough," says a person who knew him. "He felt really alone."

What Molson should have done, say analysts close to the company, was strengthen Coallier's position by hiring the best on-the-ground operational expert that money could buy. The company had the means, but once again it wanted to save money. It eventually replaced Coallier with Fernando Tigre, a Brazilian turnaround specialist (whose last name coincidentally means "tiger"), but by then the writing was already on the wall. Molson hired 1,200 salespeople outfitted with scooters, raised Kaiser's price and even changed the flavour, but the Brazilian competition, sensing weakness, moved in for the kill. Ambev, the powerful local brewer with a 70 per cent share of the market, made sure that Kaiser didn't make it into the coolers of country's countless bars and restaurants. Schincariol was equally relentless. Says an executive: "The Brazilians were exactly what Dan said they were."

So the question remains. If Molson's brass-tacks CEO went into Brazil with his eyes wide open, why did he and the rest of the company wilfully choose to be blind? The simple answer is, because they thought they could be. Molson never bought into Brazil with the intention of building a global beer empire alongside the likes of InBev,* Heineken or Budweiser. It bought into Brazil with the idea of being able to sell out at a higher price. Company executives realized that Molson had already missed its opportunity to become one of the world's global beer consolidators, so they chose the next best option: build some critical mass and try to come up with a growth strategy that would catch the attention of one of the big players. Brazil, with its huge market and the minimal presence of foreign brewers, fit the bill. Although executives acknowledge it was never discussed explicitly, the sense was that if Molson could lay claim to the country's number two brand, it would force the global brewers to pay a premium to get into the market.

"The Molson family was very old English Montreal. They were very local and only thought about investing here in Canada. They never expressed any interest in going abroad," says an executive. "But if we were to maximize the selling price, we would need to increase the value by making one or more strategic investments. So the idea was, 'Let's move fast before the big guys get all the strategic players.'"

Sound familiar? Opportunistic and imbued with a distinctive skimming-like quality, the strategy bore all the hallmarks of a National Policy mindset, only in reverse. This time, the Canadians would stake out a foreign market, forcing the multinationals, the ones who were actually *serious* about building global companies, to pay a toll fee. This dilettantish approach was further exacerbated by an overriding yet completely unrealistic expectation that Molson would continue to post revenue and profit growth quarter after quarter. Dan O'Neill had publicly committed to growing the company's net income and, by extension, raising Molson's share price. Canadian shareholders didn't want to see their investment squandered and neither did Molson management, whose performance bonuses were directly tied to net income growth and whose stock options would be negatively affected by a drop in the share price.

---

* In 2004 Belgium's Interbrew, already the owner of Canada's Labatt breweries, bought Brazil's Ambev, to become the world's largest brewery.

Molson management therefore found itself in the peculiar situation of having a salary and bonus structure that was incompatible with the company's own expansion strategy. It had a serious problem on its hands: how was it going to roll out a major investment in a hugely volatile market while continuing to post profit growth? It soon became apparent that Molson couldn't absorb Kaiser's hefty price tag *and* pay to build its own distribution system. Management realized that if it didn't find a way to cut costs, its share price would suffer. It came down to a question of distribution or dividends, and dividends won out.

Even more telling, however, is the belief among management that Molson could somehow pull it off. In hindsight the entire proposition almost defies logic, yet despite O'Neill's open acknowledgement that Canadians were like guppies in Brazil's shark-infested waters, there was obviously an underlying conviction that the company could commit just about every sin in the international business bible and still be redeemed. "There was some magical thinking that as a Canadian company we could somehow get away with it," acknowledges an executive. "We were Molson— we had the name, the history, we could make things happen."

It's not hard to see how they came to that conclusion. The Canadian beer market is a surreal place. In Ontario, the largest market, people buy their beer at the cleverly named The Beer Store, a government-ceded retail monopoly owned by Molson and Labatt. For those who haven't shopped— and I use that word lightly—at The Beer Store, they're in for an edifying experience. The product, which is handled with about as much care as a load of cod, is rolled out to the customer on a conveyor belt. The "salespeople" wear rubber gloves. As one disenchanted customer wryly wrote in a newspaper letter to the editor: "[It] is the worst retail experience in Canada; more interest is shown in the product by people selling gravel."

Not only are consumers often forced to buy in bulk because it's less hassle for the breweries than supplying individual cans and bottles, but competing beer companies have to play by the monopoly's rules if they want to entertain any hope of being consigned to the store's "discount" category. (What exactly makes Molson Canadian a "premium" beer is hard to say). The most egregious stipulation is an industry-wide standard bottling agreement, imposed by the two big breweries, that all bottled beer be sold in the same dirt-brown long-necks. Ostensibly presented as a more efficient, environmentally friendly system, the recycled bottles save the breweries a ton of money as well as the effort of coming up with any sort of attractive packaging. It's also an effective non-tariff barrier to foreign breweries looking to crack the market.

As gatekeepers to the entire market, the Molson–Labatt tag team are able to sign licensing agreements with foreign brewers that essentially allow them to skim royalties off the top of rented brands. The government helps keep the market closed with a minimum floor price for beer aimed at keeping cheap American imports out and a ten-cent "environmental" levy on aluminum cans, the preferred packaging for U.S. brewers. The industry was even singled out by Brian Mulroney's Conservative government for a five-year reprieve from the 1989 Free Trade Agreement with the United States. (Arguably it was the least the feds could do to make up for interprovincial trade barriers that forced beer makers to establish a brewery in every province or region where they sold beer, handicapping their ability to be competitive.)

The upshot? Molson never had to learn to distribute, package or market its product, and whenever it wanted to make more money, it simply raised prices, while volume growth came from imported brands. What was its reward for such lackadaisical efforts? The Canadian beer market is one of the most profitable in the world. "They have a pretty cushy ride—their costs are so low because they save so much on bottles and distribution," says David Hartley, an analyst with Blackmont Capital in Toronto. "When you come from an environment like that and you try to get something to work in an aggressive market like Brazil, it's pretty incongruent, isn't it?"

Adds a Molson executive: "The fact that Molson doesn't have to compete in Canada means that all the brains in the organization are consumed with dealing with very small operational issues, like how to get one-tenth of a point more in market share from Labatt. We are not faced with key issues of strategic growth, which pull individuals up to that next level of thinking."

So was Molson naïve? Yes, but the naïveté did not stem so much from a lack of knowledge of the Brazilian market as from the company's distorted estimation of its own abilities and of what it actually took to succeed. If anything, the experience only proved that there are tried and true formulas for tackling international markets. Those rules weren't followed, and the reaction was predictable: the Brazilians ate Molson alive.

FOR WHOM THE BELL TOLLS

While Molson executives acknowledge that the company's short stint in Brazil brought an end to the company's 219 years as an independent brewer, Molson's experience was positively civilized compared with the rape and pillage of BCI, Bell Canada's short-lived international wing, and TIW. They made many of the same mistakes as Molson did, and like the brewer, they had no one to blame but themselves.

Brazil was a cable operator's dream when Peter Legault first set eyes on the market in the late 1980s. The country's television industry, dominated by a handful of domestic broadcasters, was closed to cable, but Legault, a Toronto investment banker who had launched First Choice pay TV, planned to be there the day it opened up. When the Brazilian government began auctioning off cable concessions in 1994, Legault and seven other Canadian partners teamed up with the country's largest publishing house, Editora Abril, to secure majority stakes in ten licences covering the greater São Paulo area. The venture, Canbras Communications Corp., had barely begun raising money for the project when it attracted the attention of BCI. Legault and his associates thought they had found the perfect strategic partner: a company with technological know-how and a Canadian cachet in country general distrustful of Americans. How wrong they were.

Bell was a bully from the very beginning, issuing ultimatums to the Canbras management and dragging negotiations on for seven months before finally investing in two convertible debentures that would give it a 51 per cent stake in the company. But what was worse, say Canbras founders, was Bell's demeaning attitude towards its Brazilian partners. The

Civita family, while quietly unpretentious, were the fabulously wealthy owners of Latin America's largest publishing house. The Ugolinis, one of the original licence owners who retained a seat on the Canbras board, were the leading sugar refiners and the largest wire manufacturers in Brazil. Bell was small potatoes compared with these people, yet the BCI executives treated them like "serfs," says Legault. "They immediately pissed off our partner through their arrogance. Their attitude was, 'We're going to tell you peons in Brazil how to run a cable company.'"

Omar Grine, another Canbras founder and its CEO from 1995 to 1997, considers the experience one of the most frustrating of his professional career. "The Brazilians were so disappointed in Bell. To this day if you mention Bell to them, they go berserk," he says. "They had no interpersonal skills, no cross-cultural references or sensitivity training. They treated people like they came from the bush, as if all Brazil had was soccer and samba."

It would not take long, however, for Bell to get its comeuppance. It dug deeper into Brazil, teaming up with TIW in 1997 to win two mobile-phone licences, which were quickly followed up with local telephony concessions in São Paulo and Rio de Janeiro. In each case, BCI took minority stakes (but had operating control) in the ventures and hired contractors, consultants and Bell retirees to run them. As was the case in many of the dozen or so countries where BCI invested over the decade, there was little rhyme or reason to its strategy. Its cozy monopoly back in Canada had provided the carrier with a war chest of cash that it reportedly sprinkled around "like poker chips,"[99] investing millions without having done the proper market research or developing any discernible business plan. It repeatedly introduced technology ill-suited to the market while its people on the ground complained they were given no direction from head office.[100] "It became obvious that Bell didn't have a strategy to penetrate Latin America in the proper way," Grine confirms.

By 1999 Michael Sabia, the newly installed chief of BCI, was selling off the company's Asian assets, turning a neat profit. It was clear that BCI had never planned to stick around for the long haul—its international commitment was limited to the time it would take to flip its scattered investments.

Unfortunately, in Latin America it didn't make its getaway fast enough. In June 2000, Bell threw its lot in with Carlos Slim Helú, the shrewd owner of Mexican carrier Telmex, to create a pan–Latin American mobile phone and Internet operator, Telecom Américas. As part of the three-way tie-up, which also included SBC Communications of Texas, BCI chipped in most of its South American assets and committed to making around $1 billion in cash and capital contributions to the new venture.

It didn't take long for things to unravel. The money was supposed to come from the sale of Vésper, BCI's local telephony holding in Brazil. BCI had tried to include Vésper in the Telecom Américas deal, but Slim, who is renowned for buying depressed assets at a bargain, wouldn't pay the $1 billion that BCI executives were demanding. After trying, and failing, to play a game of hard-nosed brinksmanship with the canny Slim, BCI thought it had clinched a deal with one of Vésper's U.S. shareholders, but the deal soon fell through. Increasingly squeezed between Vésper's huge financial demands and its obligations to Telecom Américas, BCI was dangerously over-leveraged and careening towards insolvency when the telecom bubble broke. By the end of 2001, BCI was forced to write off Vésper to the tune of $86.5 million.

Telecom Américas was restructured several times, but by mid-2002, BCI could no longer stay afloat and sold its 39 per cent stake to Slim for US$366 million.* BCI was wound up, and all that remains is a shell for managing the various lawsuits launched by disgruntled shareholders. Meanwhile BCI's original investment, Canbras, went through half a dozen CEOs in as many years. In November 2000, minority investors, including the original founders, offered to buy back the struggling cable operator, but Sabia refused, saying that Canbras was extremely important to BCI's strategy in Brazil. Three years later, with Canbras facing imminent default, Bell dumped the company for the embarrassingly small sum of $32.6 million. To

---

* In 2002, Bell Canada Enterprises, BCI's parent company, also took a $7.5 billion write-down on Teleglobe Inc., the overseas telecommunications provider it had bought from Charles Sirois just two years before for more than $7 billion.

add insult to injury, Bell opted to sell Canbras's assets instead of its shares so that Bell could take a tax writeoff on the $250 million it had sunk into the operator. "They left the company as a shell, which really screwed the minority shareholders," says Legault.

Canbras's frustrated founders blame the failed enterprise on Bell's monopoly position back home and a corporate culture that combined the worst of government civil service mentality with unchecked corporate conceit. "They were used to a monopoly environment in Canada where they could demand things and worry about the consequences later, and you can't get away with that in a foreign country," says another Canbras co-founder. Bell management mistakenly believed they could parachute in for a few years, flip their investments and make some fast and easy money. "They were never committed to being international," says the one-time investor. "And as a result, bci doesn't exist anymore."

For telecom analyst Eamon Hoey, no great fan of Bell, the mighty monopoly's ignominious downfall can be distilled to one thing: arrogance. "They had a false sense of their our own capabilities and a false sense about being able to carry their Canadian experience to these countries, where there is a different culture and different ways of doing things," he concludes. "What did they know about investing in these countries? Zip, zero. They lacked the experience, and when they saw it was really hard to do, they abandoned ship. It was a lot easier to go back to Canada, throw up their hands and leave shareholders with the brunt of the loss."

Still, it's hard to say who had the last laugh. Vésper, now owned by Brazil's Embratel, is reportedly doing quite well these days. Before things went sour with Editora Abril, the Civita family had asked Bell to be its strategic partner for its entire cable platform. Bell dragged its feet and eventually turned them down. The Brazilians went with an American partner instead, and Abril, through its cable company, tva, which owns the rights to mtv in Brazil and controls the country's leading Internet provider, is now Brazil's second-largest media conglomerate. "If Bell had had a little bit more sensitivity and more competent people, it could have been one of the largest, if not the largest player in Latin America," says Grine.

Instead, that title goes to Carlos Slim Helú. Telecom Américas is now a subsidiary of Slim's América Móvil, the largest wireless carrier in Latin America, with 93.3 million wireless and two million fixed-line subscribers in fourteen countries. In contrast to BCI, Slim has followed a very deliberate strategy that combines a long-term approach with opportunistic acquisitions and a policy of complete ownership control. In 2005 América Móvil posted revenues of US$16.4 billion and profits of US$2.8 billion. In 2006 *Forbes* magazine listed Slim as the world's third-richest man; his fortune was estimated at US$30 billion.

DANCING WITH THE DEVIL

I interviewed Slim when I was a correspondent for the *Financial Times* in Mexico. It was difficult not to be in awe of a man who commanded so much wealth and power, and yet, although he had his views on how the media should cover his vast holdings, he was surprisingly approachable—one might even say hospitable. In contrast, when people met Daniel Dantas, they came away with an entirely different impression. The founder of an upstart Brazilian asset-management firm, Banco Opportunity, Dantas had the reputation for being ruthlessly brilliant and more than a little scary. Even his fellow Brazilians kept their distance from him. "It only took a few seconds for you to realize that he didn't build his empire by being nice to people," says a Canadian businessman familiar with Dantas. "It was the look in his eyes, I can't even describe it. People were afraid of him."

Yet that didn't seem to stop TIW's Charles Sirois and his shrewd right-hand man, Bruno Ducharme, from getting into bed with him. Even before TIW (Telesystem International Wireless) teamed up with Opportunity in 1998 to acquire two privatized cellular-phone holdings, the Quebecers had been warned of Dantas's wily ways. A fellow Canadian businessman who'd met with Dantas, and decided to steer clear of him, recalls warning Ducharme in 1996 to "watch his wallet" when it came to the Brazilian banker. "Ducharme never asked why, and didn't want to know," says the businessman.

Instead, TIW, eager not to miss out on investment opportunities and confident it had found in Dantas someone who shared the same goals and entrepreneurial drive, downplayed the potential risks. To speed things up, it even dispensed with the time-consuming legal formalities of signing a shareholders' agreement with Dantas. TIW figured it could cover its bases by structuring their joint venture, Telpart, in such a way as to give it strategic influence over the appointment of management and board members, in return for its 49 per cent stake. The rest of the company was divided between Dantas's Opportunity fund, which held 27 per cent, and several pension funds, with a 24 per cent stake.

"We trusted Opportunity. We figured they were like us," says one former TIW executive. "We thought, if we get into a conflict, we could challenge him because we were smart enough to take him on."

But they had no idea what they were up against. TIW never anticipated the lengths Dantas was willing to go to secure an advantage, regardless of the agreements he'd made. The banker convinced the pension funds not only to join forces and create a second company, Newtel, which had a majority 51 per cent stake in Telpart, but to give Dantas a 51 per cent stake in the new venture. As a result, Dantas's fund, with 27 per cent ownership, now indirectly controlled Telpart. TIW verbally agreed to this structure on the condition they sign a formal agreement later ensuring shared control of the mobile operator. That agreement never came about.

TIW, which had paid some US$380 million for its share in Telpart, quickly lost control over the enterprise. The two sides squared off in an acrimonious power struggle involving phalanxes of lawyers and, by one count, twenty lawsuits.[101] Ducharme, perhaps believing he could beat Dantas at his own game, reportedly helped finance lawsuits against the banker by his enemies. TIW descended deeper into the murky underbelly of Latin American magic realism when it recruited Nelson Tanure, the wealthy and well-connected owner of Rio's second-largest newspaper, to outflank Dantas. Instead, the scheme was exposed when a well-respected journalist, believed to be in Tanure's pay, was caught writing columns overtly in support of TIW. The discovery set off a massive scandal.

By 2002 TIW was fed up and sinking under the weight of its disparate holdings, which stretched from China to Romania. Highly leveraged, it was forced into a major restructuring while under bankruptcy protection. Within a year, TIW sold out to Dantas for $70 million, in addition to paying untold legal costs. Says one Canadian veteran of Latin American business: "It was the worst case of being screwed by a partner I have ever seen in my life." But according to TIW executives, there was little they could have done to avoid the ensuing disaster. While the company has been heavily criticized for failing to sign a shareholders' agreement, executives argue that legal documents would have meant little in a country where judges can be bought and the rule of law is questionable. "When things start to go sour in real life, if you need to go back to this piece of paper, it's finished, especially if you are a foreign operator," says one insider. "The balance of power is what counts."

Eduardo Klurfan, the former representative for Scotiabank in Brazil and the ex-president of the Brazil–Canada Chamber of Commerce, has a different take. "It's not the Brazilian system. The same thing would have happened in Canada if they had done the same stupid thing," says the Argentine-born banker. "Their problem was, they underestimated the Brazilians and thought themselves more knowledgeable." It's a point that TIW executives, in hindsight, acknowledge. "We thought, wrongly, that we could manage any downsides because we were so smart."

MY WAY OR THE HIGHWAY

Like Molson and BCI, Alberta's TransAlta had never set foot outside the heavily regulated confines of the Canadian energy market when it decided to take the plunge into Argentina. In the early 1990s, the land of pampas and gauchos, not unlike TransAlta's own Alberta, was alive with possibility, racking up double-digit growth under the market-oriented reforms and privatization drive being pushed by the country's silk-stockinged president, Carlos Menem. In addition to selling off creaking state-owned enterprises, the Argentines were busy building hydroelectric dams and generation plants for sale to giddy foreign investors.

TransAlta, with its Chilean and American partners, dove in, acquiring the nearly completed Hydroeléctrica Piedra del Águila, a massive 1,400-megawatt dam in the southern state of Neuquen. Although the Canadians focused on ensuring that the construction was up to spec, they glossed over crucial elements that they either didn't understand or failed to anticipate. Despite their technical expertise, they overlooked one of the most fundamental elements of any energy project—they never bothered to check whether they would be able to get their electricity to market. Perhaps used to the reliability of Canada, they assumed there was enough transmission capacity to transport the dam's electricity to the capital of Buenos Aires, more than a thousand kilometres away. There wasn't.

Making matters worse, TransAlta, which was used to the steady, regulated fixed-pricing regime at home, was operating in a highly volatile spot market where prices could change "ten times an hour." Hindered from reaching the much more lucrative Buenos Aires market, it was forced to sell into the local energy grid, which was already flooded with generating capacity, at a massive differential. Prices were depressed further by the 1994 peso currency crisis in Mexico, which devastated markets throughout the region and caught TransAlta, which was relying on short-term project financing, off guard. When its debt came due, the company was unable to secure new funding to replace it and was forced to pour more of its own money into the project, including into the construction of a new transmission line.

In 1998, TransAlta finally bowed out, taking a $72 million writedown on the project and selling its 16 per cent stake the following year.

"Why would you go from being a regulated business to investing $200 million in a country you've never been in before, with people you've never worked with, in a spot market that should terrify anyone who's never done it before?" said a person familiar with the project. "They didn't see the big picture. They came at it with an overconfident 'We know everything and we don't need any help, thank you very much' attitude."

What is harder to understand is why TransAlta followed up its Argentine fiasco by moving into Mexico and making many of the same mistakes again. This time, the private power generators being auctioned off by the Mexican government ensured a guaranteed revenue stream. The problem was (and is) that the government had to rely on PEMEX, the state-run oil monopoly, to supply the gas that TransAlta's two generating projects would convert into electricity. Not only was there was no infrastructure for getting the gas, but PEMEX was plagued by gas shortages, prompting the monopoly to play politics with the supply it did have while being forced to import higher-cost fuel from the United States.

At the same time, TransAlta also ran into multi-million-dollar cost overruns in building the generators. Despite the notorious difficulty in getting just about anything done in Mexico, not to mention its rather militant electricity workers' union, the company decided to manage the construction and initial start-up largely from Calgary, flying engineers in on shifts instead of basing them on site. Steve Snyder, TransAlta's chief executive, admits it was perhaps the company's biggest mistake. "We relied overly heavily on commuting back and forth. Culturally the engineers didn't want to move and we thought it was good enough to handle that way," he says. "But you need to be permanently on site to deal with every-day issues and develop government relations. We didn't understand that the up-front costs of Mexico are higher than elsewhere."

To veteran observers, it comes down to a failure to understand that things are *different* in other countries. All too often, Canadians hold the misguided belief that somehow things will be *easier*, particularly in developing countries, where they assume that their skills and abilities are superior. "There's this sense that five of our guys are worth fifty of theirs. They believe the farther away, the easier it is," says one Canadian executive sent to manage a multi-million-dollar project on his "stomach lining," as he puts it. "However much you think you need, you should put in double the effort; but they tend to put in half, so it's out of proportion by a factor of four. What does that do? It sets you up for failure."

Unfortunately for TransAlta in Mexico, the unanticipated cost overruns could not be passed on to its customers because its revenues are capped. "They bid into a straitjacket situation," says a person familiar with the project. "They're stuck with it for fifteen years. They can't apply a price increase, and they can't apply it to new customers. They're underwater." Snyder insists the ventures are "successful," but he is clearly chastened. "It's still a challenge. Revenue is not what we thought, and costs are higher." When it comes to counselling other companies to go abroad, he is decidedly bearish: "It's riskier, costly, and if the rewards are relatively sure in your home base, why would you do it?"

Thierry Vandal, chief executive officer of Hydro-Québec (HQ), needs no convincing when it comes to the pitfalls of international markets. Born in Germany to a French Canadian father who was born in Massachusetts, Vandal switches seamlessly from French to English thanks to having lived all over Canada following his father's military career. Although he can trace his family's Québécois roots back to 1680, the fortysomething executive is not cut from the same cloth as the typical HQ rank and file, which is perhaps why he firmly believes that the lumbering, politically influenced provincial monopoly doesn't have the constitution for international business.

"Trying to do work internationally is a fantastic challenge. You are working with different political rules, different regulatory rules," explains Vandal. "You figure you do it here, you have to do it there, but you tend to forget some of the reasons you do it successfully here—like the fact that you benefited from tariff barriers that gave you a head start. You figure it's easy, so you go elsewhere," he adds. "But international is very different and dangerous in an organization like HQ, where you need total discipline in deciding where you put your development dollars. If you have a cultural habit of spending a lot of money, that may make sense in Quebec, but when it comes to the rest of the world, it's a recipe for disaster."

Which is exactly what happened at HQ. In 1994, environmental opposition put an end to the company's proposed Great Whale hydro project and the utility was confronted with the prospect of no new development in the province. Going international seemed like the next logical step and fit in nicely with the separatist Parti Québécois's bid to assert its independence internationally. Hydro-Québec International (HQI) was formed, becoming "one of the flagships for the state of Quebec," says Vandal. Politically motivated and buoyed by an unlimited fount of investment dollars, HQI soon had more than two hundred new recruits with no international experience running amok, snapping up deals pell-mell, from Senegal to Vietnam.

"They spent a huge amount of money travelling all over the world, flying business class and cocktailing around," says one former HQI employee. "They were all over the map, paying one million here, ten million there. They had no plan, no focus and no strategy. It was disastrous." The organization invested not only in generation but in energy transmission and distribution while routinely sending unqualified employees with no language skills to manage far-flung assets. "HQ is not a world-scale distribution retailer," admits Vandal, who assumed the company helm in 2005. "When it tried internationally, it failed."

HQ's ignorance of international markets came to the fore in easy-going Australia. The Quebec utility, together with an Australian partner, built a costly underground transmission cable linking the electricity grids of New South Wales with Queensland state. Originally proposed as a private line, HQ subsequently applied to the Australian government to regulate the service, but only *after* it began operating in 2001. The slightly baffled government regulator struggled with the request because, in trying to assess what tariff rates to apply, it determined that the cable should simply "*never have been constructed*" and therefore was of questionable value. It compromised by issuing rates based on a significantly cheaper overhead cable, ensuring HQ would not see any return on its investment for the next 10 years.

Not surprisingly, within a year of the 2006 decision, HQ sold its stake in the ill-conceived venture. It's par for the course for HQ, which has sold off or exited almost every market it has entered, leaving a trail of bad blood and red ink. "I wouldn't be surprised if they have lost $200 million to $300 million in the past few years," says a former employee of HQI, which has been reduced to a shell company and employs perhaps a dozen people.

It has also been costly for Canadian companies that have entered markets in HQI's ruinous wake and have struggled not to be tarred with the same brush. "HQI came up with a lot of duds, made commitments it couldn't deliver on, and left a trail of very bad deals," says one engineering company executive. "They had too much arrogance. For them, going to another country was like visiting the colonies; they had a 'we'll teach you' attitude.'" The problem was, they'd never had to "sharpen their pencils to compete," he says. "They had the financial might, but not enough *sagesse* to compete."

That same blunt-edged arrogance also explains how another Quebec-based company, Lassonde Industries, blew its chance to become one of the leading producers of fruit juice in China. The opportunity was practically handed to Canada's second-largest juice maker on a silver platter. Like many Canadian companies, Lassonde, known for its trademark Rougement apple juice, earns a significant portion of its revenues licensing foreign-owned brands like Allen's, Tetley and Sun-Maid in Canada, where 90 per cent of its sales originate. It had never ventured far from home when, in 1993, the company was contacted by Gervais Lavoie, a Quebec native who had been living in China on and off since the mid-1970s. A former Maoist turned entrepreneur, Lavoie believed China's newly emerging consumer class would lap up the opportunity to buy fruit juice, still a relatively unknown product at the time.

Lavoie originally approached Lassonde with the idea of buying a second-hand juice machine it was trying to sell. He ended up cobbling together a joint venture in which the Quebec company chipped in the equipment while a Chinese partner supplied the bulk of the investment, some US$1.2 million, which included an idle cement factory and US$500,000 in seed money. They called the brand Rumeng, which roughly translates as "dreams of women" in Chinese, and its slick, black-labelled bottles of apricot, peach and strawberry nectars sold for US$10 a bottle in high-end restaurants.

Within five years of its 1995 start-up, the hugely popular drink line was ringing in annual sales of more than US$15 million and was the third-largest juice brand in China. The operation boasted 30 offices around the country, with 500 employees, and its ubiquitous label could be found in remote corner stores along the historic Silk Road to supermarkets in Shanghai. Lassonde had paid little attention to the faraway operation, happy to let Lavoie and the Chinese run the show—until it realized that Rumeng, representing just 10 per cent of Lassonde's revenues, was responsible for a whopping 40 per cent of profits.

Suddenly, the Quebecers decided they needed to take charge and bought out the Chinese partner in 2000. They embarked on a costly spending spree, buying new equipment and replacing local management with a Canadian chief financial officer and a marketing manager from France. "They thought the Chinese were no good at running the business," says Lavoie, who, with a 15 per cent stake, had no more say in daily operations. "We were doing too well," he says. "When the Canadians saw that the Chinese were doing better than them, they didn't like it. They wanted to get their hands on the profit and the money."

It took just a year for profits to flatline, and by 2003 Rumeng was losing money. Lavoie and the Chinese offered to buy back management of the company, but Lassonde refused, says Lavoie, who resigned soon after. The Quebecers turned down at least three other buyout offers, including one from China's largest juice company, he says. Instead, Lassonde quietly cleaned out the company bank accounts and pressured its accountants in China to write off inventory and raw materials that Lavoie says were still perfectly good. Lassonde declared a $13 million loss on the venture—a tasty little tax writeoff—and left China still owing $4 million to the China Agricultural Bank and $2.3 million to its former Chinese partner. "The Chinese thought, this is impossible, especially from Canadian people," says Lavoie, adding, "The Chinese would never do what Lassonde did to us."

The Lassonde case is emblematic of a pervasive belief shared by companies big and small that what happens outside of Canada is somehow irrelevant. And because little value is placed on foreign operations, there is a prevailing sense that other countries and cultures have little to contribute to the received wisdom of corporate Canada. Surprisingly, this is true of the country's most multinational companies, like Bombardier, which despite having operations in dozens of countries is not quite as international as its corporate profile might suggest. "The problem is, Bombardier is still a very provincial and very parochial company," explains a former executive. "They still believe you can go to Germany and tell the Germans or the Mexicans that they should do things according to La Pocatière. Instead, I think that La Pocatière could learn a few things from the Mexicans and the Germans. I think it's changing, but they never try to glean things from other countries."*

The ex-employee illustrates his point with a small but telling example. He was asked to organize a dinner in Montreal between Bombardier executives and visiting Mexican dignitaries. When a high-ranking Bombardier lieutenant realized that the employee, following the regular social protocol, had seated the spouses together with the businessmen, he became angry and told him not to put a Mexican woman beside him. "He said he didn't want to waste his time talking to women," he explains. In fact, any time the Mexicans came up to Quebec, the company staunchly advised that it would pay for no more than one dinner, and no entertainment. In contrast, the Spaniards, from rival train manufacturer CAF, did a fantastic marketing job, he says, taking Mexican subway officials on trips to Spain. "In Latin America, when you don't know how to behave you are banned," the employee says. "But Bombardier doesn't want to learn."

Wining and dining is, in fact, a sore point for Canadian companies in general. They are often criticized for being cheap and unsophisticated when it comes to wooing potential customers. They seem to put very little stock in cultivating relationships, preferring to get straight down to business, a practice that outside of the United States and Canada is not only considered crass, but unrealistic. To a large degree, the brass tacks approach can be attributed to a strong legal framework in North America that allows for a higher degree of transparency and efficiency in business transactions. There is more implicit trust, making formalities less necessary. But while to Canadians that might make more sense, it won't change the fact that the rest of the world operates according to a vastly differently set of parameters.

"The biggest mistake Canadians make is not understanding the culture of business when they are in another country," explains Mark Romoff, a former federal trade commissioner who has been posted to Japan, Mexico and Malaysia. "In most countries, relationships count first, business will

---

* La Pocatière is Bombardier's original subway manufacturing plant, located 370 kilometres northeast of Montreal.

come. For Canadians, business is first and the relationship comes later. The best price is what counts, and that's what rarely counts in most other places in the world."

So what happens? Canadians do a five-day, five-country tour of Asia and then are surprised when they are unable to drum up any business. Or they send a still wet-behind-the-ears MBA to be their marketing manager in Asia who "doesn't know how to dress, talk or entertain," says Milton Parissis, a Toronto-based corporate strategist who has worked in 114 countries. "North Americans are very self-cherishing. It's my way or the highway. They can't own up to the fact that things are done differently in other countries. And if they don't understand, they delegitimize it."

Executives with Westcoast Energy had their own brush with Canadian parochialism when they tried to strengthen ties between British Columbia, where the company was headquartered, and Mexico, where it was looking to invest. When Mexican President Ernesto Zedillo visited Vancouver in 1996, the company had difficulty persuading B.C.'s premier, Glen Clark, to meet the Mexican head of state because he assumed Zedillo was in town for "a labour issue."

In 1997, the Mexican president returned to Vancouver to attend an APEC leaders' summit, which included a dinner held in his honour with the CEOs from eighteen Asia-Pacific countries. During the dinner's opening speeches, the Canadian hosts stumbled while trying to pronounce Zedillo's name, recalls one Westcoast executive. The most embarrassing point, however, came when the head of the Vancouver Port Authority attempted to engage Mexico's minister of commerce in conversation. "Do you own a car?" she asked, followed by: "Do you live in an apartment?" (Most Mexican cabinet ministers are educated at American Ivy League schools, perfectly fluent and quite well off, and their preferred mode of transport is a black chauffer-driven Ford Explorer.) The Westcoast Energy people were already squirming in their chairs when the head of the Port Authority managed to outdo herself. As the waiter came over to fill the water glasses, she leaned over to the Mexican minister, lightly touching his elbow, and confided, "In our country it's safe to drink the water." As one company executive summed it up: "The Mexicans thought we were a bunch of yahoos."

International business veterans attribute this disconnect to the fact that Canadians simply aren't big travellers. They don't get out, so they cannot test their perceptions, either of themselves or of others, against reality. The problem is compounded by fact that Canadians are "language phobes," argues one well-heeled business traveller. After enduring years of being force-fed one of the country's two official languages, we seem to equate a new idiom with bad-tasting cough medicine. While Europeans easily glide between three or four languages, English Canadians, still haunted by high school French, struggle to string a sentence together. French Canadians, denied the right to study in English if they so choose, are similarly handcuffed. Weighted as it is with politics and history, language, instead of being Canada's window to the world, has for many become a dead end.

How else to explain why, for example, a leading Canadian window manufacturer would send two unilingual *Mennonites* to drum up business in Latin America? "They didn't speak Spanish, didn't drink and didn't smoke—in a place where wine is sustenance and a good cigar is savoured," explains a marketing executive at the company. "It's like going to Japan and not eating sushi."

One of Milton Parissis's more gruelling experiences involved a pharmaceutical firm looking to strike a distribution deal in Saudi Arabia. The Canadian company sent a female marketing manager to hammer down an agreement with a Saudi sheik. The meeting had barely started when the sheik leaned over to Parissis and asked, "How much for her?" Parissis tried to placate the sheik by giving him his gold pen, and even offering him his cufflinks. The sheik was unmoved. "Everything has a price," he said, "and I've made a request of you." Says Parissis, "It was pretty sticky. The Saudis were offended. They were rejected, and you never reject someone in his own house in Saudi Arabia. Needless to say, we didn't get the deal."

Parissis couldn't even recoup his gold pen as a business expense because he didn't have a receipt. In what he interprets as a telling indication of Canadian naïveté and his own personal pet peeve, most companies refuse to pay expenses without a receipt, even though most countries, especially developing ones, don't have formal invoicing systems (try getting a receipt from a Mexican taxi cab).

Ultimately, those in the field place the blame for Canadians' approach to international markets squarely at the feet of corporate chief executives and their boards of directors. Described by one European observer as "clubby and indecisive," Canadian executives rarely have international experience or the stomach for the raucous foreign markets so alien to cozy Canadian board rooms, where everyone knows your name. "CEOS don't have global experience," admits Michael Stewart, former head of Westcoast Energy's international arm. "I don't think the capability is lacking, but the thinking is timid and narrow." Prem Benimadhu, a corporate consultant and researcher with the Conference Board of Canada, agrees: "It's the mindset we have at the top of organizations. They find it intimidating." TransAlta's Steve Snyder doesn't dispute the problem: "It's naïve to think a board and management team which has worked exclusively in Alberta is now going to have global brains."

As a result, Canadian companies seem to make the same mistakes over and over again. Either overly cautious, seeing a potential threat at every turn, or all too trusting, they move with glacial timidity when boldness is called for, or get duped by those who don't play by the straight-laced rules. Overwhelmingly, they underestimate the importance of culture and language, routinely sending people with no overseas experience, assuming that being good at your business is enough to make it work in another country. Consequently, they overestimate their own abilities in markets that are invariably more difficult and costly to operate in—at least if one is not used to them.

"Canadians have a very immature, incomplete, biased, jaundiced view of what goes on in other countries," says Ian Mallory, president of Calgary venture capital firm Pickworth Investments. "A lot of what we take for granted about our position in the world can be traced back to a blindness at head office, from people who don't travel and don't speak the language." Adds Pierre Alarie, who worked in Latin America for fifteen years, representing both the government and the private sector: "We need to attune ourselves culturally. We should be the one people in the world able to take advantage of that, and we don't."

Even Scotiabank, which has waded into markets that the rest of Canada's banking establishment would never dare to enter, is guilty of the same lapses. While it was quite canny in its stealthy acquisition of its Mexican subsidiary, Inverlat, insiders acknowledge that Scotiabank succeeded in taking over the management of the technically insolvent bank almost despite itself. The Toronto head office sent down four rather WASPish middle managers, about as culturally attuned to Mexico as Yorkshire pudding, to take charge of more than three hundred branches and eleven thousand employees. "None of us spoke a word of Spanish. None of us had worked in Mexico. We went in there naïve as anything," admits Peter Cardinal, Inverlat's former president and Scotiabank's executive vice-president for Latin America. "We thought, where do we start? Particularly when communications is a problem."

To its credit, Scotiabank rode out Mexico's 1994 currency devaluation, known as the Tequila Crisis, but it took a decade for the bank to gradually up its stake in Inverlat to its current 99 per cent ownership. The plodding paid off, but it nearly drove the Mexicans nuts when it came to Scotiabank's attempts to buy a second bank—Mexico's BanCrecer, which together with Inverlat would have given it a 9 per cent market share in the hugely profitable and growing Mexican banking sector. But Scotiabank's dithering, compounded by the troops of lawyers and interpreters sent down from Toronto, finally exhausted the Mexicans' patience, says a bank insider. "You just don't know how to deal with us," Mexico's finance minister complained to Scotiabank officials. "You deal with us like we were North Americans. You don't know how to deal with Mexicans."

In the wave of banking consolidation that swept through Mexico, BanCrecer was picked up by another Mexican bank while Citibank, HSBC and the Spaniards scooped up the country's other major financial institutions. Despite its five-year head start over other foreign entrants, Scotiabank missed the opportunity to buy cheap when it had the chance and as a result, with its Inverlat subsidiary commanding a meagre 6 per cent of the market, has fallen short of its own stated goal of carving out the 10 per cent stake it says it needs. "You need to ask yourself, where are they now? Where were they when BanCrecer was for sale? When Banorte [another Mexican bank] was for sale? Why didn't they go whole hog and put the banks together?" asks one former executive. "They could have bought far more cheaply six or seven years ago if they had been less Canadian about it."

To be fair, Scotiabank had to weigh its Latin American ambitions against those of its shareholders. Corporate executives are often discouraged from taking global markets more seriously by Canadian shareholders who are even more squeamish than they are. When Labatt struck out in 1994 and bought a 30 per cent stake in the Mexican brewery FEMSA, pension fund managers and institutional investors went berserk, accusing the brewer of being "unfocused, undisciplined" and "too bold."[102] In the wake of a veritable coup d'état, Labatt executives engineered the company's sell-off to Interbrew, whose Belgian owners looked favourably on the Mexican investment.

To keep shareholders at bay, companies either downplay their foreign investments, burying them at the back of the annual shareholders' report, or set unrealistically high benchmarks for their return on investment. One manager of a Canadian asset in Latin America recalls how his company had gone to great pains to keep its foreign venture out of the spotlight for fear its stock price would get pummelled. The company was eventually sold, and two weeks before the ownership transfer the board of directors came to visit the asset for the first time. One of the directors, surprised by what he saw, took the manager aside, confiding: "If I'd seen this before, I wouldn't have voted in favour of the sale."

To offset the risk and assuage the market, Canadian companies routinely insist on a premium when investing abroad, usually in the neighbourhood of 25 per cent. "At that rate you might as well stay home," says Stewart. "The market is not going to allow you to earn that kind of return on a sustained basis. If you believe you need a 25 per cent return on equity to justify the premium of operating in Mexico, for example, you're better off saving your money." Which is why so many companies are ready to pack their bags and head home at the slightest hint of trouble. Before the Tequila Crisis, the Canadian bottled-water brand Naya was very popular in

Mexico. When the peso started to plummet, the water disappeared from the shelves. Naya's French and Italian rivals, Evian and San Pellegrino, stayed the course, but the Canadians have never been back.*

To be sure, Canadian companies don't have the same resources or access to long-term financing as the Europeans and Americans do (which is discussed in the next chapter), but the cost of cutting and running is often far dearer than many realize. "Commitment is a huge thing," explains Mallory, especially in developing markets, where relationships are key, and trust, in the absence of a reliable legal system and volatile economic conditions, is paramount.

Foreign businesspeople often remark that they are reluctant to get involved with skittish, attention-deficient Canadians for fear they might bolt when the going gets tough, or just lose interest. "There's an image among the Japanese that we only want to do business with them once in a while and that we can't be counted on because we are going to lose interest and disappear on them," says Chris Lindal, executive vice-president of Viceroy Homes. "They were always worried about that." Boris Rousseff, the Belgian-based president of the Canada Europe Round Table for Business, agrees. "They act like they're doing you a favour—there's an underlying sense they don't really need the business. If they are in Europe it's because of goodwill, but they don't really need it to make a living. There needs to be a 180-degree about-face in the mentality."

If not, Canadian companies will continue to falter in international markets. As it is, the track record is less than stellar. "I hear of more failures than successes," admits TransAlta's Snyder. The mistakes are not only costly, even fatal, for the companies, but with so few Canadian firms active internationally, high-profile slip-ups threaten to tar the whole country with a reputation for being a global lightweight. "It's terrible because foreign markets not only write off the company in question, they write off all Canadians," says Lorna Wright, an associate professor of international business at York University's Schulich School of Business.

---

* In 2000, Naya was bought by the French food conglomerate Danone.

Michael Lobsinger, the founder of Calgary-based technology firm Zi Corp., has had to grapple with the halo effect firsthand. In one encounter he will never forget, the Saskatchewan native was meeting with seven major money managers in New York to raise money for his new-found company. The most important manager at the table quickly made it known that he had a "financial philosophy" never to invest in Canadian companies, launching into a long litany of failed ventures. "Sweat started pouring down my face," recalls Lobsinger. "I turned around and said, 'Aren't you a fucking idiot. If you can't sort the good from the bad, that's your problem, not mine.'" The manager, perhaps impressed by Lobsinger's chutzpah, ended up buying half a million shares in the company. Still, he says with not a little frustration, "I get this all the time."

Unfortunately, as the failures mount—Molson being the latest, but surely not the last—the onus will increasingly be on Canadians to prove that they are serious, worthy and reliable foreign investors and business partners. That will mean taking a serious look at how they operate in their own back-yard—because how one competes at home is a reflection of how one competes abroad. Ultimately, Canadians will have to come to grips with the inherent contradiction in the country's economic model—one in which protective policies and regulatory environments leave companies ill-prepared to compete internationally because staying home is no longer an option.

Molson is perhaps the best example of this destructive catch-22. Since merging with Coors in 2005, there is little left of the iconic brewer that has played such an important role in Canadian history. While family scion Eric Molson is chairman of the new entity in which Molson retains a 55 per cent ownership stake, the company is incorporated in Delaware and headquartered in Colorado. The board of directors is stacked with Coors executives, who include the CEO and CFO. If *Globe and Mail* columnist Eric Reguly is right, Molson's head office in Montreal will eventually become as superfluous as Seagram's faux castle in Montreal became once the distiller built its New York headquarters.

As for The Beer Store—the monopoly that was supposed to protect two national champions—it's now controlled by foreigners.

6 | TEAM CANADA AND TEQUILA: THE PITFALLS OF GOVERNMENT TRADE POLICY, PROMOTION AND FINANCE

"This is a country that doesn't think strategically."

JOHN GRUETZNER, BEIJING-BASED
TRADE AND INVESTMENT CONSULTANT

EXACTLY ONE YEAR after coming to power as Canada's newly elected prime minister, Jean Chrétien was at the helm of arguably the most ambitious and unprecedented trade mission in Canadian history. For the first time, the prime minister, his cabinet and all the provincial premiers had joined forces under the brash new banner of Team Canada, and they had set their collective sights on landing the biggest fish of all: China.

Like Pierre Trudeau's official recognition of China in 1970—a full two years before the United States did so—the November 1994 trade mission was a pre-emptive strike that acknowledged the emerging powerhouse. The mission had vision and moxie, and it made a powerful statement to the world that Canada was ready to do business. And the world seemed to be listening. Chrétien and Team Canada hosted a glittering gala at Beijing's historic Great Hall of the People, the biggest event put on by a foreign country in recent Chinese memory. "There was a real buzz in the room," recalls Tim Reid, then president of the Canadian Chamber of Commerce. "The atmosphere was so friendly. We were so well received."

The Chinese were anxious to meet the people who had given them Norman Bethune, the beloved Canadian doctor who had treated the wounded during China's bitter war with Japan, and representatives of the nation that, in open defiance of a U.S. trade embargo, shipped them wheat during the years of starvation in the 1960s. In the 1970s Ottawa arranged for two planeloads of Canadian businesspeople to fly to Beijing and exhibit their technology, a move that proved instrumental in China's decision to end its decades of self-imposed isolation. Perhaps it was no surprise, then, that companies on the Team Canada mission claimed to have sealed $9 billion worth of contracts and letters of intent with Chinese eager to do business with them.

So why is it, more than a decade later, after the rest of the world has woken up to the Chinese juggernaut, that Canada has missed the boat? Canadian exports to and investment in China remain negligible, while decades of goodwill have lost their lustre as Mao Zedong's famous ode to Norman Bethune is eclipsed by the stampede of foreign multinationals jostling for a toehold in China.

Many argue, and rightly so, that Canadian business is largely to blame for not following up on the government's lead. It would not be the first time. As long ago as 1920, Canada's trade commissioner to China lamented: "Canada has had direct steamship communication with China from the port of Vancouver for more than thirty years, yet in all that time not a single Canadian business firm have established themselves or had agents in this country."[103] In contrast, the government agent pointedly noted, there were sixty American firms in China at the time.

Still, one has to wonder what kind of path Ottawa was paving for business into one of the world's murkiest markets. Despite the historic ties and oodles of camaraderie, the Team Canada effort never translated into any tangible trade preferences or policies. At the time of writing, Canada had yet to sign a foreign-investment protection agreement with the Chinese, an important legal recourse for would-be investors that a number of other countries have clinched. Formal ties are limited to a limp-wristed "strategic partnership" that pales alongside ambitious gambits by

Chile and Australia to strike free-trade deals.* Was Team Canada really lighting the way, or was it just digging a road to nowhere?

As Roy MacLaren, Canada's former trade minister, recalls it, Chrétien evinced little interest in the Team Canada concept when he first broached the idea with the prime minister. It wasn't until MacLaren mentioned that the ten premiers would be coming along that Chrétien suddenly perked up. The idea of having the premier of Quebec walking behind him, in lockstep with the other provincial leaders in a joint trade promotion effort for all the world to see, was immensely appealing to the PM. Even Team Canada, like so many other things, was partly seen as another tool in the pitched battle with Quebec separatists.

Over the next decade, the success of the first Team Canada trade mission to China would spawn dozens more junkets throughout Latin America, Europe and Asia. Like a travelling road show, they would repeat the same performance in every new venue, and often, as in the case of China, return for an encore. But seen as they were, through the narrow prism of the national-unity debate, the missions only gave the most perfunctory nod to the more pedestrian issues of trade barriers and investment protection.

"In the Team Canada missions to China† we did not talk about policy or trade obstacles with the Chinese," says MacLaren. "So we were in and out, in and out, without ever laying the groundwork for the future. And it turned into a sort of government circus of signing contracts."

Rather than being an inadvertent hiccup, however, the sacrificing of far-reaching international objectives on the altar of domestic politics is an enduring hallmark of Canada's deeply flawed trade policy. Slapdash strategy and political short-sightedness were largely responsible for the failure of Prime Minister Pierre Trudeau's highly vaunted "Third Option," which sought to counterbalance Canada's dependence on the United States by

---

* Chile signed a free-trade agreement with China—the first between China and a South American nation—in August 2006.

† There were officially two Team Canada missions, but Chrétien went to China a total of six times.

strengthening ties with Europe and Japan. More of a reaction to the Nixon administration's 1971 decision to tax imports than a deliberate, thought-out offensive, Trudeau's short-lived exercise was plagued by bureaucratic infighting and incoherent policy. By 1976, Trudeau had turned his attention to the looming crisis in Quebec and the international effort was all but forgotten.

It's a legacy that lives on in the country's failure to capitalize on competitive advantages and aimless efforts at promoting trade that in many cases have done a disservice to Canadian business and damaged the country's reputation abroad. "We have never had a coordinated trade policy," says Peter Clark, an Ottawa trade consultant. "Our trade policy is responding to crisis. It's ad hocery in the extreme, and it always has been."

Nowhere is Canada's filibustering perhaps more in evidence than in Europe. Despite historic trade and cultural ties, Canada remains one of just eight countries without preferential trade access to the world's largest trading bloc. It was the first country to broach the idea of a trade deal with Europe in 1972, but over the next two decades its bold overture was drowned in a sea of high-minded but toothless contractual links, political dialogues, transatlantic declarations and joint action plans. The Europeans, some say, have never been interested in a real trade deal with Canada. But just what has Canada done to convince them otherwise?

In 1994, with the ink barely dry on NAFTA, MacLaren began pushing for a North America–EU free-trade deal. But just as he began shuttling across the Atlantic for exploratory talks in London, Paris, Bonn and Geneva, Canada's fisheries minister, Brian Tobin, was ordering the arrest of a Spanish fishing trawler in international waters off the Grand Banks. It was an unprecedented move for the normally compromising Canadians, who charged that they had to defend depleted fish stocks from European overfishing. Tobin, dubbed "Captain Canada" in the ongoing Turbot War, won the hearts of Atlantic Canadians and the enduring ire of the Spaniards.

While Canada's attempt at gunboat diplomacy conveniently deflected attention from its own egregious overfishing, what was even more interesting was the unwavering support Tobin enjoyed from Prime Minister

Chrétien. There was no vacillating here, despite the clear breach of international law, the very minor role of the already moribund fishery in the Canadian economy or the cost in terms of Canada–EU relations. And the costs were high. Any chance for a free-trade agreement was scuttled by the Spaniards, who froze the Canadians out of ministerial meetings and high-level talks.

"It was badly handled," confides a high-ranking Ottawa insider. "Brussels went bananas; they went haywire over the fishing dispute. If there was any indication that Canadian trade relations with Europe showed signs of improving, Spain would step in."

Luckily for Canada, the Americans weren't ready for free trade with Europe. But that didn't stop the Mexicans, who went on to sign a deal with the EU, becoming the only NAFTA partner with a transatlantic trade tie.

Amazingly, despite the diplomatic kerfuffle, Canada got a second chance at a free-trade link-up with Europe. In 1998, talks were launched with a bloc of four countries—Norway, Switzerland, Liechtenstein and Iceland, which make up the European Free Trade Association and are outside the EU zone. It was an opportunity for Canada to redeem itself and prove to the rest of Europe that free trade, particularly in agricultural products, was not only possible, but beneficial.

A decade later the proposal is technically still on the table, but talks floundered almost immediately thanks to an encore performance by Captain Canada. The cabinet minister from Newfoundland and Chrétien dauphin pushed through subsidies on Canada's virtually non-existent shipbuilding industry. The Norwegians, among the world's leading shipbuilders and ship owners, were nonplussed. The incipient negotiations died on the vine.

So why would the prime minister allow a fisheries minister to stymie potentially groundbreaking trade deals with the Europeans not once, but twice? For two reasons, say veteran Ottawa bureaucrats. Chrétien's principal concern was to "keep a lid" on regional bones of contention, arguably at whatever cost. More importantly, he was grooming Tobin as a rival to his arch-nemesis, Paul Martin, for the leadership of the Liberal

Party. Both cases provided Tobin with a platform to not only raise the Newfoundlander's political profile, but to provide him with an instant following.

"Chrétien let Tobin introduce the shipbuilding subsidies because he thought Tobin would be a rival to Martin's leadership bid," said one insider. "The Norwegians said, 'What's this—free trade, and you're subsidizing shipbuilding?' Ottawa's reaction was, 'Well, that's too bad for them.'"

Considering Ottawa's dismal record on trade deals, however, Canada appears to be the real loser. Since 2000, Canada has dabbled in a host of free-trade negotiations with Singapore, Central America, the Andean region and Caribbean countries like Jamaica and Dominican Republic. Yet despite the relative obscurity of most of these markets, Ottawa has failed to sign a single deal. In fact, since NAFTA, Canada has racked up just three pacts, with Chile, Costa Rica and Israel. "Since NAFTA there has been virtually nothing," says Derek Burney, a former ambassador to the United States and NAFTA negotiator. "We never thought, at the time, that would be it. For a country as dependent on trade as Canada is, it's enormously shortsighted."

The United States, meanwhile, has since gone on to clinch eight deals with thirteen more countries, including Singapore, Central America, Australia and Bahrain,* and has another half dozen in the works. The American initiative is part of a global uptick in bilateral trade pacts and regional trading blocs in the face of flagging multilateral trade liberalization and a growing desire by emerging nations like China and India to flex their newfound economic muscle. Mexico has thirty-two bilateral agreements under its belt, including one with Japan, a tie-up that Canada has half-heartedly pursued for years. "We're even behind Peru," notes Glen Hodgson, chief economist at the Conference Board of Canada. "They have a free-trade agreement with Korea."

Supposedly Ottawa has hung its hat on multilateral free-trade efforts under the World Trade Organization (WTO). But while paying lip service to

---

* Two agreements, with Oman and Costa Rica, have yet to be implemented.

freer global markets, Canada actively undermined its own influence in the latest Doha round of negotiations in 2006 by refusing to ease protections on its supply-managed dairy, poultry and egg industries. As a result, Ottawa, one of the multilateral system's original heavy hitters, was shut out of high-level negotiations and replaced by Australia, with a GDP about half that of Canada's. A foil to Canada's feeble efforts, Australia has aggressively pursued multilateral trade liberalization while seeking out bilateral agreements. Since 2002, it has signed deals with the United States, Singapore and Thailand and is now brokering deals with Japan, China and the ten-member Association of Southeast Asian Nations (ASEAN), which is looking to establish a free-trade bloc to rival NAFTA and the EU.

"Canada has withdrawn from the international trade scene. We're no longer a significant player," says MacLaren. "We have been superseded by the Australians while the U.S. has suddenly signed half a dozen bilateral free-trade agreements, and they don't depend on exports to the degree we do. There needs to be a real shift. There is no policy, no nothing, coming out of Ottawa."

The main back-up plan appears to be Ottawa's "new and emerging markets" strategy, a wishy-washy campaign targeting India, China and Brazil, that has the leaders of these much larger countries rolling their eyes. "It's a joke to them—they think it's funny," says trade consultant Peter Clark. "How can you call Brazil an emerging market?" The irony has not been lost on India and China either, which together represent a third of the world's population and are among its oldest civilizations. The special minister appointed to head up the initiative—first an Ontario lawyer and then a vegetable farmer from Cape Breton, neither with prior experience in the area—only confirmed the dilettantish effort.

Undeterred, the federal government has exhorted Canadian business to invest in these waking giants while trying to coax the Chinese into buying into everything from Alberta's oil sands to pulp and paper. Yet the crucial details and overarching strategy continue to elude officials, leaving the countries in question perplexed. Weeks after Paul Martin headed his first mission to China as prime minister, the Canadian embassy in

Beijing refused travel visas for more than fifty Chinese businesspeople invited to attend a government-sponsored export fair in Vancouver. The reason? The government didn't believe they had a legitimate reason to come to Canada.

In 2003, the same year that Ottawa unveiled its emerging-markets strategy, it closed the Canadian tourism office in São Paulo, Brazil's largest city. Still, Paul Martin headed up a trade mission the following year, promising to renew long-neglected bilateral ties. Despite the Canadians' confusing signals, the Brazilians pursued a trade agreement with Canada and sent negotiators to Ottawa in September 2005 offering a bilateral deal with Mercosur, the customs union comprising Brazil, Argentina, Uruguay and Paraguay. They were politely rebuffed. In an interview, former international trade minister Jim Peterson explained that, among other things, Canada was still waiting to see what would happen with the latest WTO trade round as well the Free Trade Area of the Americas, which Venezuelan president Hugo Chávez had declared "dead" the week before.

"There is a lack of cohesion between what the government says and what it does," says James Mohr-Bell, executive director of the Brazil–Canada Chamber of Commerce. "When you talk and then don't do anything, people become uneasy. When you talk and do the opposite, then you lose your credibility altogether."

By spouting grandiose goals on the one hand and hiding behind the inevitable delays and failures of multilateral trade efforts on the other, Ottawa has perfected the art of appearing to be busy without ever getting anything done. It's a manoeuvre worthy of George Costanza, the character in the *Seinfeld* television series who passed his time trying to figure out how to keep his job while spending the day sleeping under his desk. Inevitably, George was always caught out, spouting feeble excuses no one believed.

Not even the bureaucrats are buying it anymore. "Our attention has been off the ball," admits Bill Johnston, a veteran trade commissioner recently named consul general in Ho Chi Minh City, Vietnam. "What vision is there for our role in the world? We have to get the message out there, but we have to see that vision coming down from on high. We tend to have gigantic trade missions or a new strategy for emerging markets, but if behaviour doesn't change, then what's it all about? We tend to confuse rhetoric with strategy and activity with results. These missions are like Alice in Wonderland. If you don't know where you are going, any road can take you there."

LA BOMBARDIERA

In October 1997, Westcoast Energy, together with a group of partners, won an international bid to build a US$1 billion nitrogen injection plant in the Gulf of Mexico. The plant, which enhanced the Mexican production of heavy crude oil recovered from vast undersea reservoirs, was the largest project of its kind in the world and a major coup for the Vancouver-based company. But Westcoast's celebration was short-lived. Days after the announcement, Canada's ambassador to Mexico publicly complained that Canadian companies would never be able to compete for large contracts in Mexico because of rampant corruption. Interviewed by the Mexican press, the diplomat cited the "very dirty story" of how Bombardier had won and then lost a US$360 million government bid to build subway cars for Mexico City. It was the third time the Quebec transportation company had lost out to Spanish rivals.

This decidedly undiplomatic accusation unleashed a political maelstrom in Mexico that not only prompted the ambassador's resignation, but jeopardized Westcoast's much larger deal. PEMEX, Mexico's all-powerful state-owned oil monopoly, was furious, especially since it had gone to great effort to ensure that the bid process was open and transparent. Westcoast, worried that it might be thrown out of the consortium, sought the intervention of high-ranking Mexican officials. "There was a definite air of disqualification," says Ian Mallory, Westcoast's director general in Mexico. "Our partners—the Germans, Japanese and British—thought the Canadians were beyond unsophisticated. They thought we were complete idiots."

Westcoast managed to hang on, but was treated like a naughty child at the luncheon to celebrate the awarding of the tender. The British,

Japanese and German consortium partners were seated at the head tables with senior Mexican officials while Westcoast, with a 30 per cent stake in the deal, was, with the exception of its CEO, relegated to the "kiddie table." In a speech, the head of PEMEX thanked all the partners—except Westcoast. "Why? Because Bombardier had Ottawa by the balls," says Mallory. "Their contract was a third the value of ours. Nobody seemed to care. It was all about positioning back home."

It wouldn't have been the first time that Ottawa's preoccupation with defending its national champion would come at the cost of the country's entire trade policy, not to mention other Canadian companies. Ottawa's ill-considered decision to back Bombardier in its ongoing subsidy war with its Brazilian aerospace rival, Embraer, had incalculable consequences for trade and investment, severely strained diplomatic relations and sent Canadian companies in Brazil running for cover. The question is, was it at least worth it?

The Brazilians were smarting even before Ottawa decided to challenge Embraer's subsidized jet sales before a WTO dispute panel in 1996. The federal government, bowing to domestic pressure, had been pressing Brazil to release two Canadians convicted of the 1989 kidnapping of a wealthy São Paulo businessman. The Canadian position was seen as a flagrant disregard for Brazil's justice system, particularly since the pair, though lionized at home as unsuspecting innocents, were in fact members of a Marxist terrorist group. Ottawa secured their extradition in 1988 in a prisoner exchange and within months they were freed, serving just ten years of their twenty-eight-year sentence.

Then came—at least that's the way the Brazilians saw it—the second slap in the face. Embraer had originally been part of the Brazilian air force when it went private in 1994. The company's CEO at the time met Bombardier's chairman, Laurent Beaudoin, during a luncheon. The Embraer chief suggested that Bombardier buy the Brazilian aerospace upstart in order to create a united front against global behemoths Airbus and Boeing. Beaudoin crisply rejected the offer, with words to the effect of: Don't worry, we're going to destroy you. "Bombardier was very superior about it," confirms James Mohr-Bell. "They ignored them [Embraer] and then embarked on a campaign to kill them financially or step over them."

Just as Embraer began to spread its wings, Ottawa took Brazil's national champion to the WTO. There is little question that Embraer was getting government help—although perhaps not as much as Bombardier's billions in subsidies—and shortly after winning the right to impose trade sanctions, Ottawa slapped an import ban on Brazilian beef in 2001. The Brazilians, their national pride assaulted not once but twice, went nuts. They poured bottles of Canadian Club whisky into garbage bins and hauled a Brazilian steer, dubbed "La Bombardiera," in front of the Canadian embassy. Clearly chastened, Canadian officials lifted the ban three weeks later. But the damage had been done. The one-time nice guys became known in Brazil as "the bad guys from Canada," says Mohr-Bell.

"Something failed in the Canadian system," he says. "They were letting favoured treatment of Bombardier go beyond whatever was reasonable— nobody was there to say: this is no longer in the interest of Canada."

It certainly didn't do Canadian companies any favours. Spooked by the palpable animosity, they cut any visible links to Canada, stopped advertising locally and shied away from promoting activities or public events. Brazilian officials refused to even reply to invitations to attend Canadian Chamber of Commerce events, while bilateral trade and invest-ment dried up as companies like the Brazilian oil giant Petrobras refused to buy anything Canadian. "It was the complete hijacking by one Canadian company of Canadian commercial policy," says Tim Plumptre, a former director of the Brazil–Canada Chamber of Commerce in Toronto.

And for all that pain, what did Ottawa gain? Brazil ignored the WTO ruling, and without any significant bilateral trade Ottawa had no economic leverage with which to pressure the Brazilians, says Chuck Gastle, a Toronto trade lawyer who wrote a research paper on the case. "I marvel at the lack of strategy that brought Canada into such a dispute. You have to have an end game in trade. If you don't, you have to wonder why you are doing it," he explains. "The sad reality is, it strained the relationship with Brazil at a time when it was emerging as a key player on the international scene."

The Brazilians eventually found it in their hearts to overlook Canada's transgressions, and Prime Minister Paul Martin headed a Canadian mission to Brazil in November 2004. The Brazilians even offered the Canadians a trade deal. And why not? They could afford to be generous. Embraer, the pipsqueak company that Bombardier thought was too irrelevant to bother with, is now beating their pants off in the regional jet market. "It's all forgotten and forgiven now," says Plumptre. "For one simple reason—they've won."

TEQUILA SUNRISE

It was supposed to be a fabulous entrée into the Mexican market. More than four hundred Canadian companies were slated to attend a Canadian trade fair in Mexico City that was being touted as a springboard for bilateral trade in the run-up to NAFTA. Embassy officials scrambled to coordinate the hordes of arriving businesspeople while Ottawa doled out big bucks to help pay for their plane fares, hotels and display booths. But within hours the much-anticipated event looked more like a Tijuana-style bachelor party. "Half the companies had no business being there," says one former embassy official. "By 10 AM, everyone was wearing big sombreros and drinking tequila. It was absolutely insulting."

One of Canada's leading window manufacturers didn't have any business being on a Team Canada trade mission to South America, but that didn't stop company owners from snapping a picture of themselves with a grinning Prime Minister Chrétien. The photo, which greets visitors to its corporate offices, includes a clutch of dark-suited Chileans identified as the company's newly signed local dealers. That the Chileans had no intention of representing the firm was beside the point, explains a company executive. "They got together a bunch of Chileans that they liked and took a picture with Chrétien so they could say it was a done deal. They did the same thing in Argentina," he explained. "There never was a focus, never a commitment on their behalf, but they had a picture that said: 'We're there.'"

At the most recent Team Canada trade mission to China in January 2005, the government announced the signing of more than one hundred agreements by some of the 280 companies on the junket. A cursory scan of the long list of participants, however, turned up several questionable companies and bogus announcements. JTE Environmental Resources, which reportedly agreed to buy stakes in two Chinese environmental protection companies, has a Vancouver-listed telephone number that does not answer. On its crudely constructed website, the company explains that it is "led by the Administrator, who is appointed by the President of Canada."

Another company, 3L International Corp. Group, which the government press release describes as hailing from Richmond, B.C., is not listed in Richmond or anywhere else. A third firm, Valdor Fiber Optics, appears to be a real company, based in San Francisco, although with nominal representation in Vancouver. The only problem is that its purchase of a Shanghai fibre optics manufacturer, purported to have been clinched on the mission, was actually announced five months earlier.

The stories of abuse and misuse of government largesse are legendary and may partly explain why, despite the myriad missions, fairs and schemes exhorting companies to "go global," there is so little success. In the government's zeal to produce results, many companies have copped a free ride, but this scattershot approach to promoting trade is costing them more than they realize. By emphasizing quantity over quality and short-term gain over long-term results, Ottawa discourages Canadian firms from taking international markets seriously and entrenches reliance on government support.

For John Gruetzner, a Canadian business consultant based in Beijing, the damage is particularly evident in China. The repeated missions have not only begun to wear on the Chinese, but perpetuate the idea that the world's fourth-largest economy is still a new and relatively unexplored market. By periodically parachuting in a raft of diverse and disparate firms, the unwieldy and politically weighted missions have distracted companies from the real business of meeting customers, striking up partnerships and understanding the market, he says. "The constant repetition of Team Canada prevents people from getting in and rolling up their sleeves," explains Gruetzner. Instead, the missions "are like a high school reunion that keeps coming back every year."

Rick Waugh, chief executive of Scotiabank, went on one mission to Brazil and swears he'll never go on another. "All we did," he says with tinge of exasperation, "was wait, and wait, and wait for the government sector to show up. And then we heard speeches and then we did a little bit of networking. It was very inefficient for a businessperson's time." Charlie Fischer, the head of oil company Nexen, is less sanguine. "Trade missions don't do anything. They're boondoggles, a waste of time."

For many businesspeople, the crux of the problem is the government's failure to understand what companies really need to make the difficult leap into foreign markets. Despite a dizzying array of agencies, programs and—according to one calculation—eighteen government departments with mandates to promote trade, there is a disconnect between the grand ideas dreamed up in Ottawa and practical, day-to-day business concerns. The result is a series of ad hoc and usually short-lived endeavours that lack any coherent strategy.

The Canadian Business Centre in Mexico City is a case in point. Opened in 1994, the centre, which sported a board room, office space, a secretary and imported-wood floors from Canada, was supposed to pro-vide Canadian companies, grouped together in one spot, with a collective momentum. "It was a great idea," says Pierre Alarie, a Canadian executive with long-standing ties to Mexico. But instead of having a core group of renters to pay for basic costs, the government opted to charge business travellers a daily fee. The rates were no better than those of a hotel, and after racking up several million dollars in losses the centre closed two years later. "The government should have surveyed companies in Canada first," says Alarie. "It was a huge disaster at a time when you could do no wrong in Mexico."

If business were just consulted, say those in the field, government would quickly discover that what companies want are not obscure sup-port programs that have generated an entire industry of consultants just to wade through the bureaucracy, but simple, straightforward answers. For a company looking to export ice cream to Korea, for example, that means being able to find out what the tariffs and market regulations are and how to get that information from the Koreans, explains Lorna Swift, of York University's Schulich School of Business. "The government is not getting the information, and it's not getting the right information at the right time to the right people."

In a 2003 survey done by the Canadian Federation of Independent Business, a full 80 per cent of respondents said that they did not use government trade promotion services, and that "the rare ones who do so have expressed mixed opinions on efficiency."[104] "Companies are asking for tariffs on a specific product, and instead we tell them that China has a robust housing market," explains Bill Johnston. "They ask, 'Why go to China?' And we say, 'The Chinese economy is growing.'"

Many attribute the government's inability to focus on a lack of business experience, which some say is particularly evident in the embassies and among diplomatic staff. Although some businesspeople had high praise for certain individuals—like the ambassador to Cuba who parked a Canadian-made ambulance on the front lawn of his residence and then had guests walk through it to attend a party—they were the exceptions rather than the rule. In the case of India, for example, some of Canada's largest investors in that country—and there are not many—noted they had yet to be contacted by High Commissioner Lucie Edwards, who had assumed the post in 2003. While Edwards has an impressive resumé, all too often, ambassadors are patronage appointments with little grasp of the country they are working in, say critics. "Do they speak the language? Have they ever done anything like this?" asks one well-heeled businessman. "When you look at the positions abroad, it's embarrassing."

Similarly, while Yvan Bourdeau, CEO of BMO Capital Markets, singled out the commercial counsellors at Canada's Chinese embassy as among the best trained in the world, many businesspeople complained that although neophyte staffers were "careful, courteous and polite," they couldn't spot a business opportunity if it hit them on the head. Andrew

Stodart, the former international brand director for Black Velvet whisky, uses the example of Taiwan, which had a 300 per cent tariff on Scotch whisky and a 400 per cent tariff on cognac. The tariff on North American whisky, in comparison, was just 25 per cent. "If somebody had been on the ball at the embassy, they would have written to every Canadian whisky producer," he says. "But they have no business background."

Instead, the Canadian embassy providing the most market intelligence in 2003 was in Damascus, Syria. It flooded the Trade Commissioner Service with 247 tender notifications by the Syrian government. What the service or companies are expected to do with this information is not clear. In fact, of the almost 6,500 pieces of market intelligence sent back to Canada from the various postings around the world that year, only 800 to 900 were specific trade leads, says Johnston. As to what happened to them, he says, no one knows.

By the same token, there is little rhyme or reason regarding where embassies and consulates are located. Some 20 per cent of Canada's trade commissioners and their support staff are in the United States, including six in Buffalo and seven in Minneapolis. In 2004, Ottawa opened seven new consulates in the southern U.S. states. Yet according to an internal government report commissioned more than a decade earlier, government resources deployed in mature markets like the United States and Europe garner very little return for the investment.[105] As one former government hand explains: "If you need to be supported by trade commissioners in a country like the U.S., then there's something wrong with your approach."

The real bang for the buck comes from locating consulates in developing countries, where languages and business practices are different and a government presence is seen as a sign of credibility. Charlie Fischer points out that Nexen's operations in Yemen account for 30 per cent of the country's GDP, yet Canada is the only member of the G8 without an embassy there. Instead of leveraging Nexen's success to actually "make a difference" and help Yemen in its efforts to promote civil rights and democracy, Ottawa opened an embassy in Sudan to keep an eye on Calgary-based Talisman, which was operating a controversial oil project in the war-torn country.

The government may have a role to play in ensuring that human rights are respected in Sudan, but Ottawa appears more concerned with optics than with the opportunity to make a tangible difference.

"We are the most successful foreign company in Yemen," says Fischer. "Then you have Talisman in Sudan breaking all the rules, so they put in an embassy to track them. Why doesn't the government put money where they can make an impact?"

It would be nice to know just what kind of impact government programs and services are having on Canadian business's ability to operate internationally, but there's no way to measure it. Ottawa's focus is so fuzzy that it merely tracks the number of companies that participate in missions and trade fairs but does not assess how many become viable exporters.[106] A 1992 internal government evaluation could only conclude that weak vetting procedures had helped to "subsidize more than stimulate exports" while tending to "reward failure over success."[107] A recent survey of ten thousand exporting companies listed in the government's database, WIN-EXPORT, revealed that 4,790—almost half of them—*no longer existed*.

The 1992 report made a series of recommendations, including reorganizing the many government services and activities into a one-stop shop, which companies could access through an account manager, as would occur in a bank. Ottawa has yet to implement the idea, but Australia did and within three years it nearly tripled the number of its exporting firms. In 2004, Austrade was named the world's top government trade promotion agency for its efforts to bring new exporters to market.

The Australians' highly targeted efforts were in full force at the 2005 Aichi World Expo in Japan. The government, working through its department of foreign affairs and trade, used the premiere technology fair as a platform to showcase Australian high-tech prowess in five strategic areas, including the automotive industry, biotechnology and environmental services. It then secured corporate sponsorship from companies like Toyota and mining giant Rio Tinto and followed up with a series of missions for Australian companies that coincided with business seminars and networking meetings at Australia's Aichi pavilion.

In contrast, Canada's effort was organized by Heritage Canada. The highlight was a big-screen image of the aurora borealis while the theme—Wisdom of Diversity—rambled on about the "values and principles that promote and protect our environmental and cultural diversity." There were no corporate sponsors except for Manulife, the insurance company, and no visible trade or business links.

In the government's defence, Canadian companies too often rely on public servants when it comes to the business of breaking into international markets, says Howard Balloch, Canada's former ambassador to China. "I believe the embassy should be supportive, and I also believe doing business is up to businesspeople," he says.

The aimless missions and tequila-doused trade fairs are symptoms of a larger problem, admits Bob Armstrong, former president of the Canadian Association of Importers and Exporters—one in which Canadian companies are all too complicit. "The trouble with Canada is that we all wait for the government to do it for us," he says. "We've allowed the government to drive the bus on trade instead of questioning what they do and why."

SEE NO EVIL

At the offices of one of the few private companies to offer trade-financing services in Canada, a dozen clocks display time zones from Rio to Dubai while two eight-foot-high Chinese stone statues stand guard in the lobby. On the wall, a sepia-hued map charts the three transoceanic voyages of the great British naval explorer Captain James Cook. But perhaps the most telling memento of all is the three ceramic monkeys squatting on a table in the entrance. Across the top of the figures reads the familiar adage "See no evil, hear no evil, speak no evil," a fitting metaphor for the 800-pound gorilla that weighs heavily over Canada's trade-finance industry and has arguably affected the nation's ability to export more than all the fruitless trade missions and policy procrastinations combined.

Export Development Canada (EDC) is an obscure Crown corporation that is as little understood by its government minders as it is by the general public. But from its bunker-like Ottawa headquarters, its powerful reach is felt across the country. Under the cloak of confidentiality and minimal oversight, it has gradually secured an almost uncontested monopoly over funding for companies that want to export. Originally established to bridge gaps in private-sector trade finance, the agency has metastasized into a zealously protected and impregnable fiefdom. As one observer familiar with the agency summed up: "We've created a monster."

EDC is unique among government-backed export credit agencies in that it competes directly against and, some say, actively discourages bank-backed trade financing. Whereas agencies from Finland to Australia and the United States either prohibit competition with banks or have abandoned areas already serviced by the private sector, EDC is moving in the opposite direction. It is muscling in on syndication deals, preferring to get involved in lucrative lending and insurance rather than just provide export credit guarantees. It even has overseas offices, with agents knocking on the doors of foreign firms in a bid to drum up business for Canadian goods.

Eric Siegel, the corporation's recently appointed president and chief executive officer, denies crowding out the banks, arguing that the risky and expensive business is not attractive to them. "The banks are not interested in doing lending," he says. "They could get in if they wanted, it's not a finite pie." It's an assertion Scotiabank chief executive Rick Waugh denies: "We'd love to do medium-term export financing, but how can we compete? EDC takes the business," he says. "We're in the business of lending. Why wouldn't we want to do it?"

The banks find it almost impossible to compete against EDC, which can easily undercut them by offering lower rates. It can do so because it doesn't pay taxes and can borrow money cheaply because it enjoys the same sovereign risk rating as the government of Canada. Most importantly, EDC, unlike its counterparts in other countries, is loath to provide the guarantees the banks need to backstop riskier, long-term international loans. "Why should we take all the risk if the deal goes bad, while the banks have none of the exposure?" says Siegel, with barely concealed antipathy.

Contrary to its foreign counterparts, EDC believes that by buying down foreign risk, it is giving the banks a "free ride" when it could be cashing in on the lucrative loans itself. The agency is preoccupied with its bottom line because of what insiders describe as an overwhelming need to be "self-sustaining." That it relies on its own balance sheet instead of government funding is held up as an ideal that does not cost taxpayers a cent. But the result is an often contradictory tug between commercial operations and public policy that has turned the banks into adversaries instead of allies and diverted EDC from its real mission, say industry experts and former high-ranking EDC employees (many of whom preferred to speak off the record).

"They got a little bit deluded about the fact that being self-sustaining became the end. It became the justification," explains a former EDCer. "It's an inward-looking organization that looks after itself first. It's not there to do Canadian trade policy. It's there to look after EDC." Says Glen Bays, director of trade finance for TD Securities: "They lost sight of their mandate. We view EDC unfortunately as competition. As a Crown corporation it should be filling the gaps, not competing head on with the private sector, doing everything it can to earn money." Adds another veteran trade finance banker, "EDC interests are not necessarily Canada's interests anymore."

Not every banker agrees. In 2005, EDC announced a new program to provide guarantees in co-operation with the banks. Few banks have participated, arguing EDC is still trying to control competition by dictating what fees they can charge, but Scotiabank has managed to do one structured finance deal under the program. Richard McCorkindale, the bank's director of international corporate and commercial banking–structured finance, says he doesn't have a problem sharing the risk and covering the 15 per cent of the deal that EDC won't backstop with export guarantees. (Unlike other export credit agencies that will cover 100 per cent of a structured loan with guarantees, EDC will cover only 85 per cent.) "Some banks want 100 per cent coverage, but if you are not willing to do even 15 per cent, then what are you bringing to the table?" he says.

Overwhelmingly, however, the reaction to EDC is palpably negative, and not just among bankers. In an ironic twist, the agency charged with promoting Canadian exports has blocked Canadian lawyers from acting as counsel on multilateral projects involving the Crown corporation. EDC has argued that retaining Canadian lawyers would set it apart from other multilateral lenders and export credit agencies that normally work with international law firms in New York and London. "The bottom line is, they want the cachet of being in New York as opposed to Toronto," says a Canadian lawyer. "They literally take steps to prevent Canadians from participating in international transactions. That is our export support agency—talk about confidence in your country."

The agency's reputation for being arrogant and even antagonistic with those it deals with is exacerbated by the fact that while it runs like a private enterprise, it is not beholden to any shareholders. Other than being subject to periodic parliamentary reviews, EDC operations are rubberstamp affairs. The members of its board of directors are political appointees whose grasp of the agency is dubious, say insiders. According to one senior EDCer, the last trade minister to actually understand its convoluted machinations was Roy MacLaren, whose cabinet term ended in 1996. "They are masters of obfuscation and selective disclosure," said a one-time EDC officer. "They don't answer to anyone."

Its transactions closed to public scrutiny and exempted from access-to-information requests,* EDC does not even have an ombudsman, despite repeated Parliamentary recommendations.† Whenever it must (under political pressure) finance a deal that supersedes its conservative risk profile, it dips into something called the Canada Account, an off-balance-sheet fund controlled by cabinet. "Frankly, it always surprised me the auditor general lets that slide by," says a political insider familiar with the agency.

---

* Under the Federal Accountability Act proposed by the Stephen Harper government in 2006, EDC would be included under the jurisdiction of the Access to Information Act.

† EDC has a compliance officer, who ensures that EDC follows its own guidelines. Unlike an ombudsman, the compliance officer is an EDC employee rather than being independently appointed and working out of the finance minister's office.

"The minister responsible just says, 'By the way, chaps, we're going to give Bombardier $100 zillion,' and everyone looks at the window and says, 'Next item.'"

But while everyone was looking the other way, EDC's unfettered monopoly has left Canada in the peculiar position of being a heavily trade-reliant country without any banks to take exporters international. Despite a strong, profitable financial system, the banks are either unwilling or no longer capable of providing long-term trade financing or syndicating structured trade projects. "The banks no longer have the expertise or the motivation," says one banker, while those that do have the means are busy financing exporters in other countries.

TD now has export finance operations in Baltimore, Houston and New York, and in 2004 it was named "Bank of the Year" by the Export Import Bank, the U.S. government export credit agency. That year it led the league tables with the highest number of approved transactions of any Ex-Im lender. "We now have more resources south of the border than there are in Canada, and we're a Canadian bank," says Bays.

According to one banker's calculations, banks providing loans to American exporters backed by Ex-Im guarantees earn a 35 per cent return, compared with the 14 per cent return they would make financing a Canadian exporter without an EDC guarantee. TD's Bays says this is not only more profitable for the banks, but cheaper for Canadian companies, which is why he encourages the exporters that can to source their export financing south of the border. "Canada is losing its exporting to the States because it can't provide competitive financing," he says.

Perhaps that's why, when CIBC sold its $800 million structured export finance business to the Standard Chartered Bank in 2000, there was not a single Canadian loan on its books. "Try standing at the corner of Bay and King [the heart of Toronto's financial district]—there is not a trade finance banker to be found," says an industry expert and former EDCer. "Nobody cares anymore, or they've set up operations in New York. Tell me, how's that good for Canada?"

As a result, the banks are all but absent from the highly profitable business of international project financing that undergirds big, multilateral infrastructure projects. In the rare instance that a Canadian bank is involved, the project sponsors will specifically ask that Canadian suppliers not participate for fear of becoming entangled with EDC. Such is the case with a US$300 million port facility that Scotiabank financed in the Dominican Republic. There is no Canadian content, say those familiar with the deal, because the port's U.S. builder had used Canadian suppliers in the past and was fed up with EDC. (Scotiabank's syndicated loan was guarantee by the French government's export credit agency.)

"Very often a sophisticated buyer will say it doesn't want a Canadian bank involved because it knows the bank will want to maximize Canadian suppliers, which means it'll have to deal with EDC," said a banker. "On occasion, banks have had to agree not to have Canadian suppliers."

In fact, the banks don't make a habit of promoting Canadian exports in any of their international transactions, say industry insiders. "Unofficially the banks know that once they start speaking about a Canadian supplier they are doing themselves out of a deal," says one banker. And Canadian banks aren't the only ones. With EDC preferring to direct lend (instead of provide export guarantees), foreign banks are also reluctant to back clients who want to procure Canadian goods. "My guess is that deals are being lost and Canadian companies don't even know it," said a former EDCer.

They definitely lost out in Kuwait. The Canadians helped put out hundreds of oil fires that decimated the country following the 1990 invasion by Iraq and were in line to participate in its multi-billion-dollar reconstruction. EDC offered a US$500 million line of credit to the Kuwaiti government to buy Canadian goods and services, but the Kuwaitis, looking to rehabilitate their sovereign risk rating, wanted to work with the commercial banks. EDC refused to budge, say observers, and as a result, the loan was largely ignored, essentially shutting Canada out of the lucrative reconstruction.

EDC insiders say the agency is so insistent on lending in order to boost its bottom line that it has done syndicated loans that had no Canadian content, from financing leveraged buy-outs of Bermuda-based satellite companies to the sale of Russian potash to Brazil, Mexican-made subway cars to Colombia and British-assembled telecommunications components to Algeria. EDC's Siegel admits: "There is a small percentage of [deals with no Canadian content], but we try to mitigate it by the quality of the deal."

While EDC effectively finances other countries' exports, Canadian companies are short-changed. Not only is the agency "too slow, too expensive and too difficult to deal with," say clients, but its aversion to risk and focus on investment-grade investments has shut out precisely the kind of companies that government export agencies are designed to support. And although the EDC is constantly criticized for lending billions to Bombardier, it is not prepared to take nearly the kind of risk that the company needs to compete in the heavily subsidized and risky aerospace industry.

Instead, its largest client is the forestry industry, which traditionally makes up nearly 20 per cent of EDC funding. The agency provides the forestry firms with short-term credit insurance, a service normally provided by big international private insurers like Euler Hermes ACI, which have been unable to break into the Canadian market. Given that half of EDC financing is directed at the United States, we can assume the agency is spending a huge chunk of its resources insuring softwood lumber exports to the Americans. Why multi-billion-dollar forestry firms need to use EDC instead of being serviced by private insurers remains unclear.

Meanwhile, smaller companies with new technologies or those that are looking to get into less secure markets—like China—are being bypassed. "The hardest part of being a small company is access to capital—it is the fuel," says Chris Lee, chief financial officer of Vancouver-based Nicer Canada Corp. The telecommunications company has had funding requests turned down by a number of government agencies and EDC has never responded to its overtures. "There seems to be a lack of empathy towards an entrepreneurial group that has worked very hard and succeeded or had a degree of success," says Lee. "There needs to be some range of acceptable risk for lending to young entrepreneurial Canadian companies."*

The irony is compounded by the fact that while many companies are desperate for funding, both EDC and Canadian banks are awash in cash. EDC declared a $1.2 billion profit in 2004 and is sitting on another $3 billion in provisions—funds put aside in case of loan defaults or insurance losses. The agency has obviously succeeded in being self-sustaining, say observers, but who is it helping? It's certainly not helping the Canadian financial sector support Canadian companies abroad: the leading private-sector provider of trade financing to Canadian companies is London-based HSBC.

With the banks out of the picture, how does a single Crown corporation, run by government bureaucrats with no private-sector experience, meet and anticipate the needs of all of Canada's companies? The short answer is, not very well. According to a survey done by the Canadian Federation of Independent Business, 85 per cent of respondents had never used EDC's services. In another poll cited by the federation, at least 20 per cent of business owners had never even heard of the Crown agency. According to some estimates, EDC, with its preponderance of heavy hitting clients, reaches less than 5 per cent of small to medium-sized enterprises.

"So don't be surprised if Canadian business can't get out there and compete," says one former EDC staffer. "What tools do they have to help them?"

---

* In a 2003 survey done by the Canadian Federation of Independent Business, companies identified their inability to access insurance as the biggest obstacle to doing business in foreign markets.

PART TWO

WHY ALL IS NOT LOST: HOW TO GET FROM BUFFALO TO BEIJING

7 | DRAGON SLAYERS AND DEPANNEUR DYNASTIES

"Canadians succeed when they dare. All that's missing is the dare."

STANLEY HARTT, CHAIRMAN, CITIGROUP CAPITAL MARKETS CANADA

HAVING READ THIS FAR, you might think that Canada's future isn't all that promising. But if you were to come away from this book thinking that Canadians are destined to be nameless call-centre drones or never move beyond your friendly neighbourhood bank manager, you'd be wrong. It's true that a lot of people have already written Canada off, but although we haven't accomplished half of what we're capable of and continue to squander opportunities through sheer complacency and scattershot strategies, we are still a young country, a teenager really. And teenagers, as everyone knows, like to revel in their bad habits while stubbornly keeping their redeeming qualities under wraps. It's simply a matter of growing up in time to recognize and celebrate those qualities, before it's too late.

It can be done, and the following pages will introduce the people, companies, resources and strategies that are proof anything is possible and that can help pave the way. In this chapter you will meet a handful of Canadian entrepreneurs and their trail-blazing companies. Some are multi-billion-dollar enterprises, and some have yet to turn a profit; some are stock market darlings, while others remain under the radar. They represent very different kinds of businesses, and they come from different parts of the country, but they all exhibit traits that often elude Canadian companies yet are crucial to international success. Each nurtures innovation, emphasizes marketing and branding, cultivates cultural intelligence and recognizes the need for global scope. Above all, they are doggedly persistent, serenely confident and hugely ambitious. I came out of each of these interviews inspired by what Canadians were capable of.

Some of the best expressions of Canadian moxie include Research in Motion, the Waterloo-based maker of the Blackberry handheld computer, the Four Seasons luxury hotel chain and Montreal circus troupe Cirque du Soleil. Each organization produces a unique, globally recognized product and manages to flourish in industries where government regulation can't protect them. And like Cirque, the brainchild of a fire-eating performer from the small town of Baie-Saint-Paul that now boasts more brand recognition in the United States than sportswear giant Nike, an inordinate number of this next generation of globally minded, identity-driven companies hail from Quebec.

The province is a fascinating dichotomy of the country's strongest and weakest attributes. Alternately exuberant and outgoing or chauvinistic and insular, Quebec's dual personality perfectly illustrates how a society can turn its unique set of cultural, linguistic, political and geographic conditions into a powerful advantage or an excuse to step into its own custom-tailored straitjacket. It becomes immediately obvious that where Quebecers' niggling insecurities prevail, the province fails to project itself internationally. Sectors like cheese, maple syrup, energy and forestry, all heavily regulated by government or industry cartels, come to mind. But a deep sense of identity, combined with a streak of maverick entrepreneurism, has acted as a springboard for companies to leave the province wherever the heavy hand of government hasn't held them back. Although Quebec's Aldo, the shoe retailer, and Cinram, one of the world's largest DVD and CD manufacturers, were both founded by immigrants, Quebec is also home to the country's only major international engineering and construction firm, SNC–Lavalin; Bombardier, the world's third-largest plane maker; Dorel, the manufacturer of Cosco car seats and Schwinn bicycles; pharmacy giant Jean Coutu; and Mega Brands, the toy company that is bulldozing its way through Lego's building-block empire.

That's not to say it's easy to get a lock on the next crop of international up-and-comers. As one federal trade commissioner aptly put it: "Whenever it's time for a Canadian company to go international, they put up a 'for sale' sign." The number of promising Canadian companies that were either sold or snapped up in a hostile takeover during my three years of researching this book was both mind-boggling and disheartening. The list includes Ontario's two leading governmental technology companies, Zenon and Trojan, both acquired by U.S. multinationals, as was Creo, the world's third-largest digital plate and equipment company, based in British Columbia. Renée's Gourmet Foods, the uppity maker of everyone's favourite Caesar salad dressing, was sold to food giant H.J. Heinz, while Vincor International, the producer of Inniskillin and Jackson-Triggs wines, was imbibed by Constellation Brands, a multi-billion-dollar wine industry consolidator based in upstate New York. The loss of Mississauga-based ATI, one of the world's leading graphic chip makers, bought by rival Advanced Micro Devices (AMD), was particularly grievous. But the coup de grâce had to be almost the complete appropriation of the Canadian-owned hospitality sector within a 12-month span. Fairmont Hotels and Resorts was the first to fall, scooped up by Saudi tycoon Prince Alwaleed bin Talal al Saud, who also helped himself to the Four Seasons Hotels, together with Bill Gates, the founder of computer giant Microsoft. Canada's other major hotel play, resort developer Intrawest, owner of both Whistler and Mount Tremblant ski resorts, sold out to a U.S. private equity firm. As Joe Houssian, Intrawest's chairman, explained, the company wanted to accelerate plans to move into Europe and Asia and needed the Americans to "go on to the next level."[108]

I was all set to interview BW Technologies, a Calgary-based manufacturing gem, when it was bought out by British inventors. I went ahead and met with BW's ingenious founder and CEO, Cody Slater, an astrophysics dropout who not only invented a wireless gas detector that revolutionized the industry, but through technological innovation has found a way to manufacture competitively in Alberta. Nevertheless, like many of his fellow entrepreneurs, Slater admits it was often a tougher sell in Canada than abroad. "When I would trundle around to oil companies, they'd ask, 'So where in the U.S. are you importing from?' They wouldn't believe there was a technology product made in Canada. Canadians as a whole are very self-effacing; everything has got to be better somewhere else," he explains. In contrast, when Slater went international, "The response was 'Oh, it's made in Canada—that's excellent.' This technology has been in northern Alberta at forty below. There was a real respect for Canadian technology and companies."

Which is perhaps why foreigners are more than happy to scoop up undervalued or underestimated Canadian firms. Slater says the British buyers have "always been impressed by Canadian companies because they do what they say they are going to do. There is a level of commitment there." Slater's reasons for selling are simple: "All this does is give us more strength to become a global player. And to be successful in this world, you have to be a global player."

That is the simple reality for many companies, including BioWare, the Edmonton video game developer that was acquired by a U.S. private-equity firm a year after I interviewed its founders. Odds are, other companies profiled here will be acquired by the time this book goes to print, but while my goal is to highlight what Canadian-owned companies can do, their stories, and the message they impart, remain the same.

DRAGON SLAYERS

The heaping trays of jellied worms, sweet tarts and icing-laden Danishes set out amidst the foozball tables and comfy couches in BioWare's rec room are not exactly what the doctor ordered. If anything, the hazy aquatic atmosphere at the video game developer's Edmonton office, where sunlight is shunned and doughnuts are plentiful, is more like a teenage redoubt from Alberta's fresh air and outdoor lifestyle. But then again, Greg Zeschuk and Ray Muzyka are not your average doctors.

This duo of former family physicians originally set out to start a medical software company in the early 1990s, when their obsession with video games got the better of them. Huge fans of Dungeons and Dragons, the intense, role-playing board game, the pair came up with a video prototype and began cold-calling leading game publishers, including Microsoft and Sony. "We called repeatedly until they took our calls," explains Muzyka. "The publisher we eventually went with—we called twenty times before they answered. Seven out of the ten publishers we contacted made us an offer."

Not long after, BioWare wowed the gaming world with Baldur's Gate, which became one of the best-selling role-playing games of all time and single-handedly revived the fading world of dragon slayers, sorcerers and shadow thieves. The company followed up by signing on to develop a series of *Star Wars* video games for LucasArts, the publisher owned by *Star Wars* creator George Lucas. The resulting Knights of the Old Republic, better known as KOTOR in gaming parlance, was at the time the fastest-selling Xbox game in history. The gamer developed an almost-instant cult following, with legions of fans enthralled with its intricately constructed universes, fifty-hour campaigns, realistic terrain technology and indigenous languages created by PhD linguists hired by the company.

BioWare's reputation for intensive research and high quality has helped set it apart in the hugely competitive, multi-billion-dollar gaming industry, where some two thousand new products are released every year. But although it has won numerous gaming awards, what has really distinguished BioWare from other third-party developers—the "hired guns" of the industry—is its push to control its own destiny and create its own brand. Unlike many of its peers, BioWare has its own marketing and public-relations team and an in-house production department that designs posters and game boxes, all of which sport the BioWare logo. It even has a web team dedicated to the growing online community of three million registered users, better known as Biowarians. "It's really unusual for a developer to do this," admits Zeschuk.

"But we know we are the ones best able to look after our own interest. You can't depend on other people to do that for you."

That brand equity has allowed BioWare to make the leap from being a mere developer to creating its own intellectual property (IP). In 2005 it rolled out Jade Empire, the first in a new wave of games featuring company-owned IP. The move not only affords BioWare a greater cut of the profits, but allows it to benefit from promotional spin-offs like figurines and comics. "The return is higher with our own IP," explains Zeschuk, whose rapid-fire speech echoes the short staccato bursts of his fast-paced video games. "The deals we are able to negotiate are better than ever."

The increased prestige has also helped BioWare attract hot new designers from around the world. The company receives as many as a thousand resumés a month, and almost a third of its 260-strong workforce comprises foreign workers from twenty countries. That international perspective has been key to the company's global success, says Muzyka, with 55 per cent of sales coming from outside of North America. "We've learned what does well in Germany, Korea, France and the U.K. We have people from all those countries who can provide a perspective and tell us what works," he explains. "People like complicated games in Germany, and more artistic games in France. We take that knowledge and apply it to the games' design."

BioWare is now looking at how to penetrate even further into foreign markets, particularly Korea and China, through either licensing agreements or joint ventures with local developers. Its efforts will no doubt be bolstered by its US$300 million merger in 2005 with another independent studio, L.A.-based Pandemic Studios. The new holding, which is majority owned by a U.S. private-equity firm, will allow BioWare, with annual sales of $16 million, to self-fund its new endeavours, including a new studio in Texas. As Zeschuk points out, those goals have, from the very beginning, always aimed beyond Canada. "We don't consider the Canadian market. We consider the global market," he says. "To be successful, you have to look internationally."

PETROCHEMICAL PIONEERS

Compared with dragon-slaying warriors, water dragons and werewolves, methanol has about as much sex appeal as lint. A colourless petrochemical that looks like water and is used to make a range of products from spandex, fertilizer, and DVDs to polyester carpeting, plastic bottles and plywood, methanol is the very definition of a commodity. And, for many years, that's exactly how it was treated. When Methanex Corp. was launched in 1991, most manufacturers simply sold their products through agents. "Typically the Japanese trading companies would show up with a vessel, take the product away and give you some money for it," says Bruce Aitken, Methanex's CEO. "That worked nicely for a while, but it didn't take long to realize you didn't know who your customers were, you didn't know what their drivers were and you didn't know what was important to them."

For the Vancouver-based company, it quickly became as clear as, well, methanol that the real key to success lay in not only cutting out the middleman, but somehow branding its own version of the virtually indistinguishable chemical compound. In 1994, under the new leadership of Pierre Choquette, a veteran chemical marketer who had toured the globe for Polysar and then NOVA Corp., Methanex embarked on a strategy that not only cemented it as the world's leading methanol producer but established it as the industry market maker, with Methanex's price doubling as the world benchmark.

Already in the enviable position of producing a quarter of global methanol output, Methanex wooed its customers by offering what Choquette calls "a value proposition"—security of supply and unparalleled service. The company established a network of storage facilities and terminals strategically located near each of its major markets. More importantly, it acquired its own fleet of super tankers, including the 100,000-tonne *Millennium Explorer*, the largest chemical tanker in the world, which allowed the company to establish a global distribution system and even rearrange shipping routes to supply customers. "It really was key to our success," says Choquette, who remains on as chairman after handing over the CEO reins to Aitken in 2004. "By controlling the quality and the movements of the product, we could provide our customers with a service they wouldn't otherwise get."

It also gave the company an amazing competitive cost advantage. By deploying a tanker of that size instead of a smaller ship and refilling it as quickly as possible, Methanex saves $1 million per voyage, says Choquette. Still, for the company to remain competitive compared with low-cost producers in Saudi Arabia and Iran, it knew it would have to find additional ways to cut costs. It gradually shuttered its high-cost North American operations and migrated production to massive new facilities in Trinidad and Tobago and the southern tip of Chile, where natural gas, methanol's main ingredient, is plentiful and infinitely cheaper. "You need to look at the lowest cost structure in the world, and you need to be competitive with it; otherwise you don't have a sustainable business," explains Aitken. "If our strategy had been to stay in Kitimat, B.C., and Medicine Hat, Alberta, we'd be out of business today."

What helped make the move successful was a management team that was comfortable operating globally. Every one of the company's executives has lived in at least three "geographies," says Aitken, himself a New Zealander who has lived in five countries. "That gives us a perspective. We know what it's like out there." The company takes care to cultivate relationships and acclimatize to each country where it does business. The size of its Chilean operations has resulted in a dozen Spanish speakers working at its Vancouver office, part of a targeted career-development strategy that promotes promising employees through a variety of foreign postings. "We choose potential stars, expose them to different geographies and different functions and then bring them to head office to expand their experience," explains Aitken. "We call it people development."

That's not to say Methanex hasn't learned some hard lessons about adapting to different markets. Choquette admits he's probably persona non grata in Qatar after the company came very close to doing a deal there and then backed off after getting spooked by the level of risk. "It was one of the best contracts we've had, a great location and good partners," he says. "But we never spent enough time educating each other on the risk. If we had, the company would be that much stronger today."

Still, with US$1.7 billion in revenue in 2005, about 850 employees worldwide and offices from Auckland, Tokyo and Shanghai to Seoul, Waterloo and Dallas, Methanex has managed to do what few commodity producers have: take the boom and bust out of the price cycle. "Our leadership position has affected our profitability dramatically," says Aitken. "We've gone through twelve quarters of top-cycle pricing. When you look at commodities, you don't have twelve periods of top-cycle pricing—price goes up or price goes down." But while some might attribute the buoyant returns to Methanex's significant market share, to Aitken it's what you do with the resource that makes the difference. "If you are just a seller," he points out, "you are taking whatever price the market will give you."

A PASSION THAT'S MULTINATIONAL

Jean Hurteau can't say exactly what made him decide to get into the cosmetics industry, but he knew one thing for sure; he didn't want to answer to a head office based in another country or a continent away. He'd done it before—heading up development for the Canadian operations of French beauty products giant, Yves Rocher. Hurteau learned a tremendous amount reporting to internationally minded executives in Paris, but the experience also opened his eyes to the downside of being a very small fish in a very large ocean. "When you are a small branch in Canada, your business maybe represents one day of production in France," he explains. "And your opinion doesn't mean much."

Which is why Hurteau decided to build his own multinational, based in his hometown of Candiac, on Montreal's south shore. He deliberately chose the name Fruits & Passion because it could be easily translated from French to English, and from the start Hurteau was exporting his fruit-scented bath foam and body milk to upscale retailers like London-based Harrods and Neiman Marcus in the United States. "The first criterion we came up with was that the brand had to be launched internationally," says Hurteau, smartly dressed in black pinstripe pants, matching socks and a sweater sporting tiny white polka dots. "We didn't want to be blocked by being only Quebec or only Canada focused. We wanted a concept that was international."

That he would be going up against giants like The Body Shop and Crabtree & Evelyn didn't seem to faze Hurteau, a college dropout who sold encyclopedias door to door before making his way into the retail franchise business. Hurteau opened a couple of high-end convenience stores in Montreal before selling out and going to work for the Canadian yarn-making division of French clothing designer Rodier. "It gave me a broad perspective of the potential of franchises, of branding in general," says Hurteau. "They had really made it, so I thought, why can't we?"

Whether Hurteau realized it or not, he had set himself a particularly challenging goal—consumer retail brands are arguably Canada's greatest Achilles heel (we are the world's leading producer of maple syrup, but even Aunt Jemima is American). What was more, Hurteau was convinced that the secret to success lay not in cheaper knock-offs of established international names, but of creating a distinctive, high-end product based on in-house formulas and bolstered by unique packaging. "We definitely didn't want to make another Body Shop—we wanted to go beyond just claiming to be ethical and environmentally friendly," he says. "We decided we really wanted to play the packaging card and be innovative."

Hurteau quit his job and spent a year coming up with the proper business plan and product mix. "It's important to base your business on something solid, and I think I did that," he says. It was a big risk considering the year was 1992 and the country was grappling with the worst economic recession in decades. "Everybody said, 'What are you doing?'" admits Hurteau, who chooses his words carefully and is surprisingly serious in tone despite the company's rather dreamy image. "But I was really determined. I needed to do it. I made the decision that at one point in my life I was going to take a chance."

With no salary and only his savings to fall back on, Hurteau hired the best chemist he could find and told him to come up with the best bath fragrances money could buy. He collected countless bottles from Italy and Spain in order to design just the right packaging. When the finished product finally debuted at trade shows in Toronto and Montreal and then in Atlanta and New York, the reaction, says Hurteau, was "incredible." "People were lining up to write orders." At the time, Hurteau, together with his wife and brother, were hand-mixing the formulas out of a 1,000-square-foot warehouse. But even then, they had already decided they would only go with top-end buyers. "We wanted to make sure the product didn't end up in a pharmacy or T-shirt shop," says Hurteau. "You'll never win by going cheap."

The company was profitable from day one, but to support the brand Hurteau opened stand-alone boutiques as well. The first, launched in 1995 at a Montreal-area mall, quickly became the shopping centre's most profitable store on a square footage basis, with annual sales of $1 million. "I was very happy, very proud," Hurteau says of the store, auspiciously inaugurated on his birthday. "Because I knew it was the beginning of a long journey."

That journey hasn't always been easy. Fruits & Passion's explosive growth is largely predicated on franchising its stores; it now has 150 in twelve countries, including China, Mexico, France and Morocco. For Hurteau, franchising is the safest way to protect the company's manufacturing base. But early on at least, he wasn't always discriminating with every potential franchisee that came calling. "We'd get inquiries to open up stores and we'd say, 'Let's go for it,'" he recalls. "You have to be careful because if you only go with opportunity rather than [thinking] strategically, you end up with not necessarily the best people or vehicle."

These days, Fruits & Passion can afford to be a little more discerning. Hurteau won't disclose the company's bottom line, except to say that it rings in some $100 million in sales at the retail level alone. Its extensive lines, from olive oil hand wash to eau de toilette for dogs, have been written up in virtually every women's magazine from O, the Oprah Magazine to Elle and are so popular that at the company's last annual inventory clearance, 22,000 customers raided the warehouse over a four-day period.

The company has also been courted by a gaggle of investors, eventually choosing from among seven offers, to partner with the Societé générale de financement du Québec (SGF) in October 2006. Hurteau says he went with the government development agency, which, for an undisclosed sum, took a 30 per cent stake in the company, because of its stated mission to support the international success of Quebec-based companies. With the fresh injection of capital, Fruits & Passion is looking to branch out further, either through joint ventures or wholly owned boutiques, into the United States and Europe. "Globalization is something that needs to be faced; it's a must," says Hurteau matter-of-factly. "If you don't go out, everybody will be coming here. If you don't think they need your product out there, you are done."

THE TIP OF THE ICEBERG

The idea for Iceberg Vodka came about by the "flukiest of flukes," admits senior vice-president David Hood. In the early 1990s, a group of Toronto and Newfoundland entrepreneurs hit up on the idea of harvesting icebergs to supply bottled water to U.S. troops during the Gulf War. They soon discovered, however, that they couldn't just hack off bits of berg from the massive floes making their way down Newfoundland's Iceberg Alley. As soon as the ice melted, the crystalline water became a magnet for all kinds of contaminants. Somebody suggested throwing the ice in alcohol to maintain its purity, and from there, Iceberg Vodka was born. "It was just one of those things you fall you into," says Hood, "like the pet rock, the hula hoop or Trivial Pursuit."

The novelty of a vodka made from 100,000-year-old icebergs harvested from the North Atlantic immediately sparked international media attention. But just as quickly as Iceberg Vodka's star rose, the venture sputtered, admits Hood. The company lost serious money when it went with the wrong distributor in the United States, and soon after there was a falling out among the partners, who had treated the business as a sideline. Hood and David Sachs, the president and a founding shareholder, spent the next several years slowly rebuilding the company. It hasn't been easy. With very little money and a shoestring staff of five, the company not only had to contend with the vagaries of capturing giant chunks of floating ice off the Newfoundland coast, but an even more capricious business climate onshore.

Iceberg had no choice but to manufacture in Newfoundland, which jealously guards its natural resources and forbids the export of bulk water from the province. So it teamed up with the province's liquor commission, which had the only manufacturing capacity to speak of: a fifty-year-old plant that pumps out Screech for the local population. Idle all but three months of the year, the plant was retrofitted with "rubber bands and chewing gum," says Hood, and in a testament to Newfoundland ingenuity, it was able to quadruple its capacity to 400,000 cases a year.

But the biggest obstacle the company has had to overcome is an ingrained attitude among the people that the province has little to sell that others might actually want to buy. "Our plans were said to be 'too optimistic,' at one tenth the size they are now," says Hood, who, despite being born in Toronto, considers himself an "adopted son." He speaks with a local twang after living in the province for a decade and marrying a local girl. "The attitude was, 'It'll never work, it's too big for us.'"

Hood admits that Iceberg Vodka would be a lot bigger than the 250,000 cases it currently produces if it weren't tied down by Newfoundland's many self-imposed strictures. But since that's not an option, the company is looking to turn what could be conceived as a handicap into an advantage—by using Iceberg Vodka's scarcity to project an aura of exclusivity and parlay its unique business plan into a brand. "These constraints make Iceberg what it is and ensure nobody else can do it," he explains. "There's only one place in the world where you can get an iceberg, and that's Newfoundland. That's our unique proposition."

Ironically, while the brand is predicated on being Canadian, the company has chosen not to brand itself as such, preferring that its Canadianness be implicit rather explicit. "Canada and brands, that's kind of an oxymoron," explains Hood. He notes that Iceberg used to tout its Canadian origins on the front label, but Canadians, assuming it had to be second rate, didn't buy it. As soon as the company took Canada off the label, sales went up. Internationally, Iceberg was up against the notion that all good vodka came from Scandinavian or Slavic countries. So the company's coolly packaged bottles sell the imagery associated with icebergs—purity, majesty, aloofness. "Are we marketing Canada? Yes, but we're doing it without saying 'Canada,'" says Hood.

For the most part, Iceberg has been getting the message across through word of mouth, with a few strategically placed ads in places like *Penthouse* magazine and by going to trade shows. It's a slow approach, but given the company's production limitations there's not much of a choice. The good news is, the Newfoundland Liquor Corp., finally convinced that Iceberg is the real deal, has committed to investing $2.5 million in a new production facility. Iceberg is also spending $25 million for a new water plant on Trinity Bay. After ten years and $150,000, the company finally got U.S. FDA approval in 2005 to sell its iceberg-category water south of the border.

Just back from a trade mission to the Middle East, where he was sounding out potential distributors for Iceberg Vodka, Hood plans to add the water to what he envisions as a growing franchise of Iceberg-brand products, ranging from rum and gin to flavoured coolers. He knows it will be tough to sell the vodka, which is already distributed in the United States, Mexico, Germany, Switzerland, Israel, Australia and Hong Kong, into countries like Egypt and Qatar, but just like the experience in Newfoundland, he sees it as a long-term proposition. "Even if you lose in the beginning," says Hood, "the long-term strategy has you winning in the end."

EXTREME VISIONARY

"Welcome to Extreme CCTV" reads the simple yet strangely discomfiting greeting perched atop an otherwise empty front desk. "You are under video surveillance. Visitors please sign in." Guests quickly scan the modest office located in Burnaby, British Columbia, for evidence of a camera, but there is none in sight. Yet, before leaving the lobby, Jack Gin, the company's intensely driven founder and chief executive points to an innocuous light switch outfitted with the firm's cutting-edge technology. He proudly showcases products in various stages of development and assembly: a camera, still in the testing phase, that can fit into a cigarette lighter, while another bulletproof variety is about to be shipped to Haiti. "The Vancouver police force took an M16 to it and it still worked," says Gin enthusiastically.

Like Gin, Extreme CCTV's patented cameras and infrared illuminators are suited to extreme situations. Designed to withstand harsh climes and poor visibility and, in effect, to see in the dark, the company's cameras have gone down volcanoes in Antarctica in −70°C weather and are used to monitor psychiatric hospitals and jails, where patients and inmates are most at risk of harming themselves under cover of darkness. Extreme's surveillance technology is now sold in over fifty-six countries and can be found eyeing London's Big Ben and the Egyptian pyramids. Its client list reads like a who's who of the rich and paranoid, from the U.S. department of homeland security, Saudi sheiks and Israeli embassies to *Fortune 500* CEOs, Wayne Gretzky and Jennifer Lopez.

Not surprisingly, Extreme's office is filled with the accolades that come with success. Since Gin built the company from the ground up in 1997, he has been named B.C. Exporter of Year in 2001 and Canadian exporter of the year in 2003. The province wanted to nominate him a second time, but Gin, who is not shy about promoting himself, demurred. His company, which combines patented technology and a flair for marketing with global reach, is a rare commodity in British Columbia, where exports are dominated by natural resources and foreign-owned branch plants like Electronic Arts, the California-based video game developer, which boasts a massive facility outside Vancouver, and Marine Harvest, the Dutch–Norwegian fish-farming multinational.

Gin, who approaches his business with an almost religious fervour, attributes Extreme's successful start-up to "sleepless nights," "relentless intensity" and "calculated audacity." This is not his first venture into the security industry; in the mid-1990s Gin launched the security-products division at Silent Witness, another B.C.-based company, which was later sold to Honeywell. In 1997 he was eager to strike out on his own and zeroed in on the still untapped market for "infrared illumination" night-vision cameras in North America. Gin put his house on the line with a personal guarantee, and within a few months came up with prototypes and products to sell. That year, flying to New York on Aeroplan points and staying in a budget hotel, he managed to showcase his new cameras at the International Security Conference, a prestigious industry trade fair. Within a month he'd made his first sale.

With half of Extreme's $24 million in annual sales coming from the United States and the remainder from Europe, Asia, Canada and Latin America, the company was global from the get-go, says Gin, who travels about twice a month. "Going global was the natural thing to do, because Canadians were not going to buy my stuff," he says. To compete in the multi-billion-dollar security market, Gin came up with a five-pronged strategy that included a narrow but global focus, a differentiated product, in-house engineering and a "team of passionates" to bring it to fruition. "Teamwork is not about helping each other out, it's about individual excellence," says Gin of his hundred-member staff on four continents. "It's not about going as fast as the slowest guy, it's about winning."

As for the last prong in the strategy—branding—it's all about being "noisy." "We have no fear about talking to anybody," says Gin, who admits aggressive marketing might not come naturally to many Canadians. "Maybe a lot of Canadians don't do that because we are reserved." His advice: "Just be brave."

DEPANNEUR DYNASTY

It's easy to miss the headquarters of North America's second-largest independent convenience-store chain. Tucked away on the second floor of a nondescript low-rise in the industrial outskirts of Laval, there's not even a sign outside to mark the retail empire that in 2005 rang in $10 billion in revenue. "I'm allergic to head offices," admits Alain Bouchard, the ebullient founder and chief executive of Alimentation Couche-Tard. His low-key quarters, a ménage of cluttered paperwork and proudly framed press clippings, are a stark contrast to the retailer's sleek, eye-catching outlets. But like the company logo—an owl sleeping with one eye open—the unassuming ambience belies an entrepreneurial energy that never sleeps.

Bouchard was already dreaming of building a variety-store operation as a teenager growing up in the small northern town of Baie-Comeau. At eighteen he was stocking shelves at a Perrette depanneur, and at twenty-eight he had his first franchise. Within ten years he'd expanded to 115 stores. But, he says, he always knew he would venture beyond Quebec and even beyond Canada. "I always had in mind to grow and go outside of Quebec and eventually out of Canada," says Bouchard, who, like Methanex's Choquette, didn't learn to speak English until he was an adult. "It was natural to me, the same way as I see it as natural to go outside North America."

But what seems to come easily to Bouchard doesn't to many Canadians. The hugely competitive U.S. market has been a retail graveyard for all too many Canadian brands, from Canadian Tire, Mark's Work Warehouse and Future Shop to Birks, Second Cup and People's Jewellers. Not surprisingly, when Bouchard started making plans to push into the United States, one of Couche-Tard's major shareholders, mutual fund company Fidelity Investments, opposed the move. Bouchard held tight for a couple of years, buying the Mac's chain in Ontario and Western Canada, before cautious investors were finally convinced that he was up to the task. By 2003 he'd acquired half a dozen U.S. chains. Among his acquisitions was the spectacular $1.1 billion purchase of some 2,290 Circle K outlets and affiliates.

Analysts and the business media immediately fretted that he'd bitten off more than he could chew, but the ever-optimistic entrepreneur never looked back. He slashed costs by half at the Circle K stores, introduced a decentralized management structure and brought in scanners to track sales in order to better tailor the merchandise mix to each individual outlet. The overriding philosophy, he says, is to adapt to each new market and empower each store manager. "These folks are the people that run the business and create value," explains Bouchard. "The most important people, after our customers, are our store managers." As part of the company's emphasis on marketing, it also began implementing its successful multi-service-centre concept in U.S. locales, co-branding with fast-food outlets and offering an eclectic mix of gourmet coffee and high-speed wireless Internet access. "I love the U.S. market," says Bouchard. "I see so many opportunities."

With Couche-Tard's 3,000 U.S. stores in 23 states generating 75 per cent of its revenue, the company is now gearing up to go farther afield—into Asia, where there are some 3,397 Circle K licensees in Japan, Taiwan, Hong Kong, mainland China and Indonesia. "We want to build on Asia," says Bouchard excitedly. "We want to do joint ventures in China with licensees—start with a small base, learn how to develop China and, after the first couple of years of testing and fine tuning, roll out a big platform."

In addition to expanding deeper into the U.S. market, Bouchard believes it's only a matter of time before Couche-Tard overtakes Japanese-owned 7-Eleven to become the world's leading convenience store chain. "There is no doubt in my mind we will be larger," says Bouchard, who does not rule out the possibility of one day buying his bigger rival. And why not? For the boy from Baie-Comeau, anything is possible—and that goes for Canadian companies across the board. Says Bouchard: "Wake up, the market is there, just take it. You're good, and you'll be better in the States, or anywhere else. It's clear, clear, clear."

8 | MULTICULTURAL MEAL TICKET, OR MULTIPLE SOLITUDES?

> "Canada has all the nationalities, all the languages, all the cultural understanding you need to have. We should be the best in the world in this, and we are not."
>
> DESZÖ HORVÁTH, DEAN, SCHULICH SCHOOL OF BUSINESS, YORK UNIVERSITY

"DON'T TALK TO me about China," mutters a prominent businessman from his well-appointed office in downtown Calgary. He's done deals across the globe and travelled the world over, but when talk turns to the emergence of the Asian giant, his face puckers into a dark scowl. "It's horrible. So big, everything so staged, all that protocol," he complains. "You have to talk through an interpreter and you never know what the hell is really going on." His experience reflects that of many who have tried to penetrate the notoriously difficult market. Between the language, the politics of face and *guanxi*—the power of personal relationships—the real wonder, say those familiar with the market, is that we manage to do any business at all.

It's even more true for Canadians. Rarely venturing beyond the northern United States for business and never having colonized another country, Canadians are less adept than many at deciphering the finely spun layers of cultural nuance. "I don't think most Canadian businessmen understand what it's like to work in China, what it takes or how it works," confides a prominent Toronto Chinese-Canadian entrepreneur. Mainland Chinese seem to have the same impression. Edy Wong, director of the Centre for International Business Studies at the University of Alberta School of Business, says he's always asked the same two questions on his frequent trips to the People's Republic. "The first is, why is it that Canadians don't come here, and second, when they do come here, why is it they have absolutely no idea how to work here?"

Yet the key to solving the Chinese puzzle may be closer than many Canadians realize. Just a few short kilometres southeast of downtown Calgary, Simon Feng is senior metallurgist and director of R&D at Standen's, a century-old leaf-spring and suspension-parts manufacturer. To Feng, who immigrated to Canada in 1998 from China and speaks with a heavy Mandarin accent, manoeuvring through China's seemingly inscrutable business culture is as natural as eating with chopsticks. "I find it very straightforward, very easy," shrugs the engineer, who is now spearheading the company's plans to set up a manufacturing base in Xuzhou, a transportation hub midway between Shanghai and Beijing.

While many foreign companies are worn down by China's heavy-handed bureaucracy or duped by unscrupulous local partners, Standen's has quickly clinched deals and secured approvals as a result of Feng's vast network of contacts. A former professor at Jiaotong University in Xi'an, Feng also worked in the private sector, heading up the first joint venture for Mazda, the Japanese automaker, in China. When it came to drumming up business for Standen's in China, he tapped former colleagues and students to find out which companies were using what products. As it turns out, Feng's former students are high-level managers at five companies that are all now Standen's customers.

"One of the advantages for me is I have a lot of connections. I was a professor for ten years, so whatever city or company I'm dealing with, somebody knows me," he explains. "It's very easy to do business because my friends are managers, and the Chinese really respect teachers."

Feng's case is unique because he was among the first Chinese youth to attend university after the upheavals of the decade-long Cultural

Revolution, during which post-secondary schools were closed. At the age of fifteen, he won second place in chemistry and a fourth in physics in nationwide competitions, and was among two dozen high school students, known as the "genius class," chosen from across China to continue their education. Feng was offered a scholarship to do his graduate work in the United States before the Chinese government sent him to Japan's Osaka University, where he earned a PhD in material science and engineering. Despite his credentials, however, it wasn't easy to find work when he first arrived in Canada. For the first year that Feng lived in Toronto, he worked for a former student repairing tires as well as for a lumber company. Through other friends from Japan, he got a job rebuilding mechanical equipment for resale to China. Like many new immigrants, he found he couldn't get a job in the mainstream without Canadian experience.

"It was very frustrating," says Feng, now in his forties. "They kept asking if I had Canadian experience. That's really stupid. I have so much experience all over the place, what difference does it make if I have Canadian experience? So what if I got six months of Canadian experience? Is it worth anything? It's amazing—I find it very hard to understand."

Eventually in 1999, Feng saw an ad asking for a metallurgist at the Standen's plant in Calgary and applied. He got the job and, being the most educated person in the company, quickly moved up the ranks. It didn't take long for him to realize that the manufacturer would have to start seriously thinking about moving into China if it were to remain competitive. A number of Standen's customers in the United States, where the company does most of its business, had built plants in China and were looking to the Calgary parts maker to supply them locally. Feng saw that if Standen's didn't make the move, local Chinese manufacturers would copy their products in no time and then sell them at half the price. "If we don't produce in China we're going to be in big trouble because not only will our customers buy in China, but they'll import from China to North America, and then we'll lose everything," he says. "If we build in China, it lowers our costs and opens up a big market for our product."

But while moving to China seems like the obvious answer to Feng, he has encountered heavy opposition from within the company. Although some managers and staff, particularly those who have been to China, are embracing Standen's bid to establish a supply-chain complex together with its U.S. customers, others continue to resist the venture, fearful of China, afraid of the risk and of what it will mean for their jobs. Feng has worked hard to change the mindset, but he admits it's slow in coming, particularly when time is of the essence. "Everybody agrees we don't have much of a choice," he says. "But people are still nervous because they don't know China very well and they don't want things to change." Since setting the process in motion in 2004, Feng hopes the company will finally begin construction on a seventy-acre plot at the end of 2006. Ironically, while outsiders often complain of China's endless red tape and interminable decision-making process, it's the Canadians that Feng can't figure out.

THE HIDDEN ADVANTAGE

There is arguably no other city in the western hemisphere as intuitively Asian in feel as Vancouver. You see it in the throngs of shoppers walking along Robson Street, you can taste it in the myriad restaurants burrowed into every downtown nook and cranny and you sense it in the sinuous architectural lines of gleaming new high-rise towers and condominium complexes. In 1997, at the peak of the influx of Hong Kong immigrants to the city, *Time* magazine christened Vancouver "Asia's new capital." Already the world's fourth-most-multicultural city, with 37 per cent of its residents foreign-born, Vancouver's Asian flavour is expected only to deepen as mainland China and India continue to be the leading sources of new immigrants to Canada. By 2020, half the people living in Vancouver and in Canada's largest city, Toronto, will hail from abroad, including a disproportionate number from the world's fastest-growing and most dynamic economies. The question is, what are we doing to harness this resource?

Since Canada is home to two of the most culturally mixed cities in the world* and boasts the second-highest proportion of foreign-born residents after Australia, multiculturalism is arguably the country's most defining feature. To many, it's also Canada's most powerful asset. Equipped with the language skills, cultural knowledge and contacts that so often elude native-born Canadians, new immigrants might be the missing link that could pave Canada's way into hard-to-penetrate markets. With one foot in Canada and the other in their country of origin, these cultural double agents have the ability to act as trade bridges, either by filling in knowledge gaps and lowering the fear factor involved in foreign ventures or infiltrating ostensibly closed societies and forging relationships, while reporting back home in a language Canadian companies can understand.

Daisy Wai, the former president of the Richmond Hill & Markham Chinese Business Association, is a long-time advocate of tapping into the Chinese Canadian community. "They already have the connections, the *guanxi*, they know where, they know who. Business is like a chess game in China, and they can play it; the Canadians cannot," she says. "We can read their behaviour—it's beyond words and very hard to explain, but we understand it." Pradeep Sood, an adviser to the Indo-Canada Chamber of Commerce, has also worked hard to promote cross-cultural business ties. "We can tell you all about corruption in India. We've been through it, so you don't have to spend thousands of dollars to learn it," he says. "We're able to provide connectivity—the people-to-people linking can be brought to the table by us."

Yet while Canada is in an ideal position to mine this multicultural resource to gain competitive advantage, the opportunity has largely languished. Like an invisible vein of gold running through the heart of the country, multiculturalism is changing the face of Canada, yet paradoxically remains what the Asia Pacific Foundation of Canada describes as a "hidden advantage."[109] "The concentration of Canadian Asians in a few cities,

---

* Toronto is the second-most-multicultural city in the world after Miami.

especially Vancouver, will, over time, stand out as the distinguishing feature of Canada," the think-tank wrote in 2002. However, it noted, "Whether this pool of immigrant talent translates into more and deeper Canadian business ties with Asia is still unclear."[110]

In fact, as Harvard professor Michael Szonyi wrote in a paper for the Asia Pacific Foundation of Canada in 2003, there is "a striking disjuncture" between the huge migration flows from South Asia and Canada's limited economic links to the region.[111] Canadian trade and investment remain minimal, while nascent efforts to connect ethnic business groups with mainstream Canadian companies have largely fallen flat. "Toronto's Chinese community is a wealth of knowledge when it comes to doing business in that part of the world," says Tim Reid, former president of the Canadian Chamber of Commerce. "Have we taken advantage of the fact that we have this tremendous knowledge base and family connections? We just haven't mobilized the resource."

In 2002, Vancouver's largest Chinese community group, the United Chinese Community Enrichment Services Society, using government funding, attempted to bridge the divide through an innovative program called Gateway to Asia. It assembled a database of 650 recently immigrated Chinese businesspeople, 40 per cent of whom had or continued to own a business in China. They were given training on how to do business in Canada and were taken to trade fairs and missions around the province in a bid to take advantage of their connections back home. For the most part, however, the Canadian companies they contacted did not respond to their emails or return their telephone calls, says Albert Yu, the program director. "It's been very slow in coming. Canadians are not big adventurers."

Even more striking is the inordinate number of highly skilled immigrant professionals who are unable to find jobs in Canada. Stories abound of engineers and computer programmers working as taxi drivers and cleaners. In a 2004–2005 survey of 245 Chinese households in Vancouver, over 60 per cent said their employment situation in Canada was worse than it had been in China. The poll, conducted by researchers for the

Vancouver Metropolis project, found that 44 per cent reported earnings of less than twenty thousand dollars a year, even though 73 per cent had post-secondary education, including 27 per cent with a master's or doctoral degree.[112] Other sources also showed that 25 per cent of recent immigrants with university degrees were working at jobs that required a high school diploma or less.[113]

In fact, educated new immigrants are faring worse than the Portuguese bricklayers and Ukrainian farmers who arrived in Canada thirty years ago. Their unemployment rate is double that of native-born Canadians, while those with jobs earn, on average, 40 per cent less than Canadians with the equivalent qualifications. The Conference Board of Canada calculates that the failure to maximize immigrant skills costs the Canadian economy up to $5 billion a year.[114] The cost to the immigrants is incalculable. "There are a lot of Chinese Canadians that are suffering," says Wai, who counsels at her local church in the Toronto suburb of Richmond Hill. "They make a lot of sacrifices to come here, they are in the prime of their life and their skills are not being used. They feel useless and ashamed. They spend their time in the mall doing nothing or watching television at home. Some are even committing suicide. This is not a life people want."

The worrying trend has prompted researchers to investigate the root cause of what Li Zong, a sociology professor at the University of Saskatchewan, describes as "a complete waste of human capital." What they have found is that it can almost entirely be explained by a near-blanket disavowal of foreign work experience; as a study by Statistics Canada in 2005 revealed, foreign experience garnered a zero return on immigrant earnings.

Why Canadians put so little value on foreign experience is hard to explain. Some observers point to systemic discrimination and have coined phrases like "democratic racism." But if you place the problem within Canada's historical business context, it actually makes perfect sense. Entreated to stay home and build walls while telling themselves that they produced the best world had to offer, Canadians naturally assume their skills are superior. More importantly, there has never been a need or a frame of reference for attaching value to skills and abilities outside the Canadian context. Which is why, when the world is globalizing at a dizzying rate, employers are concerned with how "Canadianized" immigrant employees are rather than with the new skills and languages they might bring to an organization.

It's as if Finland's tiny population of five million people decided they didn't need to speak any language except Finnish to get along. They'd be stuck in Finland. Which is why the Finns and the Dutch and the Swedes speak three or four languages. With 33 million Canadians in the world and 1.3 billion Chinese, "the Canadian Way" will likely not prevail as a standard for global competitiveness. Instead of trying to figure out how an immigrant will fit into their organization, companies should be looking at how new Canadians can help them fit into the global marketplace.

Unfortunately, Canadians' inverted view of the world is reinforced by boards of directors and executive management that continue to be overwhelmingly dominated by, well, white guys. According to the Spencer Stuart Board Index, visible minorities made up just 1.7 per cent of Canadian boards of directors in 2003. In a 2004 survey of seventy organizations, the Conference Board of Canada found that just 3 per cent of executive positions were filled by minorities. Without people from different backgrounds involved in the actual decision-making process, it is difficult for any organization to open itself up to new concepts and ideas, let alone have the confidence or wherewithal to bet the company's future on the banks of the Yangtze.

"We have this amazing diaspora of smart people from India, China, Russia, and if we could find a way to plug them in, they might be the key that unlocks the door," says Glen Hodgson, chief economist at the Conference Board. "But we haven't found a way to use them. We don't have them as senior advisers on boards. They're doing their own thing and some may be doing fairly well, but they are not integrating into our society."

Since immigrating to Canada from Hong Kong in 1966, David Fung has done exceptionally well. Starting out as a penniless young student in Montreal, where he earned a doctorate in chemical engineering, Fung went on to become a research manager at paint company c-i-l before heading up Chemetics International Co., a $200 million outfit with chemical plant projects on six continents. In 1989 he launched his own company, ACDEG International, which essentially capitalizes on Fung's cultural adaptability in acting as a high-end middleman between Canadian resources, European technology and Asian money. He now spends much of his time "writing cheques" to various philanthropic causes and sitting on the boards of numerous institutes and associations.

Not surprisingly, multiculturalism is a cause that's near and dear to Fung's heart. The only Chinese Canadian on the board of the Canadian Manufacturers and Exporters Association, he goes around the country giving speeches on the need to bridge the divide between native-born Canadians and their immigrant bedfellows. But after all this time, Fung, who lives in Vancouver, concedes that it's a fine line between multiculturalism and "multiple solitudes." "We are our own biggest hypocrites. We profess this ideal, but internally we don't embrace it," he says. "The 'hidden advantage' is only an advantage if you use it. Otherwise it's no advantage at all."

SQUARE PEGS AND ROUND HOLES

In 2003 the Bank of Montreal (BMO) became the first foreign institution to acquire a stake in a leading Chinese mutual fund company, and in 2006 it was among six firms chosen from around the world to underwrite the Bank of China's US$10 billion IPO, one of the country's biggest to date. That same year it also became the first Canadian bank to be given approval by Chinese authorities to provide banking services in Beijing in local currency. BMO boasts a small, three-person investment banking unit in Beijing, as well as branches and representative offices in Shanghai, Guangzhou and Hong Kong. It may not be diving full bore into the Chinese financial market, but at the very least it is dipping a very serious toe, if not an entire foot.

In testing the waters, the bank has relied heavily on a network of Chinese-born, Canadian-trained bankers to read the tea leaves of China's constantly shifting financial horizon. Roger Heng, BMO's Beijing-based managing director for China, was born in Guandong province and grew up in Hong Kong before attending boarding school in London, Ontario. He went on to receive an economics degree at the University of Western Ontario and a commerce degree from the University of Windsor. Also in Beijing is Tony Choy, responsible for investment and corporate banking, who was born in Hong Kong and educated in the United States before moving to Canada in 1989 to work for the bank. Their colleague in Shanghai, Lisa Xia, immigrated to Canada in 1999 and worked for BMO in Toronto, returning to her hometown in 2003 as BMO's representative. Frankie Li, general manager of the bank's Hong Kong branch, immigrated to Canada in 1988 and worked in commercial banking before being sent back home to head up BMO's corporate side in 1996. "We have to rely on very competent local nationals to be effective," explains Yvan Bourdeau, chief executive of BMO Capital Markets. "If you really want to be competitive, you need that."

Bourdeau has had more exposure to Asia than most Canadian executives. Having lived in the Far East for fifteen years, with postings in Tokyo, Singapore and Seoul, he has twenty-five years of experience working with China. Yet he acknowledges that he would miss a lot of the nuance critical to deal-making without the support of a Chinese-Canadian team that is fluent in the business cultures of both countries. "I know how to structure a deal. But it's a different thing to structure it in China," he explains. "They never say no, but sometimes you don't know what they are saying."

During a recent trip to Shanghai, Bourdeau recalls trying to line up two potential partners for a deal. He could sense resistance from one of the parties, but could not pinpoint the problem. His Shanghai representative, Xia, approached the Chinese during a break in the meetings and learned that they were also negotiating with a third party. "I relied on her very heavily to give me signals as to what actually was being said and where we were heading," Bourdeau said. "During the breaks she would go and talk to them informally, which is something they would not do with me."

With several thousand Chinese Canadians already working for the bank back in Canada, Bourdeau expects that BMO will have no shortage of new recruits as it looks to expand further into China. Recently looking for currency and derivatives traders and market-risk specialists to staff its offices, the bank did a scan of its trading floor for Cantonese and Mandarin speakers and found three employees interested in going back to work in China. "Toronto particularly has a very large pool of Chinese talent that is probably proportionally greater than that of any other city in North America," says Bourdeau. "We have a great talent pool."

The trading floor was also where Peter Beck turned to when he decided to expand his Toronto-based brokerage business, Swift Trade, internationally. An immigrant from Hungary, Beck figured there would be plenty of other new Canadians who would jump at the chance to make good back in their native countries. At the same time it would be an inexpensive way to grow the company. "There's lots of these expats looking at ways to get back," says Beck. "For us it was essential to realize that we can market this. It's easier to get people here, and so much simpler when it comes to setting up the business abroad."

Beck designed a licensing package that included all the necessary online trading technology and instructions for starting up an office. To get the word out, he approached some of his foreign-born Toronto traders who went back to their respective communities with the idea. When it came to the Chinese community "it was almost like an avalanche," says Beck. "China is booming, and everybody is looking at ways to go back and take advantage." As of February 2006, Swift Trade had seventeen offices in China, with another fifteen set to open up, making it the company's second-largest operation after Canada. "It's been excellent," Beck says. "China has proven to be a great opportunity for us."

Swift Trade's strategy echoes that of many successful immigrant entrepreneurs in Canada who have combined a desire to return to their roots with the ability to see opportunities others might miss. Austria-born Frank Stronach established Magna's European headquarters in Graz, not far from his hometown, while Linamar's Frank Hasenfratz operates three plants in his native Hungary. Less well known is Alex Schnaider, who oversees a vast empire from the anonymity of suburban Toronto. Born in

Russia and having immigrated to Canada via Israel as a teenager, Schnaider capitalized on the break-up of the former Soviet Union, scooping up Ukrainian and Russian steel plants, a Moscow casino and a power grid in Armenia. Now worth an estimated US$1.4 billion, Schnaider emerged from obscurity in recent years to bankroll Toronto's Trump Tower and buy his very own Formula One racing team. As one magazine article noted, what distinguished the thirtysomething entrepreneur from other Westerners trying to get rich on the collapse of communism was the fact that he spoke Russian. "Language helped me understand the mentality and what was really going on," Schnaider told *Report on Business*. "We were able to make decisions that others might not make. Take bigger risks."[115]

For Tim Plumptre, a one-time director of the Brazil–Canada Chamber of Commerce, language and cultural affinity are critical competitive advantages. A long-time banker in Latin America, Plumptre recalls Team Canada missions to the region in which, of 450 participants, perhaps four or five were Hispanic Canadians and fewer than a dozen actually spoke Spanish. In comparison, he says, American missions were chock full of Hispanics who routinely head up the export departments of U.S. firms. "To try to develop business in a foreign country, you are cutting your chances in half by not speaking their language," says Plumptre. "And I don't just mean Canadians who took a night class in Spanish. I am talking about Hispanic Canadians—a Mexican Canadian who knows how they do things."

Sometimes the combination of Canadian know-how and local finesse is not a function of one person, but a matter of a few individuals combining their skills. When Gary Comerford, a marketing executive with Sun Life Financial, stepped off the plane in India for the first time in 1996, he was overwhelmed. Tapped to spearhead the insurer's re-entry into India after a forty-three-year absence from the market, Comerford had travelled to the United States and United Kingdom on business, but had never really worked outside of Ontario. India was a whole other world.

Which is why teaming up with Vijay Singh brought him such "incredible reassurance." While Comerford knew Sun Life like the back of his hand, Singh not only had international experience working with IBM in Singapore, but was born and raised in Delhi before immigrating to Canada in 1978. Singh became Sun Life's country manager, stick-handling government relations and red tape, and in 2001 headed up its newly launched life insurance joint venture, Birla Sun Life. "He was my security blanket. There was a comfort, caused by his knowledge and expertise that he'd been there and done that before and knew the culture," explains Comerford, now vice-president of international operations and general manager for India. "I would bring my Canadian jolly-good-fellow attitude, and he was far more skeptical and critical, and that was absolutely required."

Although Singh is quick to point out that cultural affinity is only one tool in the international business arsenal, he admits it did come in handy when getting to the point in India's sometimes eager-to-please business culture. "I don't hesitate, in talking to people, to point out bluntly what I think I need to tell them. My colleagues, who are white Irish Catholics, have to be careful not to rub the wrong way," says Singh. "I speak the language and look like them, and if I behave properly I get entry into their minds much more easily. I'm accepted as one of them, and that's a huge benefit. The other guys have to earn it."

Still, like any tool, if not handled carefully the culture card can cut both ways and cause more harm than good. While it's almost expected that Westerners will commit cultural faux pas, if a Chinese Canadian makes a mistake, it's considered "unforgivable," says Carla Kearns, who runs a Mandarin school in Toronto. Similarly, some Chinese may prefer to deal with Westerners because it affords them a certain amount of face or status, rather than using an intermediary from Hong Kong, for example, who may be looked upon with some suspicion. In the case of India, many locals are resentful of a returning diaspora that is parachuted into the country by large multinationals and given cushy expat packages. "There is a real sense of pride in India these days," says Comerford. "They feel they've stayed, they're educated and they're as smart and can do as good a job. So you've got to be careful how you handle it."

Jealousy is a significant factor, acknowledges Michael Schaffer, a general manager with SGS, an inspection and testing services company. The firm's Toronto office, which counts nine nationalities among its thirty-member staff, routinely exploits its multicultural mix in securing sales and service contracts from Mexico to China. But while Schaffer copies the company's Polish employee on anything related to Poland, even if he isn't involved in a particular project, the company is more cautious when it comes to the South African engineers. "In South Africa, whites who leave are seen as traitors," he explains. "So there is a fine line separating when you can use ethnic or cultural affinity and when you shouldn't."

Milton Parissis, president of Parissis Partners in Toronto, recalls the case of a Canadian military supply company that was trying to sell fire extinguishers to a German firm. The Canadians thought they were being smart by sending a German employee to make the sale. They didn't realize he was from the folksy southern state of Bavaria whereas the company was based in the northern trading hub of Hamburg. To the German eye, says Parissis, it was like sending a peasant to call on the captains of a rather hierarchical industrial complex. "He didn't have the sophistication, the history and, as a consequence, he didn't have stature. The Germans felt insulted," says Parissis. "You gotta understand who you are dealing with."

And that is the crux of the matter. Turning multiculturalism into a competitive advantage involves more than simply matching up compatible skin colours and language skills. Canadian companies also must do their part to deepen their awareness and grasp the subtleties that define and distinguish each country and community. In the same way that someone from Arkansas would have little instinct for doing business in Newfoundland, an ethnic East Indian born in Kenya wouldn't know much about conducting himself in Calcutta. To the Canadian eye, Peruvians and Ecuadorians are virtually indistinguishable, but to these nationalities there is an ocean of difference that has triggered wars and continues to stoke simmering animosities.

In order to make those distinctions, companies first need to resist the temptation to use multiculturalism as a "crutch" when doing business in abstruse foreign markets, advises Margaret Cornish, executive director of the Canada China Business Council. It's often far too easy, she says, for a company to palm off all its China business on its Chinese Canadian employee without ever bothering to understand the market. As a result, the market knowledge and information gleaned by its Chinese Canadian hire may never be absorbed throughout the organization, and the company runs the risk of never integrating its foreign business into the corporate structure. The foreign subsidiary remains an orphan, and when business goes bad is easily axed—along with all the contacts and market intelligence it has built up. It's better to get a handle on the market and then pick the right person or partner, says Cornish.

At the same time, when it comes to working with ethnic Chinese immigrants, Canadians must first understand that there are significant differences between businesspeople from Taiwan, Hong Kong entrepreneurs and professionals born in mainland China. Not only the product of different waves of immigration, they represent different social strata, skill sets and motivations. Some, like the University of Alberta's Edy Wong, see more obstacles than opportunities in aligning the business interests of these groups with mainstream Canadian companies. Many Chinese prefer to work for themselves, whereas those who are willing to work for someone else may not understand Canadian culture, he says. Similarly, mainland Chinese who grew up under communism may not have the same entrepreneurial instincts as people from Hong Kong. "It would be wrong to assume all Chinese Canadians have knowledge of the Chinese market," cautions Kenny Zhang, a senior researcher at the Asia Pacific Foundation of Canada. "Not all have a willingness to promote trade, and not all have the business skills."

Having said that, a lot more would be accomplished, say those in the community, if companies were better able to recognize the skills and resources that immigrants bring to the table. A university graduate from mainland China may not speak perfect English, but her Mandarin would be impeccable and her father might be a high-level bureaucrat in the Chinese health ministry. "For a Canadian pharmaceutical company looking for a licence to sell in China, this woman has influence," explains Ken Kwan, a Vancouver businessman who worked for fifteen years in China representing U.S. multinational Honeywell. "Companies have got to be patient and understand their background."

More to the point, it comes down to both sides adjusting their expectations about how business can and should be done, explains David Fung. The Vancouver entrepreneur attributes much of the disconnect between the Canadian mainstream and the Chinese community to "a fundamental difference in business outlook." While many Canadians tend to operate on the basis of black-and-white ideas of right and wrong, the business ethics of recent Chinese immigrants, still preoccupied with matters of survival, may come in many shades of grey. As a result, mainstream white Canadians are often distrustful of those Chinese who seem willing to do just about anything to get ahead. The new immigrants, in turn, are ghettoized, confined to doing business solely with their own community.

To break the deadlock, says Fung, each side needs to make an effort to understand where the other is coming from. "In China, despite everything, only 250 million people have emerged out of poverty. There are still one billion in poverty. We must understand the background in which they were raised and what they've come through," he explains. "When survival is important, your values change. Some business ethics may come second. Is it right or wrong? Well, it depends on how you were raised."

Until now, Canadians have been quick to assume that it's the Chinese immigrants who must change. At the same time, many immigrants continue to employ business practices that clearly don't fly in Canada. "They have to understand that if they behave in a certain way which may be fine in their own community, it may not be acceptable in the Canadian community. They will never make it," says Fung. "On the Canadian side, we need to understand that we are not going to change the way a Taiwanese has been brought up."

Fung believes, however, that between these two disparate realities lies common ground and an overlapping set of values. He suggests structuring a joint venture in a way for the Chinese partner to earn so much money that there's no incentive to endanger the partnership and both sides can come out on top. "We cannot change people's values. That is a futile exercise. But we need to understand their values and then try to create what I usually call a square hole for a square peg," he says. "Currently we are not using the ethnic-Asian minority because they are square pegs that do not fit into our round holes. And right now we say: if you don't fit, we don't play. It's a tremendous waste of resources."

NOTCANADA.COM

For most of its fifty-year history, Viceroy Homes, a family-run company operating out of Port Hope, Ontario, built its traditional wood-frame homes almost exclusively for the Canadian market. Then in the early 1990s, the Japanese, looking for more earthquake-resistant, energy-efficient housing, began scoping out Canadian homebuilders. "They wanted to see the factories," recalls Chris Lindal, Viceroy's executive vice-president. "They would come by the busload; it was quite something." While others treated the Japanese influx like a bit of a bonus on top of their regular business, Viceroy made a deliberate decision to stake its future on the new market. With some 60 per cent of its sales coming from across the Pacific, Viceroy is now North America's largest exporter of house packages to Japan.

How did Viceroy do it? "We took the view that Japanese customers might be farther away, but they are every bit as concerned about issues and details and service as the guy next door is," explains Lindal. "So you give them the same level of service." Lindal immediately began taking Japanese lessons, and one of the first people he hired was his language instructor, to translate all the company's material into Japanese. A decade later there are at least fifteen Japanese speakers working for the company, the majority Japanese-born Canadian citizens or permanent residents. A few are even Chinese nationals who have worked in Japan and are trilingual to boot. "Some have serious degrees from a Chinese university who went on to Japan to get an architectural degree and work for five or ten years in a Japanese architecture firm or housing company," says Lindal. "That's a rock-solid resumé. We see that and we want to talk to that person for sure."

But while Viceroy ships its homes halfway around the world, it didn't have to venture far to hire its multinational workforce—just down Highway 401 to Toronto. That's also where it found Andrea Bermudez, a trilingual Colombian-born architect with post-diploma degrees from two French architecture schools. Bermudez, who immigrated to Canada in 1999, is charged with opening up new markets for Viceroy in Europe and Latin America. She even handles its Quebec business. But though she loves her job, when her friends back in Colombia ask her about immigrating to Canada, Bermudez tells them not to bother. "Unless they have perfect English and certain contacts they should not come," she says. "Not because they won't succeed, but because of the immigration process."

Bermudez estimates that maybe 3 or 4 per cent of Canadian companies are willing to hire a qualified immigrant. Most companies demand two to five years of Canadian work experience and rarely, if ever, ask about international experience, she says. For a professional couple with children, that means scraping by for three to five years before their incomes are even on par with what they made in their home country. "I see a lot of discouragement; you have to be really brave to do it," says Bermudez. "I know doctors and lawyers working as security guards—it just breaks my heart. I've seen people come here and leave a year later."

In fact, many of the best and brightest new immigrants are leaving in droves. Between 1980 and 2001, some 380,000 Hong Kong immigrants, mostly wealthy business investors and skilled professionals, arrived in Canada. Many came with the express purpose of acquiring a Canadian passport as an insurance policy against the transition from British colony to Chinese rule, but a significant number were also disappointed by the meagre business opportunities, onerous regulations and lack of job prospects they found in Canada. According to a Statistics Canada study of economically active Hong Kong immigrants between the ages of 20 and

45 who arrived since 1991, 40 per cent have either returned home or moved on to a third country, usually the United States. In Hong Kong there are now an estimated 200,000 to 300,000 people holding Canadian passports—the largest single source of foreign passports in the territory. "An inordinate number move on," says Don DeVoretz, an economist at Simon Fraser University who is tracking the Hong Kong immigrants. "It's astounding, really."

A number of surveys conducted by DeVoretz and others have found that while many Hong Kong natives may prefer Canada's more relaxed lifestyle, they largely see the country as a place to retire or send their children to school. They certainly don't see it as a source of wealth creation. "I would never think of doing business here," one survey respondent was quoted as saying. "I would like to work in Hong Kong and sleep in Canada," responded another.[116] All in all, the research concludes, Canada largely serves as an "entrepot" for migrants, offering language training, education and a passport before they move on to the rest of the world.

The more recent influx of mainland Chinese are expected to follow the same course. Many who were unable to obtain a visitor's visa before making the decision to move to Canada now feel duped. They are packing up and moving back. "They knew Canada was a stable country, but they didn't realize the environment was so bad," explains Albert Yu, who works with Chinese immigrants in Vancouver. "They can't get a job, they can't start a business. If I am Chinese and I come over here to do a mid-level job, I would be disappointed." DeVoretz and the University of Alberta's Shiboa Guo, in their poll of Chinese households in Vancouver, found the immigrants "experienced deep dissatisfaction with Canada and planned to move on." They went on to predict that "both the necessary and sufficient conditions exist for a continued large-scale emigration of post-98 Chinese immigrant arrivals."[117] The predictions may already be coming true; a 2006 study by Statistics Canada found that one in six young, highly educated immigrants leave Canada within a year due to the lack of job prospects.

The disillusionment has become so widespread and, in some cases, so visceral that a number of disaffected immigrants have even launched a website—www.notcanada.com—to document their travails and warn other potential newcomers against the perils of moving to Canada. The growing backlash doesn't bode well for the country's reputation or its urgent need to up its annual immigrant quota to 1 per cent of the population by 2010. Canada is the only developed country that actually wants more immigrants than it currently receives—by 2011 it will need to rely on newcomers to supply 100 per cent of its labour force growth—yet some 30 per cent of Canadian immigrants eventually return to their home countries or move on to a third country. "We risk losing our reputation as a tremendously welcoming place," warns David Pecaut, a partner with the Boston Consulting Group who has spearheaded efforts in Toronto to better integrate immigrants. "We have this great reputation, but if that starts to change it could really hurt us. We absolutely need these folks for the economy's sake."

And not only as an important source of labour. As we have seen, immigrants are the driving force behind a disproportionate number of successful Canadian companies. It's a phenomenon that is not unique to Canada. By one count in the late 1990s, 41 per cent of all Ottawa-based, publicly traded technology companies were headed by immigrants;[118] in California's Silicon Valley, close to a third of dot-coms were launched by Indian and Chinese entrepreneurs. According to Richard Florida, a professor at Pittsburgh's Carnegie Mellon University and author of *The Rise of the Creative Class*, the flow of global talent to the United States is the impetus behind much of the nation's high-tech supremacy; its leading Internet giants, including Google, Hotmail, Yahoo! and eBay,* were founded by foreigners. In this "creative age," as Florida calls it, the drive to attract top talent will outstrip competition for jobs, technology and investment and will spell the difference between progress and stagnation.

---

* This cadre of foreign-born Internet entrepreneurs includes Canadian Jeff Skoll, the first president of eBay.

The high proportion of foreign-born residents in Canada's largest cities has prompted Florida to put Canada in the winner's category. On paper, it all adds up quite nicely; but dangling a Canadian passport and the opportunity to learn English in a safe, clean environment is becoming less and less of an incentive to stick around, especially as countries like China and India are making aggressive bids to lure their overseas diasporas back home. As these countries move into a stage of hyperactive wealth creation, they have identified these pools of foreign-trained nationals as a strategic asset, and China is now offering its overseas academics free airfare and accommodation and even building specially dedicated scientific parks for returning researchers. "In China there are a lot of opportunities opening up, while in Canada they are still treated like second-class citizens," says the University of Saskatchewan's Li Zong, who's spent years studying the problem.

Ironically, one of the things that makes these overseas nationals attractive to their native countries is the fact that they've had Canadian education and training and exposure to a different way of doing things, and as a result bring a new skill set with them. It allows them to think outside the box and be more innovative—qualities that Canadian companies surely could use. Instead, Canada has helped equip them to create wealth *elsewhere*. "It may not matter at the individual level, but it does matter for the country as a whole," explains Kenny Zhang of the Asia Pacific Foundation of Canada. "If we don't use this advantage wisely and our competitor does, then Canada is not in a good position to compete."

ALL THE INGREDIENTS FOR A MEAL

Some observers, like John Wiebe, former president of the Asia Pacific Foundation of Canada, who have spent years fulminating over the issue have reluctantly concluded that connecting the Canadian mainstream with immigrant communities is "wishful thinking." He may be right. Or maybe we just need to learn how to recognize the signposts—the ones that point to the maze of bridges that circle and weave all around us but that only a small subculture of transnational migrants, itinerant expats and globally minded companies have figured out how to drive on.

It reminds me of the 1999 motion picture *The Matrix*, in which a stealthy band of travellers moves between the simulated world and reality using portals. They are usually located in the most unassuming, ordinary places—a public telephone booth, an abandoned apartment, a back alley. In Toronto, the portals connecting Canada and China are so obvious they are almost invisible to the naked eye: the Toronto Stock Exchange (TSX), the University of Toronto and the teeming alleyways of the city's Chinatown, to name just three. It's a matter of recognizing their transportive qualities and then punching in the right coordinates.

Spadina Avenue is always a hive of activity, crowded with merchants hawking cabbage and designer knock-offs from their curbside stores. But the real deals in Chinatown are being made under the radar, with everyone who can hopping on board the Chinese gravy train and heading back to pan for their nugget of gold. Retired teachers are building massive, 85,000-square-foot restaurants in Shanghai, former insurance salesmen are managing the expansion of North American hotel chains on the mainland and Communist Party secretary-generals are flying into Toronto incognito to seal $100 million investment deals. "When I go to a Chinese banquet, two out of ten people at every table are doing business in China," says one prominent member of the community. "Businessmen are going over there every single day. It's the gold rush all over again."

A few blocks away, the atmosphere on campus at the Rotman School of Management is unabashedly white collar. But don't be fooled by the excess of blue blazers and carefully cropped hair. Close to half of the students graduating from the MBA program in 2007 are from outside Canada and the United States—the largest group coming from India and China. There's even a Chinese MBA students' association, and many alumni now hold down influential jobs in Canada, the United States and back in China. "In ten years these kids will have this country licked so fast it isn't even funny," says a Chinese Canadian businessman. "If I were a Canadian business, I would go meet them, find who the premier students are and get hold of them."

Moving deeper into the heart of downtown, a century-old mid-rise is easily missed amid the skyscrapers crowded around King and Yonge streets. On the eighth floor, at the end of an empty hallway, is the Canadian headquarters of Hanfeng Evergreen. The sparsely decorated office, with its whitewashed walls and token Canadian and Chinese flags, doesn't look like much of a gateway, but Hanfeng is one of a growing handful of truly transnational companies that has operations in China and is listed on the TSX.

A combination of the word *Han*, meaning ancient Chinese heritage, and *feng*, Chinese for maple, Hanfeng was founded by Yu Xinduo, a former Chinese government official who made his fortune in the jewellery business before immigrating to Canada in the early 1990s. Impressed by the urban greenery in Canadian cities, Yu believed there was a tremendous business opportunity for landscaping in China's booming centres. He opened a nursery business in his home town of Dalian using Canadian technology and products. In 2003, with the help of capital raised in the Toronto Chinese community, Yu engineered the reverse takeover of a Canadian company, listing Hanfeng on the exchange.

With sales of $40 million in 2005, the company operates four fertilizer plants and has more than three hundred Chinese employees. Hanfeng's Canadian contingent includes an almost entirely local board of directors and a small but surprisingly multicultural staff. The company's chief financial officer immigrated to Canadian from Dalian a decade ago. The public-relations rep, though Canadian-born, is half Norwegian and half Japanese, while executive director Kim Oishi, who describes himself as "half Japanese, half Jewish" is from Dawson Creek, British Columbia. One of only two native English speakers at the company, Oishi communicates with Yu through a translator.

Like many "astronaut" businessmen, Yu spends most of his time in China. But his ties to Canada are strong, not only because of Hanfeng, but because his wife and two children live here. "He wants to have a good reputation in Canada—his family is here," explains Oishi. "So if Canadians can convince Mr. Yu, or they can find individuals like him, to introduce them to China, it will go a long way. He understands China like the back of his hand."

Of course, for any of these portals to work, immigrants will also have to do their part to meet the mainstream halfway. On the one hand, that means recognizing the value of the skills they bring and promoting them to Canadian companies that may not know what to look for. It also means making more of an effort to integrate. Yu is a case in point: after a decade in Canada, he still doesn't speak English. "The weak point of the Chinese community is they don't make enough of an effort to integrate, and they're not as patient because it's not as easy to make money," says Ken Kwan. "Mindset is very important. In Canada you have to keep on trying."

Ultimately, however, capitalizing on Canada's "hidden" advantage will depend on first recognizing that we fail to see it. Like a picture concealed within a holograph, it's only by making a conscious effort to adjust our focus that the jumble of seemingly random patterns crystallize into a conceptual whole. And the more often we do it, the more quickly and easily the picture emerges. In the same way, says David Fung, adopting a different perspective can only come by learning to respect different cultures and ways of being. The key, he says, is exposure. Twenty years ago Fung and his wife made the conscious decision not to attend a Chinese church, and instead opted to worship at an Anglican church in the mostly white enclave of West Vancouver. They were the only ethnic Chinese couple there, and people were astonished at first, he says, but now, he and his wife are just part of the congregation, like everyone else.

"To make use of this hidden resource, I think a lack of cultural respect and understanding are probably the biggest stumbling blocks. Both communities may need to take a step towards each other to make the connection," says Fung. "I believe Canada really has this tremendous opportunity. Whether we, as individuals, take advantage of it will require more exposure, education, discussion, and more debates within our communities. But we have all the elements. It's like a chef in the kitchen. Do we put these ingredients together to make a meal, or do they stay separate forever? It's up to us."

9 | THE MEXICAN LUNCH, OR A MUG'S GAME?

"In one thing people are the same—find out what it is they want and
what they need. Once you scratch off the veneer, we are all the same.
If you realize that, there are great opportunities to be had."

CHARLIE FISCHER, CEO, NEXEN

IT WAS THE EARLY 1990s, the Alberta economy was in the doldrums and a
local consulting firm was casting around for new business opportunities.*
The U.S. government had decided to backstop Latin American debt with
Brady Bonds, and momentum was building for a North American free-
trade agreement. It seemed like only a matter of time before business
would begin migrating to Mexico. The Alberta firm figured it could get a
head start on the competition by opening an office in Mexico City to
represent companies hoping to expand into the low-cost, emerging market. Little did it know that this seemingly savvy decision would mark the
beginning of a harrowing, decade-long odyssey fraught with embezzle-
ment schemes, blackmail and corruption.

Things seemed to go awry almost from the get go. A senior member
with the firm flew down to Mexico City to launch the business. His first
stop was the Canadian embassy, which referred him to a local adviser
who could provide him with on-the-ground knowledge of the market. He

---

* The company has chosen to remain anonymous to avoid further legal problems.

paid the adviser, a former Mexican chief of police armed with a letter of recommendation from the embassy, and flew back to Canada. When several months passed and almost no work had been done, the consultant returned to Mexico City to confront his wayward man-on-the-ground. The two met, but no sooner had he begun asking questions than the ex-cop pulled out a gun and placed it on the table between them. Needless to say, the meeting went nowhere and the money paid to the cop-cum-adviser was never recouped.

And that was just for starters. Undaunted, the firm forged ahead, opening up a rep office, only for its Mexican bookkeeper to pilfer fifty thousand dollars from the company by filing false account claims in cahoots with a local bank official. Then a three-way joint venture to build a multi-million-dollar industrial plant in northern Mexico turned sour when one of the partners, a leading Mexican engineering and construction company, went bankrupt. The financially insolvent firm was in breach of the development agreement but refused to exit the project unless it was bought out of the venture. The Mexican firm was quite practised in the art of manipulating the Mexican judicial system, and the Canadian consultancy, despite a costly legal battle, was unable to enforce its contract in the Mexican courts. "The judicial system was just a circus," says an executive with the firm. "We spent more money than we ever should have. Every day a thousand bucks was going out the door." Between the lengthy delays and legal shenanigans, the project eventually fizzled.

It sounds almost too absurd to believe, but in the midst of the chaos surrounding the Mexican construction company's dissolution, its in-house legal counsel raided the company files and stole the project's promissory notes. He then attempted to blackmail the Canadian consultancy, demanding fifty thousand dollars for their safe return. The Canadians refused to pay, and eventually the lawyer slunk off.

While the consultancy did have some success in Mexico, by the late 1990s the Alberta economy was rebounding. Senior management began to wonder whether its Mexican operation was worth all the headache when a nasty labour dispute with its Mexico City office confirmed their suspicions.

A couple of senior employees had quit to set up a competitive business, then turned around and sued the Canadians for unjust dismissal. Ensnared in Mexico's archaic labour laws and dragged, yet again, through the country's capricious court system, the consultancy spent tens of thousands of dollars vainly trying to defend itself against a less than impartial justice system. "It's like a spider's web," says a member with the firm. "It seems like they see you coming and say, 'Here comes another sucker.'"

After everything the company's been through, it says it can't, in good conscience, advise its clients to invest in such a corruption-riddled country. Besides, between the legal charades, wasted time and management hassles, it's not worth all the anguish and effort when there's easy money to be made right here at home. Many would agree. As far as Dick Haskayne is concerned, going international is a "mug's game." Says the chairman of TransCanada PipeLines, "'International' sounds romantic and glamorous, but it's very, very expensive, and people have no idea about the cost of operating internationally. Unless it's highly profitable, it's a disaster."

Strolling along Alberta's petroleum-paved streets, it's not hard to wonder why you'd bother wading into the morass of international markets when there's meat-and-potatoes money to be made in the comfort of home. Except, of course, what do you do once you've picked all the low-hanging fruit? If you don't know how to climb to the higher, more precarious branches, you starve. Brian Kelsall and Ella Plotkin, top-ranked international project finance lawyers with Ogilvy Renault, say they are constantly asked by fellow Bay Street lawyers why they bother working in obscure countries like Uruguay and Romania when they could be doing the latest income trust in Toronto. Their response would turn out to be remarkably prescient given the federal government's decision in November 2006 to effectively shut down the income trust industry. "You might do this year's income trust and next year's, and even the one after that, but how do you know that in ten years you are still going to have these income trusts and that there will be enough of them to go around The Street?" says Plotkin. "There won't be. If you don't keep pushing the envelope and looking for new markets—if you ignore the fact that Canada is part of a world community—then all you're doing is regionalizing yourself, you're shutting yourself down and you're just opening up the opportunity to somebody else."

To be sure, scaling global heights is not for the faint of heart. It takes persistence, conviction, smarts and huge personal sacrifice—but it doesn't have to be a crapshoot. There are ways to mitigate the risks. According to a poll conducted in the early 1990s by Lorna Wright at the Schulich School of Business, Canadian companies gave five main reasons for not going abroad: (1) too far, (2) too expensive, (3) language barriers, (4) different business culture and (5) the United States is closer. "The only thing that still holds true today is that the U.S. is closer," says Wright.

Going global is like learning to climb a tree: you have to know which branches will hold your weight and how to identify those that look healthy from the outside but are rotten below the bark. Even then—after you've planned your climb, bought the proper gear and calculated the risk—the task still requires a certain leap of faith. In many ways it's not unlike marriage: you can date a person, live together first and meet the parents; but, even then, there are no guarantees. Either you decide you want to be married and take the plunge, or you opt to remain single. Sure, the risks are greater, but so are the rewards. "If you break it down into its component parts, it'll worry you," admits Kelsall. "Forget that stuff. It's no more difficult than anything you do here. Don't focus on each individual problem but on the opportunity as a whole. Our mantra is, 'Just do it.'"

Admittedly, that's a scary proposition for most Canadians, who, some argue, are "attitudinally ill-equipped" to grapple with the cultural complexities, cut-throat competitiveness and corruption that characterize foreign markets. "If Canadians want to become international they're going to have to change their attitude," sums up Hong Kong–born Vancouver entrepreneur Ken Kwan. It's as difficult—or as easy—as that. Rick Ricker, the general manager of Reichmann's fifty-five-storey Torre Mayor skyscraper in downtown Mexico City, perhaps explained it best. I asked him how he was able to build such a monumental edifice, coordinating the arrival of tens of thousands of truckloads of material and equipment through the city's snarled streets, while navigating the thicket of municipal politics and combative unions. Without missing a beat, he said simply: "It's what you're used to."

FOR SOME CANADIANS, doing business internationally comes as naturally as eating maple syrup and back bacon. These people are like hidden gems that once you know where to dig, begin popping up in the most unexpected places. Their experiences and insights are invaluable not only to first-time exporters and foreigner investors, but even to companies already doing business out there. Based on their recommendations, I have compiled a list of dos and don'ts and added a few observations of my own. Some of these observations will seem obvious, some might surprise you; but one thing is clear: it's all within our grasp.

BEFORE YOU GO ANYWHERE

Have a plan

According to a 2004 report by TD bank, 46 per cent of small and medium-sized exporters surveyed began selling overseas as a result of unsolicited inquiries.[119] Astoundingly, only 37 per cent had any kind of plan in place to export. A subsequent poll by KPMG of Canadian exporters into the Indian market found that only half had done any kind of planning.[120] Michel Charland, director of the federal government's International Trade Centre in Montreal, estimates that about a third of companies go international as a reaction to deteriorating domestic conditions; once the Canadian economy bounces back, they forget about exporting. Another third sell overseas because someone called them. Of those that proactively export, a third are gone from the market within a year and another third last two years before folding up shop and heading home. The sum total: only 11 per cent are successful long-term exporters.[121]

Before you even think about what countries you might want to do business in, you need to come up with an international business plan that includes clear goals for your company as well as criteria for evaluating whether there is a market compatible with those aims. The plan would set internal targets for international sales and identify the products and services that would be competitive in markets outside the United States. Calgary-based oil company Nexen calls it "global characterization"—a template of eight to twelve technical and commercial drivers that acts as a litmus test for assessing market suitability. Above all, a company needs to recognize its own strengths and weaknesses and come up with a strategy that plays to its strong suit.

If you don't have the time or staff to come up with a plan internally, hit up the nearest group of MBA students, a group just itching for the chance to put their skills to use. York University's Schulich School of Business runs a global leadership program in which students provide language and strategic support to companies hoping to break into new markets. The school has eighty exchange partners worldwide, from Sweden to mainland China, who liaise with Schulich's students to develop market-entry strategies and identify local suppliers. The program is popular with European and even Israeli firms but, so far, not with many Canadians.

Global doesn't mean global

Telecom carrier TIW learned the hard way the dangers of spreading itself too thin. At one point the company had investments in a dozen countries spanning four continents. How many were successful? One.

Rather than trying to fan out across the globe, narrow your list of potential markets to one, two, three, maybe four countries. Your search should zero in on countries where you have a comparative advantage and a greater probability of success. Engineering firm SNC–Lavalin, for example, has successfully honed in on French-speaking northern Africa, "where the Americans are not," and local skills are in short supply. "In Mexico, a lot of locals can do the job, but not in Algeria," explains Michael Novak, executive vice-president. "In Algeria, we have one chance out of three of winning a bid, and we beat the Americans hands down. In Mexico, we have zero chance."

In larger, more complex markets like the United States, China and India, your search should be further refined to particular regions, provinces and even cities. China has thirty-four provinces, regions and centrally administered municipalities, each as distinct and diverse as the countries that make up the European Union. The United States, too, is deceptively diverse. "If you say you want to sell your product to the States, you've probably already lost," says Chris Lindal of Viceroy Homes. "Which state? Which part of which state? Which segment of the market?"

Do you really want to get into bed with Hugo Chávez?
Once you've whittled down the field of potential candidates, learn everything you can about the countries in question. Beijing-based Canadian business consultant John Gruetzner recommends spending at least one day on the Internet for every day that you intend to visit the country. Find out everything you can, from GDP per capita and the current account deficit to the peculiarities of the tax and labour laws, local ownership requirements, trade treaties and restrictions on taking foreign currency out of the country. There are plenty of information sources, from the government to myriad business associations, the banks and private consultants.

After you've done your initial homework, go to the country that's caught your eye. When you think you have it all figured out, go there again. Get the embassy to set up some initial introductions, but don't limit yourself to government contacts. Get in touch with potential customers, local government officials, suppliers and other Western firms. Hire well-respected local consultants to provide you with on-the-ground analysis of the competition, logistics and distribution challenges. If you think you can figure this out on your own, you are sadly mistaken. As many a veteran of international business points out, "You don't know what you don't know." Assume you need all the help you can get.

What you really want is to get the most accurate picture possible of the country's business and political risk and then to run that risk against the potential reward. Was it worth the effort for Hydro-Québec to go to

Guinea, where every time the power failed the police picked up the utility's local representative and threw him in jail? In Nigeria, Nexen went so far as to take a toehold in a small offshore project just to see whether it could operate in the country without paying bribes. It soon learned it would need to steer clear of the mainland for the sake of security and to operate according to its "value system." Ask yourself if are you willing to gamble that Russian mobsters won't help themselves to your mobile phone company. Or that a somewhat deluded Venezuelan ex-general-turned-president might decide to nationalize your mine.

ONCE YOU'VE DECIDED TO TAKE THE PLUNGE

Get the board on board

Getting any international venture to work requires the unwavering commitment of the board and senior management. That doesn't mean you need to sugar-coat the challenges and complexities to get the brass to sign off on the deal. On the contrary, build every possible catastrophic scenario into your business plan, advises a former executive with Molson. "Show them the huge risks, and then ask them: 'Do you sign with your blood?'" Otherwise, when things start to go wrong, head office is liable to get cold feet and cut off resources precisely when the venture needs it most.

Take the long view

There are no quick hits in international business. If you think you can visit five countries in five days and start selling overseas, save yourself the cost of the plane ticket. The returns can be significantly higher in fast-growing, emerging markets, but they may take years to be realized. Be prepared for the long haul; relationships have to be nurtured, and obtuse government regulations must be overcome. Simply incorporating a company in Brazil, complete with notarized documents in quadruplicate, takes six months compared with a few hours in Canada. Nevertheless, Brookfield Asset Management (formerly known as Brascan) is hugely successful in Brazil. Operating there for more than a century, it is Brazil's oldest foreign-owned company. Brookfield doesn't disclose what percentage of its revenue comes from Brazil, but its assets include twelve hydroelectric plants, two major shopping centres and high-rise condominiums, a bank, twenty thousand hectares of timberland and seven sugar cane and beef ranches.

Don't dabble, and don't dither
When U.S. window maker Pella decides to go into a new market, it finds the best trade show in the region, stakes out the best piece of real estate smack-dab in the middle of the fair and puts up an eye-catching display. "They get an immediate reaction," says Roberto Amaya, Latin American sales manager for Loewen, the Manitoba window and door manufacturer. "It's been three years, and Loewen is still thinking about whether to send down a $10,000 display to Mexico."

It's a weakness even Canada's biggest companies are guilty of. Quebec-based Bombardier does a booming business building trains for China's expanding infrastructure, but its airplanes have failed to take off with the country's fast-growing aviation industry. The reason? The manufacturer, fearful its technology might be stolen, deliberated for a year over whether to strike a joint venture with local manufacturer Harbin Aircraft Industry to build planes in northern China. Bombardier's arch rival, Embraer, came knocking and within a month inked a deal with Harbin; a year later the Brazilian-Chinese–made planes were in the air.

All too often, Canadians "don't take the first bold step," admits TransAlta's Steve Snyder. There are no halfway measures in international business. Frittering around the edges won't get you anywhere, so either go big or go home. That doesn't mean throwing money around on half-baked projects. You still need to make careful and considered decisions, but once you decide you are going to do it, then go all the way. "Don't just put your toe in the water," says Nexen's Charlie Fischer. "Either you are committed or you're not."

Being committed also means not sitting back and waiting for the phone to ring. "We need to stop being reactive and start being proactive," says Jean-François Vinet, vice-president of Tecsult International, a

Montreal engineering firm. "You want to be the first one to hear about something, not the last." Adds Fischer, "When we decide it's the right thing, we do everything to capture it. We know what we are waiting for, and we are not waiting for someone to come to us." In fact, as countries like China grow by leaps and bounds, few people these days are waiting around for Canadians to make their minds up about going global. "The most common mistake is hesitancy," says Howard Balloch, Canada's former ambassador to China, "and not recognizing that China has arrived and has to be taken seriously."

No more nine to five

Nobody said international business would be easy, and overseas work takes a lot of personal sacrifice: phone calls in the middle of the night, appallingly early morning meetings and endless travel. "The people who have succeeded in China or in Asia have done it with personal sacrifice," says Phil Hodge, a former vice-president with Westport Innovations in Vancouver. "No matter how much you don't like being away from your family for weeks at a time, that's inevitable. There's just no other way to make potential sales in China. If you see the people who have done well there, you can trace it back to a few who spent a lot of time in China." Joan Vogelsang, the president of Montreal's Toon Boom Animation, is on the road at least half the year, regularly working nights and weekends. But while she acknowledges the sacrifice, there's also a huge personal gain. "There's an opportunity to learn, to meet people from different cultures," says Vogelsang, who was born in England and raised in the Caribbean. "It's very fulfilling, especially when you succeed."

THE EXECUTION

Change comes from the inside out

Your Canadian operation should reflect its new international dimension. From the very top of your organization to the very bottom you need people and structures in place that can respond to different languages, laws and ways of doing business. That includes everything from translating brochures and having people able to take orders over the phone in a different language to retaining a law firm and an accountant with international capability. Similarly, your company needs board directors and senior management with international experience. "You have to have a management team comfortable with operating globally. Don't make any compromises when it comes to that," recommends Pierre Choquette, chairman of Methanex. "I don't know how Canadian management with no experience globally, no cultural fluency and no exposure to other geographies would be successful."

Put your best foot forward

If you sell six product lines, don't try to sell all six in your new target market. Choose the best one. "That way you can work on a small but achievable success and build on that," says Ella Plotkin, lawyer with Ogilvy Renault in Toronto. Sometimes, however, your best product isn't the one most suited to the market. Manitoba's Loewen liked to promote its wood windows and doors by putting a picture of an archetypal Canadian log cabin on the front of its brochures. The problem was that in Latin America, as in much of the world, wood is considered a substandard housing product: only poor people live in cabins. For Loewen to be successful, it had to graft its high-end windows and doors onto the kind of homes that appeal to people in Latin America.

Be there

Approach any new market with the same level of engagement that you would for Canada or the United States. If anything, assume that the farther away your market is, the more attention you need to pay to it. Parachuting in from time to time is considered little more than a social visit by your potential customers. "You have to make them think you live there," explains Alan Davitt, president of Tri-Star International, which helps companies make overseas business contacts. You may want to start out with an agent or distributor that represents a number of companies and then move to a "sub-office" where you share office services with a handful of other companies. Ideally, you need to "become local," says Robert Schad, who eschews agents to represent Husky Injection Molding abroad, instead relying on an in-house sales and distribution network. "You get a lot more out of your own people in a couple of markets than from agents in a ton of markets," he says. To John Gruetzner in Beijing, anything short of completely ensconcing yourself and providing the same level of customer support that you would in Canada—from inventory, financing and marketing to customer service, payment terms and techno-logical approvals—is a recipe for failure. "This is not an air war, it's a ground war," he says.

Don't partner with someone's mother's sister's brother
So many companies have been burned by their joint-venture partners that they prefer to go it alone. But for those who could benefit from the local know-how and resources that a partner can bring to the table, it's imper-ative, say veteran businesspeople, to make the right match. Howard Balloch, who runs his own investment boutique in Beijing, recommends looking at every potential partner and then shortlisting eight or ten, of which four may make the cut. "Too many people go into China and say, 'Anybody know someone I can partner with?'" he says. "And you get some guy saying his mother's sister's brother knows somebody. It becomes a real crapshoot."

When assessing partners, do as exhaustive a due diligence as possible. Check for any history of bribing or litigation and whether their *guanxi*, or personal connections, are as good as they say they are—but not so good as to get you into trouble. In China, companies often keep two sets of books, so make sure they show you the real books and that they are in compliance with the law. Ensure that your value systems and goals are aligned. Ultimately, you need to rely on a sharp gut instinct that can dis-tinguish pretenders from the real deal. A strong personal relationship based on trust is often your best defence in countries where contracts are not worth the paper they are written on. "When you've got that close relationship, people don't want to let you down," explains Toon Boom's Joan Vogelsang. "Nobody wants to steal from a brother."

But even brotherly love is no guarantee. If you want a little more reassurance, look for leverage, and keep the balance of power in your court. Observers recommend retaining at least a 51 per cent majority control of any venture in order to ensure that your business plans are executed. When TIW went into Romania, it conducted thousands of interviews and, as the first foreign investor to arrive in the country to scope out the telecommunications sector, had its pick of potential partners. Its ultimate choice of partner helped the venture (MobiFon) survive three changes of government, but it was TIW's iron-clad control that ensured its success. TIW not only held the financial reins, but ensured that Westerners and Canadians occupied the top two layers of management. "If we hadn't had control, it could have really jeopardized the operation because the Romanian partners didn't care at all. They were just looking for any way to make a fast buck; they told us so," says a former TIW executive. In 2005 TIW wrapped up its short-lived international jaunt by selling MobiFon, together with its Czech cellular operations, to Vodafone for US$3.5 billion.

Get the best people, not the B-team

Some say it's so obvious it shouldn't be included as a recommendation, but since so many companies seem to commit the same mistake, it has to be said: don't plunk someone in to run your new overseas venture who doesn't have any international work experience. Technical expertise does not make up for a global mindset, nor does it necessarily transfer to another country. And, whatever you do, don't send that individual into a harsh new environment all alone, without any back-up. In perhaps the most extreme case I came across, Roger Belair was sent to head up Transcontinental's new printing acquisition in Mexico. He had to single-handedly manage 1,100 Mexican employees and go without a salary for seven months because the company had neglected to come up with a system for paying him. "We should have had six to ten people on the ground," he says. "We should have come stronger."

Once you've established your operation and set the wheels in motion, you are best served by having well-trained local management in place. Try to hire the top managers the market has to offer—people you can trust, with local standing, who understand the rules and regulations. If they have international experience, that's a bonus. "The most important thing you can do is hire local managers and train them to take over," explains Aly Nazerali, a Vancouver-based entrepreneur who has an ownership stake in Bolivia's largest cable company. "It gives them pride of ownership, and all the cultural problems disappear."

That does not mean that you should leave your local team unsupervised. Senior management or board members should check in regularly and spend a few days with employees to get a sense of what's really going on. "Spend time with the people in the company—eat with them, sleep in their city. They will start to open up to you and tell you their concerns," explains a former TIW executive. "After the board meeting, stay one or two days more, see what management does, how it digests decisions and brings support. When you see them for only twenty-four hours, everybody is nice; they put on a great show, wave goodbye and know they have another month left to their own devices."

Get good advice

Set aside a pool of seed money to retain fiscal and legal advisers. There are fifty-seven different taxes in Brazil, notes Eduardo Klurfan, Scotiabank's former rep in São Paulo, and you can't be compliant with all of them. These consultants can also advise you on how to hedge against currency fluctuations and structure your investment so as to exploit preferential tax and tariff treaties. India, for example, has treaties with Mauritius and Cyprus that allow offshore investors to avoid paying capital gains tax. Barbados also promotes itself as a base from which to conduct international business and is the favoured jumping-off spot for Canadian companies. They represent the "vast majority" of some five thousand foreign firms to register for the island's favourable tax and treaty benefits, including zero capital-gains tax and a maximum corporate tax of 2.5 per cent. The real lure, however, is Barbados's double-taxation treaties with countries including the United States and China, which, when combined with provisions in the Canadian tax code, exempt companies generating active income in those treaty countries from paying Canadian corporate tax. (This explains in part why Canadian investment in Barbados is so surprisingly high.)

In some countries, particularly those with heavy state involvement in the economy, it is also worthwhile retaining a political adviser to run interference on touchy matters involving government licences and unions. Westcoast Energy, for example, retained the former Mexican head of Monsanto, the U.S. agricultural-products company. He was key in helping Westcoast choose a union to build and operate its nitrogen-injection plant, says former executive Michael Stewart. "He was well respected in the business community and could transcend political lines," Stewart explains. "That respect allowed access and provided standing. Someone with a political affiliation, on the other hand, may help you get in one day but not the next."

You pay peanuts, you get monkeys
One of the most common complaints about Canadian companies is that they are cheap. They are simply not willing to pay the cost of entry, and invariably try to cut corners—only to find that they have to pay the price of admission twice over. Don't, as one Saskatchewan company did, get a homemaker to translate your documentation, and don't think you can save money by not hiring a professional translator in China. And you're definitely not going to make a go of it "with two men and a dog, or just the dog," says Simon Gwatkin, vice-president of strategic marketing for Mitel, an Ottawa telecommunications company. You not only have to keep cash in reserve in order to maintain a presence in the market and pay for professional services, but you must also be prepared to lose money

for a significant amount of time. Whether you're thinking of doing business in China or Ecuador, you should prepare for at least three to five years of negative cash flow. "People don't understand how much money it takes, so they give up halfway through," says Schulich's Lorna Wright. "If you aren't prepared for the negative cash flow, don't go."

Expand your Rolodex

For Mitel's British-born Gwatkin, the most important tool for doing business abroad is his Rolodex. As the saying goes, it's who you know. Canadians, however, don't invest nearly enough in networking, preferring to remain in their comfort zone, limiting themselves to the small circle of contacts they already have. "If you look at Europeans and Americans, they have their own clients plus they develop new clients out in the market," says Omer Ozden, a lawyer with Hodgson Russ in Toronto. "The Canadian model generally has been to go out with one or two of their Canadian clients and, when those deals are finished, close up shop because they haven't developed anything new." It's the main reason Canadians haven't been as successful in China, adds Ken Kwan. Well-connected wheeler-dealers eschew the limelight, he says, and Canadians don't even know who they are. There are plenty of ways to network, but one easy way to start is by responding to overseas inquiries instead of ignoring them. That doesn't mean you have to jump into bed with every middleman that comes your way, but you never know when that contact might come in handy.

Don't be a sucker

Canadians are trusting folk, and they and tend to assume the best about people—which makes them particularly easy to take advantage of. Stand your ground, be skeptical and, when someone is ripping you off, don't assume it's the cost of doing business. "We are very nice, well-meaning, good partners, and we tend to be a little too malleable and manageable," says Ian Mallory, the Calgary-based venture capitalist. "You have to be able to blow the whistle." James Klotz, a lawyer with Davis & Co. in

Toronto, recalls how one of his clients discovered that his Chinese partner was double-invoicing and cheating the company by 15 per cent. The client was unperturbed, however, because he'd planned on 20 per cent. "That's not smart," says Klotz. "What if the Chinese partner had been stealing 40 per cent? It should have been zero per cent, and it could have been zero. That's just unwise."

Think in 3D

Once you've spent time and money coming up with a well-defined business plan, be prepared to change it. Your ability to adapt to change, improvise and think outside the box could very well mark the difference between success and failure. In dynamic markets like China and Brazil, conditions never remain static. They are constantly shifting: hyperinflation, currency devaluations and political instability can radically alter the business calculation from one day to the next, and what might be an attractive proposition to your business partners today may not appeal to them a year from now.

"It's totally unpredictable, and you need a disposition and an ability to respond with a positive attitude," explains Gary Comerford, Sun Life's vice-president, international. "If you think this is the plan, my experience in developing markets tells me, 'Not a chance,' because things change daily. The deal you negotiate is not the deal you have. You have to realize it's about relationships, it's about seeing it through, it's about continuity. Things elsewhere are much more fluid than in the Canadian environment, and it can be terribly hard."

For Roger Heng, BMO's managing director for China, the key is being able to wrest opportunity from the continual churn of events. The possibilities present themselves much like the patches of blue sky that emerge between clouds on a windy day. "When I'm looking at China I see a horizon of gaps. In time they change in magnitude—some get narrower, some get bigger and some are eliminated," Heng says. "What you need to do is identify the gaps, appreciate them and profit from them."

Hone your above-ground skills

The oil might be underground, but you have to make the real investment on the surface, says Nexen's Charlie Fischer. Wherever it operates, Nexen invests in the community, buying books and desks for schoolchildren or providing access to potable water. When a flood contaminated oil wells and destroyed infrastructure, the company hired local Yemenis to rebuild rather than mobilizing expat oilmen to do the job. They not only got paid, they felt they were part of the process. As a result, unlike the experience of other foreign oil companies, Nexen's Yemen facilities have never been sabotaged and its employees have never been kidnapped by Muslim radicals or tribespeople. "They don't think we're exploiting their country or taking their wealth. Rather, they think we're creating jobs and helping with infrastructure," explains Fischer, who feels as comfortable walking the dusty streets of Yemeni villages as he does strolling in downtown Calgary.

Arrogance is ignorance

Eduardo Klurfan describes it as "the Achilles heel of Canadians." The fact that a country is poor doesn't mean that its businesspeople and government officials are not sophisticated. As a general rule, the elite in developing countries are wealthier, better educated and much more worldly than the average Canadian businessperson. "You cannot overestimate your skills and come in with a patronizing attitude," says Klurfan. "Brazilian businesspeople are very smart, very intelligent. They survived hyperinflation, manoeuvring in difficult economic situations that would drown most Canadians."

Adds Charlie Fischer: "The people who horrify me are the ones who think we're better, think people from developing countries are not educated and come from the backwoods. Actually, they are very global and very well educated. We need to give them the respect they are due. Face is a huge issue around the world. If you treat them fairly, people reciprocate. If you take advantage, you get your comeuppance."

THE CULTURE OF DOING BUSINESS

In addition to these general tips for conducting business abroad, two issues that are particularly thorny for Canadians require special attention. They are the twin sisters of culture and corruption. Many people tend to underplay the importance of the culture of doing business. It can't be quantified on a spreadsheet or calculated into a business plan; it's elusive and difficult to grasp, with no measurable impact on your bottom line. Yet it's the basic building block on which business is structured, influencing everything from management styles and contractual obligations to decision-making. But doing business globally, wherever it occurs, involves more similarities than differences, and most business around the world is predicated on a few fundamental tenets: trust, respect and mutual understanding. Would you do business with someone in Canada or the United States with whom you did not share these three principles? The difference is that other parts of the world, especially those where the rule of law is not as entrenched, have different modes and methods for ensuring that foundation exists.

While you may think you are being an honest, straightforward Canadian, to others your behaviour may be an encrypted code they cannot decipher. The key to cracking the code and making the connection is what Methanex's Pierre Choquette refers to as "cultural fluency." You may never be *hermanos* with your Mexican colleagues or more than a *gweilo* to the Chinese, but you need to be able to identify certain cultural signposts and respond accordingly. "If somebody from Sierra Leone or Pakistan came to Canada and tried to apply their business methods, you can imagine how successful they would be," explains Omer Ozden. "So why would Canadians think their approach would be successful in China? You have to wipe the slate clean and learn how things are done."

It goes beyond merely versing yourself in the strictures of protocol and etiquette. It comes down to an openness of mind and an ability to accept what is different and to work with it. If you can do that, you will amass immeasurable goodwill, not to mention a huge competitive advantage.

Learn a little R-E-S-P-E-C-T

Language is the starting point for all communication, so learning the language of the country where you are doing business is an immense advantage. "You never have the whole picture unless somebody in your company speaks the language. Otherwise you're only hearing half the story," says John Powles, managing partner with Pacific Bizlinks Trade Consultants in Vancouver. Learning the language also earns you a lot of goodwill. "They always appreciate it, they always remark on it," says Chris Lindal of his Japanese customers. The fluent Japanese-speaker is able to go out to dinner with his clients without worrying about the disruption of a translator. "It allows for a higher level of sophistication and mutual understanding between us and our customer."

But although linguistic fluency is important, language is only window dressing without a solid understanding of a country's culture and history. The Chinese have a long memory, the saying goes, and every decision has a historical context. Learn as much about the local civilization as you can. Become familiar with its underlying worldview, which may be based on concepts like face and hierarchy. It's also always a good idea to brush up on local protocols, ranging from how to handle a business card in Japan to the intricacies of banquet seating arrangements in China. Never, for example, hold your glass higher than your hosts during a toast or start eating before your host, advises Ken Kwan, who, before every trip to China, reads *The Art of War* by military tactician Sun Tzu. Written around 500 BC and a favourite of Chairman Mao, the treatise explains how to get what you want without conflict and how to win should a dispute arise.

Of course, gaffes are inevitable, but ultimately what matters are your intentions. Respecting differences instead of judging them will pave the way to an understanding that goes beyond linguistic fluency. "It's important to learn the protocols, but that's just hygiene," says Sun Life's Gary Comerford. "Very quickly you will find yourself in a situation where you are over your head and you don't understand the cultural nuances. Admitting it or being respectful lets you get away with a ton of stuff. When you try to dictate your values, that's when you get in trouble."

The Mexican lunch

Outside the English-speaking world, relationships are significantly more important and the lines between business and personal life are often blurred. In the absence of enforceable laws, personal relationships are a proxy for trust and the best guarantee against getting ripped off. Which is why, in many cultures, people want to get to know you and assess your value as a person before discussing business. Latin Americans, in particular, are keen to establish a personal rapport; Mexicans have turned it into an art form, with four-hour lunches and copious tequila shots. If they invite you back to their home, you know you are in business.

"They want to meet, have a meal and, if they like you, they will take you to their house. And all that time they are doing business, the Mexican way," explains Loewen's Roberto Amaya. "If they invite you and you say no because you want to relax in your hotel and call home, to them you are refusing to do a deal. You refused to get to know them, therefore you are not interested. In your mind it's 'Let's meet at nine tomorrow morning,' but the Mexicans want to date before they do anything else. They want to know how many kids you have, if you're married, if you go to church. The cultural ideas Mexicans have are part of their business. It's not a separate function and it includes their social life."

In China, they have a word for it: *guanxi*, the power of personal relationships. Instead of being encouraged over a shot of tequila, it's cultivated over an expensive dinner and copious shots of baijiu, the fiery Chinese vodka. "In Canadian culture, after 5 PM everybody goes home—in China after 5 PM, people get active," Ken Kwan explains. "It's after-hours when people start to talk business, and the next morning they go to the office to sign the contract. Every company offers a good price, good service and a good contract—that's surface stuff. The question is, how do you make your company outstanding? It's the relationship."

Dress to impress

Because so much in business is based on personal relations, the way in which you present yourself is almost as important as product and price. Personal aesthetic, poise and sophistication are a proxy for business acumen, so leave the "frump factor" back in Canada. "The Chinese value protocol—how you introduce yourself, how smart and sophisticated you are," explains the University of Alberta's Edy Wong. Adds Ken Kwan, "Within the first three minutes a Chinese buyer already knows whether he will sign a contract with you. He is judging your body language, eye contact, even the way you sit. If you want to sell a product, you have to sell yourself first."

Let me entertain you

Navin Chandaria, the charismatic owner of Toronto-based Conros Corp., goes to extraordinary lengths to impress his customers. When he was looking to co-brand his LePage tape products with the U.S. Postal Service, he brought the U.S. postmaster general for a tour of St. James's Palace in London, England, and introduced him to his good friend, Princess Sophie. "We don't bribe, we entertain," says the Kenyan-born entrepreneur with an expansive open-arms flourish. "I will do anything for my customers—isn't that what it's all about?" Not according to most Canadian businesspeople, who subscribe to the straight missionary-style sales strategy of product plus price. "Sometimes it's embarrassing," admits Viceroy's Andrea Bermudez, who's had to explain to surprised customers arriving from abroad that there's no car to pick them up at the airport in Toronto.

To Canadians' credit, a Protestant ethic underlies much of Canada's business culture. Unfortunately, it is accompanied by a propensity for cheapness and a rigid rectitude that leaves little margin for less formal approaches. It's also really boring. Doing business in most of the rest of the world is about wining and dining, and Canadians need to learn how to court their customers. When clients are visiting from out of town, don't just take them to lunch at the local family eatery—show them around town, or invite them to your home for dinner. If you have a sales rep overseas, make sure his expense account covers bottles of fine wine and single-malt whiskies. "It costs a lot to a company," admits Bermudez, "but it's worth it."

Time is time, and money is money

One of the things that most distinguishes cultures is the concept of time. Patience is a virtue, and you will need it, because very few countries are as preoccupied with how time flies as Canadians are. Yvan Bourdeau, the CEO of BMO Capital Markets, estimates that it takes twelve to eighteen months before the Chinese will trust an outsider. Then, of course, there's all the bureaucracy and consensual decision-making. "Whatever time it takes is the time it takes," says Neil Tate, a special adviser to BMO on Asia; "Money is separate." Still, your patience need not be limitless, and knowing when to call time is important, says Phil Hodge, formerly with Westport Innovations. "Sometimes we defer too much. We tell ourselves it takes time, we need to wait, but they also want to do business," he says. You can only talk nicely for so long—you need to figure out where the tipping point is."

When yes means no

Canadians aren't great at confrontation, but they are bullies compared with most cultures. In some countries being told "no" is about as frequent as a lunar eclipse, but that doesn't mean they aren't turning you down. It's important to tune out the obfuscation to hear what they are really telling you, in the politest of terms. "There's no such word as 'no' in China. It's always, 'I'll see what I can do, I'll look into it,'" says BMO's Neil Tate. "There's usually a sunset period, so if you haven't gotten approval within a certain period—it's no." Similarly, Sun Life's Gary Comerford has learned he's got to phrase his questions in a certain way if he wants to get a real sense of what's happening at the insurer's Indian subsidiary. "I can get a yes to 100 per cent of my questions," he says. "Business is always 'great,' and it could be the most horrible month known to man."

Look below the surface

The Chinese invented paper two thousand years ago and have been using it to write reams upon reams of rules and regulations ever since. Which is why, if you abided by the letter of the law in China, you would never get anything done, explains Gervais Lavoie, an anthropologist and entrepreneur who has spent twenty-five years studying the Chinese market. To circumvent the prodigious bureaucracy, which has perfected the art of theoretical if not reality-based rules, the country has come up with a pragmatic alternative that, to the foreign eye, may seem absurd, but in practice makes perfect sense. "People get confused because they look at what they can see, but in China the surface is only there for show," says Lavoie. "If you applied the rules word for word, you might as well close the country."

Scratch below the surface and you'll find an entire underground system of well-organized civil servants dedicated to getting things done, either by "extending, ignoring or discreetly applying" the rules. That's how both Starbucks and the French supermarket Carrefour managed to open hundreds of outlets in China that, at least according to the law, are technically illegal, says Lavoie. The key to deciphering what appears to be a confusing morass is simple enough: "Their value system is upside down, so the whole system is upside down. When you see white, it's black and when you see black, it's white," says Lavoie. "It's easy to understand—it's the opposite of what you see."

Learn to play chess

Chinese children start studying the art of negotiation in Grade 1, says Neil Tate, who compares dealing with the Chinese to playing a game of chess in which they're always three moves ahead. "Before they put anything on the table, they've thought about the first move, what your response will be, what their next question is going to be, what your response is going to be and how they will handle the next one before they ever ask the first question," he says. "Wall Street may think it has smart negotiators, but when you hit the Shanghai people you'll understand they are the most advanced, sophisticated negotiators in the world."

Tate recommends reading *The Asian Mind Game* by Chin-Ning Chu to get a handle on Chinese strategy. He also advises keeping your cards close to your chest. "If you play all your cards at once, the Chinese will think less of you," he explains. Persevere, press your advantage and, when necessary, stand your ground; the Chinese will respect you for it, say observers. But while direct and confrontational is sometimes appropriate, being a "bull in a china shop" won't get you far, says lawyer James Klotz. "There are many situations where you need to know what the underlying issues are on the Chinese side. It's not a matter of negotiating politely or not, it's a matter of knowing why they are asking for the things they are asking for and what's motivating them."

Women and Saudi Arabia don't mix
When doing business in a foreign culture, there are some things you can't change and others that you can. The key is to distinguish between a country's general business culture and those practices specifically related to your company, and then to pick your battles. You can't, for example, change the fact that Mexicans eat lunch at 2 PM, explains Roger Belair, but you can keep them from stopping the production line every other day to celebrate a birthday party. You need to face up to the fact that women can't do business in Saudi Arabia or that a lot of businessmen like to talk shop at the nudy bar. If you are not comfortable going there, send a local representative who is. "The point is, it's their culture," says Mark Romoff, a former trade commissioner in Japan. "We're not going to convince them they should do business our way."

Don't count on your contract
Vancouver entrepreneur David Fung recalls how one Canadian company that he worked with in China spent two years and $1 million to draw up what it considered an iron-clad contract with its Chinese partners. The

tome-like volume had nineteen appendices, but in a country where you're lucky to find a judge with legal training, the odds of being able to enforce a contract are not in your favour. It's better to think of a contract like a marriage certificate, explains Ken Cai, a Chinese-born Vancouver businessman. "A lot of people sign an agreement and think they are done," he explains. "But it's like a good marriage. You go to the church for the wedding, but then you spend a long time—the rest of your life—working together on the marriage. In the same way, signing an agreement is not the end of a deal; it's the beginning."

Instead of suing when a contract is broken, advises Fung, sweeten the pot. "It's no different from doing business in British Columbia when you want the First Nations on your side," he says. "You say: 'Let's talk to them, offer them something,' and then everybody moves on. Yet outsiders won't do that in China. A contract is signed, and if it's not abided by, they sue. The Chinese don't care. These are not corruption issues. This is how society operates, and if you refuse to accept it, why get in?"

Keep your patents to yourself

New technologies in China are not seen as proprietary, but rather as a tool for the common good. So if you don't want someone borrowing it, don't lend it. Software company Zi Corp. works with eighteen Chinese cell phone manufacturers but keeps the predictive-text technology under lock and key in Calgary, while Westport Innovations relies on third-party suppliers such as Germany's Bosch or Siemens—internationally recognized firms against whom it has legal recourse—to manufacture some of its more sensitive technology in China. When Montreal's Toon Boom discovered its animation software had been pirated by a Chinese studio, it provided technical support and convinced the studio to become a legal customer and pay for the technology. "It's better for us to know who they are than for them to stay underground," says president Joan Vogelsang, who estimates company revenue would double if its products weren't pirated. To counteract the problem, Toon Boom plans to come out with a special Chinese-language version of its lower-end software to see what business it can drum up.

You're not Marco Polo

Ultimately, as culturally different as another country may be, people are still people. Whether they are Chinese, Czech or Canadian, they are all motivated by the desire to do business and make money. So while certain behaviours may baffle you, let common sense prevail and never lose sight of your goal. You wouldn't sign a contract in Canada with someone you'd never met, so why would you do it in China? "Learning Mandarin was important, but it wasn't the thing that helped me the most," explains lawyer Omer Ozden, who spent a decade working in China. "It was understanding instinctively how to deal with people. Any good businessperson in China can see immediately whether you are a waste of time or if they can have their way with you. So just make friends, develop a rapport—and get down to business. Don't waste six months shaking hands and drinking tea; you're not Marco Polo. In the end, everybody wants to make money."

BUT WHAT IF PART of doing business involves what you would consider, at least in Canada, questionable practices? How do you distinguish between culture and corruption? Many people interviewed for this book argue that bribes, payoffs and "facilitation fees" are just the cost of doing business; everybody does it, and being a prude only hamstrings you when it comes to competing against more accommodating Americans and Europeans. Others counter that you always have a choice, and once you've slid down the slippery slope of corruption, it's difficult to pull yourself back up. Whatever your take, however, the maze of government bureaucracy and the survival ethos that pervade so many countries requires a certain manoeuvrability that has no equivalent in Canada. In Brazil they call it *jiego de cintura*, which refers to a soccer player's ability to bob and weave around unexpected obstacles. Without that flexibility he might never be able to get past the clutch of defencemen blocking his path to score a goal.

In Brazil, there are so many obstacles to getting things done quickly and expeditiously that they've given it a name: *el costo Brasileiro,* the

Brazilian cost of doing business. The World Bank produced a two-volume report documenting all the difficulties, from delays in acquiring work permits and incorporating companies to applying convoluted salary scales. Having three levels of government whose rules and regulations often directly contradict each other, Brazilians pride themselves on figuring out ways to manoeuvre through the morass that border on illegal. These "shortcuts" are called *jeitinhos,* and the better able you are to grease the wheels, the smarter you are. Think of it as driving into a massive traffic jam that will take hours to unsnarl. You could wait patiently and lose valuable time, or you could take a short detour, driving the wrong way down a one-way side street. A block later, you're free and clear. That's a *jeitinho.*

For many veteran businesspeople, the key to survival is being able to distinguish a *jeitinho* from real corruption. Canadians in particular, they say, often apply a very narrow set of moral standards to situations that require a certain flexibility and are the result of a radically different frame of reference. David Fung compares it to playing by the rules of hockey, when in China everyone is playing soccer. Why would you insist on court protection in a country that can't provide it? It's like insisting that everyone use their hands to play soccer. "This is refusing to accept that we are playing a different game with a different set of rules. Then we think the Chinese are bad. Well, what's bad about soccer?" says Fung. "We play hockey and we say there is a red line and a blue line. The Chinese ask, why? There are reasons for it, but if you take out the red line and the blue line, you can still play the game."

"It is not a case of right versus wrong," he adds. "It's about, how do we make things work? Of course we all have a moral line of our own. That line in the sand is up to us to draw. Everybody will have a different line, based on their upbringing, based on their cultural background. In the case of Canada, we've drawn the line so far back that we totally ignore the value of the other society."

What makes it harder is when others, including Americans and Europeans, are more disposed to playing by different rules. While Canadians will balk at taking Asian businessmen to nightclubs, Americans may simply pay an agent to do it. When Ken Kwan worked at Honeywell in China the company routinely paid consultants a fee. "The attitude is that for big contracts you have to do that. If you don't, then the opportunity will go to someone else," he says. The Europeans are allegedly even more freewheeling, armed with generous public-relations budgets and equally accommodating governments. "Bribes for Germans used to be, and probably still are, marketing expenses. How can you compete against that?" says Andres Darvasi, a Chilean Canadian businessman based in Mexico. "Americans are a lot more flexible. If they have to give a bribe, they will find a way do it."

Still, many businesspeople with a long history of working overseas maintain that honesty is the best policy and it even has a certain cachet—like when you're the only one wearing a bikini at a nude beach. While everyone else is letting it all hang out, you retain a modicum of mystery and your privates don't get burnt. "We don't take bribes, we don't bribe anywhere in the world, nothing," says Robert Schad, chairman of Husky Injection Molding. "Our competitors do it extensively; we don't. It works very well because we stand out in the way we serve our customers."

You have to be persistent, acknowledges Nexen's Charlie Fischer, especially when the French government is giving airplanes as gifts to the Yemeni government. But the oil company counteracts less scrupulous competition by winning over the community with jobs and providing public services. "We're often called naïve, but we're clean and we don't go to jail," he says. "You can bribe people in power for a time, but it's not sustainable. Once you cross the line, people know you have a price, and they'll be at you again and again."

That doesn't mean that you can't be crafty when it comes to protecting your interests. Take Bombardier's decision to publicly denounce what appeared to be a corrupt government tendering process in Mexico. "It demonstrated a lack of effort to manage the politics behind the deal," concludes Miguel Juáregui, former chairman of the Canada–Mexico Business Committee. "You don't tell Mexicans they are a bunch of crooks. A better approach would be to have made it politically impossible for the Mexican government not to follow transparent channels." Similarly, Molson could have levelled the competitive playing field in Brazil by discreetly alerting authorities to the fact that rival brewery Schincariol was evading taxes. "You have to bring know-how," explains Eduardo Klurfan. "But it has to translate into issues that are acceptable in the marketplace you are operating in. You need to understand the rules of the game locally."

Of course, you can minimize the problem by avoiding countries or regions where it is essentially impossible to do business without bribing someone. Nexen doesn't operate on the African mainland because it has found corruption to be unavoidable. Russia and neighbouring satellites like Kazakhstan and Belarus are another region of the world to be bypassed for the same reason. Canadians and others have been repeatedly rough-housed in the former Soviet sphere, where corruption often commingles with violence. Maritime businessman Ken Rowe dubbed Russia "hope-lessly corrupt" after his Halifax-based IMP Group International was forceably evicted from the Moscow hotel it co-owned by a private security force in 2004. Bernard Isautier, the savy French-born oilman, described Russian energy giant Lukoil as a "monster" before being bullied into sell-ing his wildly profitable Calgary-based PetroKazahkstan to the Chinese over disputes with Lukoil and Russian government regulators.

According to one well-placed observer, Scotiabank could have avoided its costly exit from Argentina, including a $540 million writedown of its Quilmes subsidiary, by merely paying a bribe. "I know for a fact that a few million to the president's office and it would have been dealt with, but Scotia decided it wasn't going to play jiggery-poke," said the insider. "One could argue that if you are not willing to do that, then you don't go into markets that require you to do those sorts of things. There are certain sectors where it is very, very difficult to be morally upright. In certain countries it's a matter of routine and, let's be honest, it's tax deductible. It's only in certain, rarefied parts of the world where it's not like that."

For a quick guide to a country's corruption quotient, Transparency International, the German-based non-profit, writes up an annual list of the world's worst offenders. If you decide to take the plunge anyway, bear in mind that bribery was made a money-laundering offence under the Canadian Criminal Code in 2001 and is considered the equivalent to trafficking in heroin, advises James Klotz, who heads up the international corporate governance practice for Davis & Co. There are also additional implications for Canadians who may one day want to sell their companies to American buyers, whose lawyers are increasingly on the look out for so-called "agency payments" as part of their due diligence. Being "wilfully blind" as to where these payments go is no longer an adequate defence, warns Klotz. "Canadian companies just cannot pay bribes right now. It's not only commercial suicide potentially, but there's a five-year prison sentence."

THE CANADA CARD

Canadians are by no means as pure as the driven snow. Toronto-based Acres International became the first prominent Western engineering firm to be sanctioned by the World Bank in 2004 after it was caught paying bribes in Lesotho. One of the most notorious scams in recent Chinese history was pulled off by two brothers, Barry and Stuart Hansen, from London, Ontario. In the mid-1990s, the pair was promoting an exclusive US$500 million golf club and housing development on the outskirts of Shanghai. To get a clutch of international investment banks to finance the deal, the brothers faked documents showing they had paid the land use rights to the five-hundred-acre development and forged leases indicating multinationals like Exxon and General Motors had already signed on to house their expat employees at the upscale estate. Millions of dollars disappeared, touching off an ignominious legal battle spanning nearly a decade and involving half a dozen countries.

But although many Canadians' carry-on luggage includes the proverbial "suitcase full of money," Canadians generally are considered to be more honest, straightforward and reliable than many other nationalities. In a world where personal trust regularly usurps contractual obligations, Canada's reputation for fairness and decency is an invaluable commodity. Free of the lingering ill-will that follows former colonizers like France and

Britain, and combined with a non-threatening demeanour, it's a tremendous calling card, one that Canadians do not avail themselves of often enough. "No country in the world starts off with so much goodwill behind it, bar none," says Tim Plumptre, a long-time champion of Canada–Latin America trade. "It's a major competitive advantage, and of course we don't realize it because we're Canadian."

In China, Canada still starts out with a "huge" advantage, say observers, despite the waning trade and investment ties between the two countries. The Chinese are taught about the heroism of Norman Bethune* in school, and many of them, drawn by Canada's reputation for tolerance and safety, have either immigrated or sent their children to study here, including leading officials of the Communist Party. In 1998 Chinese premier Zhu Rongji called Canada China's "best friend," and that friendship, combined with Canada's traditional approachability in the wake of China's increasingly thorny relations with the United States, is a significant opportunity just waiting to be mined. "Canada has a great brand in China and a lot of links with the Chinese," says lawyer and Sinophile Omer Ozden. "We're in a great position. With the advantages we have, we could be a major force in China."

Michael Lobsinger, the chairman of tech firm Zi Corp., agrees. He has refused to move the company's Calgary head office to the United States despite pressure from his New York investors. While heading south would make sense financially, especially given the fact that Bay Street has never bothered to give him the time of day, being seen as a Canadian company in China is worth more. "I was under huge pressure from the pension funds to move to New York," explains Lobsinger. "'What have the Canadians given you?' they asked. 'You got no help, no assistance, nothing.' But in a foreign country, when we're not embarrassing ourselves in Ottawa, they trust us."

In fact, while Canadians seem to spend a lot of time seeking approval from Americans, not being American is perhaps their greatest asset. On

---

* The Chinese government plans to air an epic twenty-part TV series, one of the most ambitious in the nation's history, on the life of the Ontario-born doctor.

the one hand, Canadians have the technology and best practices associated with the United States, along with the credibility of having to compete and collaborate in such a sophisticated market. Yet they do not have the Americans' battering-ram mentality, which has left so many with bruised egos. "I've always said it's a pleasure to compete against Americans around the world," says Methanex's Pierre Choquette. "They rarely change their stripes. They go in and operate as if they were in North America. The Canadians I have been exposed to are much more respectful of different cultures."

The distinction between the two countries seems to be appreciated in Mexico, which has its own history of grievances with its northern neighbour. In a revealing example of the power of Canada's reputation, Paul Brent recounts in his book, *Lager Heads,* how Labatt CEO George Taylor was able to convince the Mexican owners of Femsa to sell to the Canadians instead of to Milwaukee-based Miller, which already had a small stake in the brewery. "There is no way I could compete with Miller unless I could convince the Mexican family that we were better guys, we were nicer guys, than the Americans," Taylor is quoted as saying.[122]

Loewen's Roberto Amaya has also benefited from Canadian goodwill in Mexico. Unlike his American competitors, who have to "bribe" their Mexican distributors with all sorts of free materials and reassure them with exclusive sales agreements, Amaya doesn't need a contract to sign on a Mexican distributor, and they pay him for promotional material. "When I tell them no one else will sell in their area, they believe me and spend forty thousand dollars on a showroom without a contract," he says. "We have a huge competitive advantage you can't build, you can only tarnish. How is it you have trust before you actually meet the person? You shake hands and they are already smiling, because you are *Canadian.*"

Many countries are, in fact, very appreciative of Canada's displays of decency and tolerance. Andrew Stodart was amazed by the reception Black Velvet whisky got when it was launched in Hungary. The head of international branding for the Canadian liquor label had no idea that Canada was held in such high esteem by Hungarians, many of whom had

271

sought refuge in Canada after Hungary's failed 1956 uprising against Soviet rule. Within two years of entering the market, Black Velvet became the leading imported whisky in the country. But while it was one of the rare instances of a brand being promoted as Canadian, for the most part it is Canada's chameleon-like qualities that earn it kudos internationally. Without an imposing sense of national purpose and a still-congealing identity that lacks the personal ticks associated with old age and cultural homogeneity, Canadians are better able to blend in.

In the case of Sun Life Financial, that means adopting an Indian mentality, work ethic and purpose when operating in India, says Gary Comerford. "We're not a Canadian company doing business in India. We're an Indian company owned by a Canadian company." That fluidity, sensitivity and ability to downplay origins allows many firms to assume whatever identity suits them best in a given situation. Canadian companies will often pretend to be American when competing in the United States, only to switch tack and tout their French or British connections when in Europe. "I'm your best compromise," says Philippe Huneault, former vice-president of strategic opportunities for TIW. "If you want me to be French, I'll be French. If you want me to be American, I'll be American. I'll be the flavour you want. We're somewhere in the middle, and that's an advantage."

But the real advantage of Canadians' reputation for respect and quiet modesty is the fact that nobody expects much from you, says Jeff Swystun, global director for Interbrand. "We are the last people to beat our chests. We almost wait for someone else to recognize our accomplishments—which is a flaw in practice, a nice thing in character," he explains. "Yet underlying all that, we want to compete. Anytime I tell people about my roots in Canada or Winnipeg, it's greeted with a chuckle—until I drive them under the table." Fellow Winnipegger Rick Waugh calls it the Canada Card. The Scotiabank CEO is not convinced that Canadians are necessarily "nicer or better," but one-on-one they're just as good and not as threatening. "I used to do business with very powerful companies and people in New York. We'd leave a little bit on the table while the Americans would go for the jugular. I used to call it my Number Two Strategy. I'd say: 'You can deal with the American guy, but we're a good alternative. Keep us at the table, and we'll adjust.'"

Another advantage that Canadians don't always exploit is—wait for it—the government. Although there is plenty to fault in the plethora of disjointed government strategies, schemes and initiatives, part of the problem is how businesspeople wield the tools made available to them. In the same way that you can't use a hammer to drive in a screw, many companies fail to understand the nature of government resources or how to exploit them in a way that will render maximum results. Accessing state support should not be an enigma wrapped in a conundrum, but almost without exception I found that while native-born Canadians complained about turgidly bureaucratic and misguided programs, new Canadians marvelled at the generous array of opportunities. I suspect the reality lies somewhere in the middle.

Take the Team Canada trade missions. Arguably the most misunderstood of the government's trade promotion policies, they are now a metaphor for Canada's missed opportunity. Consultants like Beijing-based John Gruetzner advise against going on the missions because they prevent managers from rolling up their sleeves, understanding the market and meeting customers. But the missions, despite their penchant for multi-million-dollar signing ceremonies, were not meant to be a substitute for grassroots reconnaissance. "Team Canada is grossly misunderstood," says Howard Balloch. "They are PR, a great way to draw attention. It's like appearing in a beauty contest where you get everybody to look at you. It's not a place to find partners or negotiate a deal."

In fact, the missions can be very useful, if you know how to use them to your advantage. Toon Boom's Joan Vogelsang took advantage of a trade mission to China headed by Quebec Premier Jean Charest to present her Chinese customers with awards. In China, where government officials command a high degree of respect, Charest's presence was a great honour, and the ceremony was carried on Chinese television.

A 2001 Team Canada mission to China provided a definite boost to the power-plant project that David Fung was working on. He capitalized on Prime Minister Chrétien's presence to arrange for a picture to be taken with himself, various high-level Chinese officials and Canadian executives involved in the project. Coordinating the travel arrangements of so many important people cost a cool $100,000, but the picture is the best insurance policy that Fung could have against corruption. "Every junior official looking for trouble sees this picture and decides there are better candidates next door. It tells them I have access, and they don't want their careers jeopardized," he explains.

As a rule of thumb, in countries where the government wields significant influence over the economy, having the Canadian government on your side can be an important asset. The embassy in Beijing has been extremely helpful to Westport Innovations in securing meetings with senior Chinese officials, says Phil Hodge. In some cases, particularly when Westport is dealing with state-run enterprises, embassy officials will not only sit in on the meetings, but be the guests of honour. "In China, having the Canadian government sit beside you is a very strategic thing to do, especially if you are not a big company—it adds a lot of credibility," he says. "It's an interesting dimension that I don't think Canadian companies give enough credit to. It's a huge benefit."

Of course, you have to have a strategy. You can't arrive at the embassy's doorstep and say you sell specialized water-filtering equipment, and please set up five meetings. You need to know who you want to see and why. It also helps to have a little imagination. In the case of Mitel, the Ottawa high-tech firm had a very important business meeting in Australia and wanted to make an impression. It arranged to have the get-together at the Canadian embassy, which boasts a sumptuous view overlooking Sydney Harbour. "It didn't cost us a bean," said Simon Gwatkin, Mitel's vice-president of strategic marketing. "If this had been the U.K., it would have cost thousands of dollars."

There are innumerable ways in which the government can help, says Alan Davitt, a former international business team leader at the Canadian Commercial Corp., a federal international contracting agency. It's not always easy or obvious—nor should it be, he argues. While getting government support can be akin to "prodding an elephant," if it were a cakewalk many companies would feel even less compunction than they already do to plan ahead before going international. "Business isn't easy; why should government be?" asks the president of Tri-Star International, which specializes in helping companies access federal government support. The key is to approach government not as a bureaucratic black hole, but as any other business problem that requires sales and marketing finesse. "Canada is unique in terms of the help exporters can obtain from their own government," says the U.K. native. "It's a matter of learning how to use and access those resources and build relationships in Ottawa, just as you would with customers abroad. The disconnect happens because companies don't know how to utilize government effectively."

TIME TO FIND SOME COJONES

So you've got international goodwill and government support that, while not always entirely focused, can be valuable tools. What are you, the Canadian businessperson, going to do with them? What contribution will you make to this equation? How are you going to help build the foundation for a globally aware, savvy and sophisticated business culture?

A good place to start is within your own company. One of the biggest failings I have come across in corporate Canada is the inability to appreciate, nurture and exploit international work experience. Few companies seem to invest in international training or have a strategy that includes overseas postings as part of an employee's career advancement. In contrast, the German multinational, Siemens, has a deliberate policy of sending its most promising workers abroad. Its Canadian subsidiary even sent an employee to Japan for his master's degree, notes Schulich's Lorna Wright. "Can you imagine a Canadian company doing that?"

Quite the opposite. Not only do Canadian companies tend to send retirees, B-teams and otherwise irritating personnel abroad, but they often have no mechanism for reintegrating them into the corporate ranks or profiting from their experience. "Canadian companies are notorious for not using the experience and knowledge that people bring back," says Wright. A study of Canadian energy companies conducted as part of a thesis project for the University of Calgary found that a third of repatriated employees left their jobs within two years of returning to Canada (usually to work for the competition).[123] The reason? They felt their international experience was not valued or put to use back at head office. "It's like putting an axe to your career," acknowledges Pierre Alarie, who returned to Canada after fifteen years in Latin America working for various Canadian companies. "You don't realize that when you return home there's no formal process to reintegrate you, and you lose money because your spouse can't work. What's the incentive for going abroad?"

Canadians who have worked for foreign institutions overseas get an equally cool reception when they try to return home. Although there is a serious shortage of international experience among the very domestic rank and file, Canadian returnees are often rebuffed rather than embraced—considered a threat by the closed-shop mentality that pervades many institutions. "It's not a welcoming culture," admits John Hancock, a trade counsellor with the WTO in Geneva, who says his foreign experience is considered a "liability" when he's looked at finding work in Canada. "The attitude is, 'Why did you leave? What do you know about the fiscal imbalance?'"

Given such a parochial environment, companies at the very least should invest in language and cultural training for workers engaged in overseas business. "At least then they wouldn't put their foot in their mouth," says one European-born Canadian executive. All too often the shortcomings of the Canadian education system become painfully evident when Canadians routinely make the kind of embarrassing gaffes that they love to fault Americans for. "Very often they say things and you just want to disappear," he laments.

Of course, it's difficult to create awareness within an organization if its leadership doesn't have a global mindset. Not only should a company's board of directors include members either from other countries or with international experience, but in this day and age it's hard to believe a chief executive could be qualified to run a major operation such as a bank, mining company or forestry firm without having worked overseas. It's not enough to know the technical ins and outs of an industry—this means nothing if you can't apply it in another context. In the same way that a CEO can go from selling household cleaning products to flogging beer, there is a method to international business that you cannot learn without living it. As operational leaders, CEOs should be obliged to have this skill set, just as they should be obliged to speak at least two languages. The prime minister of Canada must be bilingual, and the head of a globally competitive company must speak more than one language.

Canadian companies, particularly the handful of larger, more global ones, should also encourage their Canadians suppliers and service providers to join them overseas to provide them with valuable international experience and exposure. Unfortunately, Canadian multinationals often discriminate against their compatriots for fear they will appear less professional in foreign eyes. Lawyers Ella Plotkin and Brian Kelsall, for example, often find it easier to get work with international clients than with big Canadian companies. The firms argue they would have a tough time explaining to their foreign partners why they are using Canadian counsel on an overseas project. "It's endemic in Canadian corporations, even at the top levels," says Kelsall. Adds Plotkin: "They're often not confident enough to convince somebody else that this Canadian experience is good enough, even when they are the major participants. Canadians can be their own worst enemies."

Canadian companies can also give themselves a leg up by investing in resources that will support their international endeavours, by providing either valuable networking opportunities, market intelligence or fora for developing policies and marketing initiatives. Think-tanks, which can supply research on international macroeconomic policy, are woefully under-appreciated in Canada, whereas many business groups, such as the Canadian Council for the Americas, are little more than one-man shows. Others, such as the Canada–Japan Business Conference series, dissolved in apathy. If Canadian business wants to get serious about being globally competitive, it needs to help build a sophisticated hosting environment, including establishing a serious international network of Canadian chambers of commerce. The U.S. chamber operates high-level delegations that actively promote and influence policy initiatives in foreign countries, going so far as to organize committees to write position papers on specific legislation. "They are so competent and reliable that when a civil servant in the European Community has a problem, they go to the American chamber," says Boris Rousseff, a European trade expert. "The Americans so heavily influence the legislative process that they almost dictate what the Europeans put in the legislative norms. Imagine the competitive advantage that offers."

The Canadian equivalent, in contrast, is little more than a patchwork of forgotten outposts and country clubs. The chamber of commerce in Germany is reputedly made up of a lone Canadian lawyer. The country doesn't even have a chamber of commerce in China. The closest thing to it, the Canada China Business Council, is headquartered in Toronto and lacks the standing and profile afforded to officially registered chambers in China. Founded by high-powered operator Paul Desmarais, chairman of the multi-tentacled Power Corp., the council is overseen by his son André, who is its honorary chairman and son-in-law to former Prime Minister Jean Chrétien. While the council (vainly) tries to drum up Canadian business interest in China, it has largely operated as a vehicle for organizing social events and Team Canada trade missions. "The Americans in China are very well supported, not only by the embassy and consulates, but by strong business groups who seem to have the ear of government," explains a Canadian trade commissioner formerly posted in China. "The Canada China Business Council is not a policy group; it was often nothing more than a way for Chrétien to organize Team Canada missions. With Desmarais as his son-in-law, it was all very cushy."

Last, but not least, corporate Canada needs to help forge the next generation of globally minded Canadians. Terry Clifford, a former school principal and member of Parliament, has spent the last fifteen years trying to do just that. At the age of sixty-seven, he still tirelessly crosses the country collecting donations and meeting eager young adults who vie for a chance to join the ranks of Global Vision. Every year a handful are chosen to participate in a trade mission. To qualify, they must get a company to sponsor them to the tune of four thousand dollars, in exchange for the market intelligence and trade leads they pick up on the trip. Clifford has led missions to Brazil and China, and was even invited to George W. Bush's ranch when he was governor of Texas. "It shows the world we're serious about our young people and that our young people are ready for the world," he says. "And not merely as spectators—they're ready to lead."

The "kids," as Clifford calls them, are invariably offered jobs in every country they visit, and Global Vision graduates fan the globe—proof, Clifford says, that "if you show Canadian kids a different way of doing things, they'll do it." Still, the irrepressible optimist admits he can get depressed sometimes. "I've made a conscientious effort to develop Canadian talent and bring it not just to the national stage, but the international stage," says Clifford, who was awarded the Order of Canada for his efforts. "It gets recognized around the world, but we have a hard time getting accepted by business in Canada."

He doesn't have to convince Pierre Choquette of the need to create Canadian global citizens. Since retiring from Methanex, Choquette has established a family foundation that awards twenty scholarships a year to students interested in spending a term studying abroad. The scholarships, which are divided between the University of British Columbia and the Université Laval, are each worth ten thousand dollars. Once a year, Choquette meets with the recipients to hear what they've learned. He believes that if Canadians could couple their inborn advantages with a global mindset, it would make for an unbeatable combination.

There's just one thing missing. The Mexicans call it *cojones*. The polite translation would be chutzpah. Mauricio Ospina, a Colombian-born trade facilitator with Ontario Exports, put his finger on the problem with a simple comparison: "At a trade show a Canadian will stand inside his kiosk and hide behind the computer, waiting for someone to approach him or for something to happen. An American will stand in the middle of the corridor and be in your face," explained Ospina. "I like Canadians, but they need to be a bit more assertive."

It's great to be nice and understated, but if you don't capitalize on these qualities, what is the point? As Howard Balloch explains, "Being Canadian gets you in the door, but it doesn't get you the order." If anything, that lack of assertiveness, that shy, retiring quality that some Canadians have, can be a real deterrent to doing business. Customers, whether they are Canadian or foreign, naturally gravitate to those sellers who make it easy for them to buy. Call it the path of least resistance. Asians, for example, prefer to deal with Canadians, explains Lorna Wright. "Canadians are not as aggressive, and they don't carry all that political baggage," she explains. Despite their preferences, however, "Asians say it is easier to deal with Americans because they want the business," Wright says. "The Americans come to them, they say, and Canadians don't. The Americans push, and Canadians won't."

What's worse, some foreigners interpret Canadian reserve as either haughty condescension or lack of character. Considering the goodwill that precedes Canadians, it's disappointing for foreigners who expect more and don't have the interest, patience or incentive to take the time to try and figure them out. "Canadians need to develop a bit of an ego," says one European who is somewhat exasperated with Canadians. "They suffer from a lack of presence—they have no image. Canadians don't have a style of their own. Who are they? What do they want?"

It's a problem that seems to particularly plague English Canada. Interestingly, in Lorna Wright's research, she found that one of Canadian companies' greatest competitive advantages was having a project manager from Saskatchewan—the prairie province is a seemingly rich repository of low-key, good listeners and all-round "great people." Yet English Canadians seem to have more difficulty acclimatizing than do French Canadians who have ventured abroad. Mexico-based Quebec entrepreneur Bruno Perron described it this way: "English Canadians don't adapt, and they aren't in your face either. You have to be either obnoxious like the Americans or compatible like the French, but you can't be in between." John Wiebe, president of the Globe Foundation of Canada, an international consultancy based in Vancouver, has a similar take: "The problem is, we are not international marketers, we've never had to be. We don't wine and dine and we're not ruthless."

The reasons why are complicated and go to the very heart of Canadian identity. This is not the place for diving down that particular rabbit hole, but as complex as the Canadian psyche may be, one thing is pretty clear: Canadians have every reason to be confident. The more international work lawyer-duo Ella Plotkin and Brian Kelsall do, the more they are convinced it's true. Usually the lone Canadian contingent to bid on international project finance deals, they regularly compete against U.S. and British-based global law firms—and they win. "There is nothing they know that we don't know. There's nothing they do that we as Canadians can't do," says Plotkin (who happens to have been born in Russia).

That doesn't mean Canadians have to be arrogant, in-your-face or tacky self-promoters. They can be confident in their own way. I liken it to the difference between Donald Trump and Paul Reichmann. Whether it's books, television shows, clothing lines, perfume or spring water, there is hardly a product Trump, the U.S. real estate mogul, wouldn't put his name to. Canada's Reichmann has never put his name to anything, not even his own buildings; but that doesn't mean he doesn't have a brand. When asked by the *New York Times* what he thought his legacy would be, the media-shy magnate admitted he'd never thought about it. "Hopefully, in each city, they [the buildings] will last a long time and be meaningful for the city," he said simply.[124]

In Mexico City, Reichmann's Torre Mayor recalls the ancient ruins of the Aztec Templo Mayor, or Great Pyramid, an iconic landmark located in the geographic and foundational heart of the country's capital. In comparison, Trump's eponymous Towers sound a little prosaic, not to mention self-indulgent. Reichmann may be more modest than his flashy U.S. counterpart, but his accomplishments are not.

10 | A NEW APPROACH TO PARENTING:
WHAT GOVERNMENT CAN AND SHOULD DO

"I don't understand why you have a plan for a company but you
don't have a plan for a country."

CARIN HOLROYD, SENIOR RESEARCHER,
ASIA PACIFIC FOUNDATION OF CANADA

I WAS IN MY last year of university and, like everyone, was short of cash, when
I clinched what I thought was a cushy job working for the government. All I
had to do was come in for a few hours every morning and photocopy newspaper articles containing the words "prosperity" and "competitiveness." For a
generous hourly wage, I highlighted the critical watchwords and then struggled to staple together the thick tomes of photocopied articles that were to be
delivered to various cabinet ministers and high-level bureaucrats before the
start of the working day. The endeavour was part of Prime Minister Brian
Mulroney's ambitious "Prosperity Initiative," launched in 1992 with the goal
of making Canada more internationally competitive.

But as I trolled the empty government corridors to kill time, wasted an
unimaginable amount of paper on botched photocopying and compiled
stacks of papers that I knew no one would ever read if they had a real job,
the whole exercise struck me as just a bit incongruous. Even in my university naïveté, I remember thinking: "This is the path to prosperity?" *Not.* My
suspicions were confirmed when I graduated in the summer of 1992 to face

one of the worst recessions in recent memory. A journalism graduate, I had two options: wander the endless purgatory of small-town newspapers, getting paid $17,000 a year (which was not enough to cover the gas to get to my assignments), or leave the country. I chose the latter.

Now, nobody's perfect and Canada isn't the first country to grapple with the discomfiting challenges of globalization. There is no question that Canada's future looks a lot more promising than, say, Italy's. But I think it would be instructive to look at how other countries, particularly Finland and Australia, have confronted these same issues and compare their responses, not only with Canada's, but even with its *ability* to institute similar policies.

Let's take Finland. Much has been made of the tiny, geographically inhospitable country's competitive prowess. Just the southern city of Tampere and its surrounding area, population 300,000, is home to a dozen global companies, from Nokia to Metso, that are market leaders in their fields. Observers of the Finnish miracle attribute the country's success to a few key elements: a spirit of collaboration; technical expertise; a history of outward-looking, internationally minded companies; and leadership. In particular, they point to the mutually supportive, virtuous circle of industry, academia and government.

As early as 1970, Tampere city officials were formulating a business development strategy, investing in science parks and development companies and hiring an industry ombudsman to coordinate policy with business. Local business leaders took a personal stake in shaping as well as supporting those policies while the university in Tampere not only churned out highly skilled, specialized engineers, but encouraged its professors, with their substantial industry experience, to act as a bridge that tailored research to the needs of industry. To top it off, the initiatives in Tampere were tightly linked to Finland's national policy and institutions throughout the country.

Could Canada apply a similar strategy? The answer lies in the basic building blocks of the successful Finnish model. To begin with, Canada doesn't have a history of globally oriented companies, nor does it have much in the way of homegrown corporate leaders: most are American. So what about a government that embraces business and sees its role as that of a facilitator in the pursuit of wealth creation? Once again, that's a tough one. Almost without exception, businesspeople in Canada report a sense of ambivalence if not outright animosity on the part of government. That suspicion was amply illustrated in May 2006, when former EnCana CEO Gwyn Morgan was publicly eviscerated by a Parliamentary committee. The retired head of the $14 billion oil company had offered to chair a parliamentary oversight commission for the token sum of one dollar a year, only to be summarily dismissed by contemptuous Liberal, NDP and Bloc Québécois MPs. He "doesn't reflect Canadian values," said the NDP's Peggy Nash of one of the rare Canadian-born heads of a major corporation.[125]

Not surprisingly, that sophomoric anti-business ethic has filtered down to the universities. Benoit Labonté, the former president of the Board of Trade of Metropolitan Montreal, recalls the virulent opposition a decade ago when the city's leading business school, École des hautes études commerciales, decided to build a new campus and name the classrooms after companies. "We need a better integration of universities and companies, which is not the case right now," he says. "It's a question of culture." That culture has helped foster a gaping disconnect between Canadian industry, the education system and students. The University of British Columbia didn't open its centre for advanced wood processing until 1996, marking— after centuries of logging—the country's first and arguably only hands-on bachelor's-level program focused on furniture and wood manufacturing.

"If you look at the typical education level in a Swedish or Finnish pulp mill, there are very few people without a master's degree in chemical engineering or pulp and paper engineering," says Clark Binkley, the former dean of UBC's Faculty of Forestry. "If you go to a typical Canadian pulp mill you are hard-pressed to find anybody with a master's degree. The educational system here has just not been organized to do that. Think about this industry and how important it is—and you don't have a single program? You've got to wonder why."

Binkley believes the answer lies with a visit he made to a high school in Kelowna to give a talk on the forestry industry. "I asked them, 'What worries you about the forestry industry?' And they all said, 'Clearcuts—they're bad.' I asked how many students had ever been to a clearcut, and only two of the fifty kids raised their hands. Their teachers had never taken them to one and explained it to them. I just couldn't believe it," he says. "Here's a quintessential timber town where kids were completely disconnected from the circumstances in which they found themselves. I have never been in a Finnish high school, but considering the approach they take to the industry I honestly don't believe you'd find the same thing there. I believe the Finns see the industry as much more integral to their future."

With the education system, the government and corporate Canada seemingly ill-fitted to the Finnish model, we are left with the two guiding elements that could arguably overcome any systemic shortcomings: co-operation and leadership. Sadly, I don't know which one Canadians are worse at. Let's begin with co-operation. While the New York and European stock exchanges are combining forces across the Atlantic, Canadian provinces can't stop squabbling long enough to agree on a single securities exchange regulator *for the country*—giving Canada the ignominious reputation of being the only industrialized nation without a national regulator. There are so many interprovincial trade barriers, the Conference Board of Canada concluded, that "their sheer numbers present a daunting obstacle to any attempt to compile a full list or estimate the cost."[126] Since each province comes up with its own certifications, regulations and monopolies on everything from milk to liquor and energy, Canada is the most decentralized federation in the world—and it shows.

Meanwhile, the rest of Canada looks on and, like a child, is condemned to relive the sins of the parent. The enmity between East and West continues to percolate while petty rivalries among companies domestically spill into global markets and prevent them from being able to co-operate internationally. "We are one of the most bitchy sandbox players I have ever seen," says business consultant John Wiebe. "We don't know how to get together and take on the world. Everybody is looking for his share of the pie, and it's all about getting money out of the government. There's this zero-sum-game we all play, and we all end up losing in the long run."

This is not to say that the government isn't aware of the problem or hasn't made efforts to confront the country's nagging productivity concerns and lacklustre record of innovation. Following Finland's example, Prime Minister Jean Chrétien unveiled the Liberal government's Innovation Agenda, allocating an estimated $4 billion a year to fund research chairs, centres of excellence, national research labs and generous tax credits with the goal of placing Canada among the top five nations in the world for R&D spending by 2010.[127] During his economic and fiscal update in 2005, Finance Minister Ralph Goodale mentioned some variation of the words "competitive" and "innovative" nineteen times. Goodale's successor, Jim Flaherty, also took a run at the problem during his November 2006 fiscal update, though he opted to use euphemisms like "quality of life" and "sustainable growth." But so far, despite the grand speeches and wads of cash thrown at the problem, nothing seems to be working and many observers are left scratching their heads, wondering why.

It's no great mystery. Aside from the reasons mentioned above, we've got to ask a very basic question: What fuels innovation? Why would a forestry company invest in new silviculture methods? Why would a Manitoba farmer plant new wheat varieties with higher yields? Why would a Canadian bank offer its clients new services, such as being able to withdraw money from accounts denominated in any number of worldwide currencies? Why would a Newfoundland fishery invest in state-of-the-art, labour-saving technology or diversify into the aquaculture business?

One thing is for sure: it's not because of more government-funded research labs. According to the OECD, public R&D spending has no statistically significant effect on economic growth. On the other hand, an increase in business spending from 2 per cent to 3 per cent translates into a 12 per cent jump in real GDP per capita.[128] There's only one reason why business would deny itself a short-term dividend in favour of longer-term returns: because it has to. As Roger Martin, dean of Toronto's Rotman School of Management, argues, it's not a problem of supplying more scientists, it's a question of more demand on the part of business.[129] And where does that demand come from? From the incentive fuelled by a competitive environment. Without that competitive drive, public investment and business are like two toddlers who, despite being put in the same room, continue to parallel play—they may handle the same toys, but they never interact.

So how do we create more demand for innovation? There's no need to reinvent the wheel. To be innovative doesn't mean having to build whole new industries from the ground up in sexy-sounding sectors like nanotechnology and biopharmaceuticals. Innovation is all around us. Rolf Penner is a third-generation grain and hog farmer from Morris, Manitoba. He'd love to feed his own grain to his hogs and "work up and down the value chain," but since the Canadian Wheat Board blocks him from growing cheaper, higher-yield varieties, it's more economical for him to import corn and soybeans from the United States. He'd also love to diversify into processing chicken, which is a more popular meat than pork, but because of a strict quota system on chicken production he can't. "When I look around the Prairies, all I see is potential—all this space, all this grain and not a lot of people," he says. "Any yet, everywhere I look, I see roadblocks to fulfilling that potential."

LEAD BY EXAMPLE

Government in Canada has a huge role to play in fostering global competitiveness. But to do that it must first have a strategy, and that strategy has to be based on a clear goal. Blurry concepts like productivity, innovation or even global competitiveness, per se, are not the goals, but merely a measure of whether the goal has been achieved. The fundamental question that government policy-makers should ask themselves is, how can Canadians graduate from being telemarketers, middle managers and commodity producers to not only running, but *leading*, globally oriented enterprises? "If the goal of every government is to have high-end jobs, industrial competitiveness comes from leadership. If you stop producing corporate-level people, that expertise, those jobs, disappear," explains business consultant John Gruetzner.

It requires nothing short of a radical shift in the Canadian mindset, and the starting point should be our perspective. We need to adjust our depth of field and, even more importantly, to look at everything we do in Canada through the lens of international markets. During the last review of the federal Bank Act in 2006, legislators honed in on shortening the critically important time it takes to process a cheque, but mundane issues of the banks' international reach or viability were never addressed. Despite all the money flung at the Innovation Agenda, a connection was never made between innovation and international markets. "There was no real understanding of what innovation was, and no theory of how it fit internationally," says Toronto lawyer Chuck Gastle. Montreal-based pharmaceutical tycoon Francesco Bellini could never use the $70 million made available to his company, BioChem Pharma, through Technology Partnerships Canada because it was conditional on conducting drug trials in Canada. "To sell a global drug you need global trials," he explains.

For this strategy to work, the concept of "international" needs to infuse every aspect of government oversight, from education and taxation to immigration, trade policy, the financial system, labour laws and energy policy. "Canada is in a great position, but it needs people (in business and government) with a more global perspective to really leverage that and really push the country to the next level," says Dr. Xiang Bing, the Canadian-educated dean of China's Cheung Kong Graduate School of Business. "If Canadians don't work together to build up their global capabilities it could jeopardize their current position, because everybody else is moving up so fast. There's a new league coming, a super league of countries and companies, and you have to be ready for it." It's a tall order, and many of the people interviewed for this book expressed doubt that Canadians, together with their government, can pull it off. Here's to hoping they're wrong.

PROMOTE WINNERS INSTEAD OF PROTECTING LOSERS

Industrial policy is a dirty word in Canada, and no wonder. Like an experiment in alchemy that explodes in your face, what was supposed to produce the golden nugget has turned into a lump of coal. The government grand wizards cast the spell backwards, producing the opposite and inverse of what they had originally intended. By blocking the foreign ownership of Canadian companies in certain sectors, while at the same time prohibiting foreigners from competing against those companies in the domestic market, government created the worst of all possible worlds. Without any real competition, it had to resort to manufacturing competition. "The brilliance of the stupidity of the banking policy in Canada is they want competition, but they want it to be Canadian," says David Bond, the former chief economist for HSBC Canada. "Is God going to create new banks? It's absurd; they want competition, but they don't want foreigners, especially if they're gringos. It's inconsistent and irrational."

But instead of reversing the spell, government architects spun a very elaborate web of checks and balances in a bid to cleave together what is an inherently contradictory construct. They forced Canadian investors to buy Canadian stocks to make up for the fact these companies' stocks were penalized because they couldn't raise funds internationally. They conjured up the CRTC to rein in the massive monopolies they had created, only to have the regulator impose a "plethora of restrictions...never applied in any other industrialized country in the world."[130] Until now, the government has tried to defend a host of odd mutations that persist in the Canadian economy as evidence of how we are "different." I would counter that it is damning evidence of an underlying malignancy that pervades the economy.

These ill-conceived policies not only alienate consumers* but also foster animosity between the government, companies and would-be entrepreneurs, giving rise to the country's pervasive bitchiness. There is no love lost between the CRTC and the big telcos or the banks and Export Development Canada. The acrimony fuelled by the Canadian Wheat Board has pitted farmer against farmer on the Prairies. What's even more destructive is the message government sends to Canadians: it is telling them that *their own*

---

* In 2006 the CRTC announced that the phone companies had overbilled Canadians by $650 million, but instead of returning the money to customers, the regulator decreed the money would go towards providing service to remote areas.

government thinks they wouldn't survive without protection. Why? Because the competitors outside Canada are better than they are. Canadians seem to have taken the hint. As Roger Martin notes, in any sector where there is heavy government protection, Canada has produced no global leaders. It would seem that basing industrial policy on nationality rather than competitiveness is perhaps the most unCanadian thing imaginable. "We are like Gulliver—we've tied down our multinational companies and made them less competitive," says John Hancock, a Canadian trade counsellor at the WTO. "In the name of protecting our sovereignty, we've diminished it."

Which is why Canada should work to shed its mantle as one of the "most restrictive" countries in the OECD in terms of barriers to foreign investment. The government should either allow foreigners to compete in the market or remove the ownership caps on telecommunications, media and airline operators. It should also bid the Canadian Wheat Board a fond farewell, along with the dairy, egg and poultry marketing boards, and auction off a good percentage of Crown land to forestry companies. The Conservative government of Stephen Harper has made some positive inroads in this regard; Industry Minister Maxime Bernier, an unabashed freemarketer, has taken on the CRTC and many of its most stunting regulations, declaring: "Our goal is to reshape telecommunications policy so that it supports an internationally competitive and robust telecommunications industry in Canada."[131] Chuck Strahl, minister of agriculture and agri-food, has pledged to dismantle the Canadian Wheat Board's monopoly and proposes introducing a dual marketing system that gives farmers the choice of selling their wheat and barley either independently or through the board.*

With these restrictions removed, the Conference Board of Canada estimates that Canada could up its share of foreign investment from its current 3 per cent stake of global inflows to 9 per cent. "We should have a wide-open market. Let's have an industrial strategy aimed at creating home-grown, global multinationals," says Hancock.

---

* As of the writing of this book, the proposal was being fiercely opposed by the Wheat Board and new Liberal Party leader, Stéphane Dion.

Key to encouraging global champions is making certain the nation has a fully functioning financial system, the backbone of any successful economy. When banks don't participate in export-trade finance, don't have an international presence that would allow them to support Canadian companies in developing markets and don't even recognize foreign assets as collateral, something is very wrong. The solution, says Carleton University trade guru Michael Hart, is simple: "Reduce the regulatory barriers on banks, and they'll provide export finance." With restrictions on foreign ownership removed, there is no reason why banks should not be allowed to merge.

This is not to say that government should get out of the way entirely. While some argue that the market should be allowed to operate unfettered, there is a role for supporting strategic industries. That doesn't mean simply throwing money at desperate cattle ranchers or softwood lumber producers who are blocked from exporting to the United States. A good example of a successful strategy is the co-operative approach taken with the Ontario automotive industry. The industry found itself in a highly precarious position: not only had Ontario been bypassed for nineteen of the last twenty car plants built in North America, but the big vehicle manufacturers, despite being among the country's largest companies, don't even make the list of top 100 R&D spenders. To clinch it, as Michael Grimaldi, GM Canada's CEO, pointed out, "While a student today can obtain a degree in aerospace engineering at Ryerson University [in Toronto], we still do not have an integrated degree in automotive design and engineering offered in any Canadian university."[132]

So the industry, together with the union and the federal and provincial governments, joined forces to find a way to lure new, cutting-edge investment. Between 2004 and 2006, $1 billion in government funding clinched $7 billion in industry commitments, much of it tied to next-generation flexible manufacturing and the establishment of research centres, including a new, GM-sponsored Canadian automotive centre of excellence in Oshawa, which will feature Canada's first bachelor's program in automotive engineering.

The failure of Canadian industrial policy has been one of intent, says the WTO's Hancock. Instead of "promoting winners, it's always been about protecting losers." There is no reason government can't pick winners, adds Gerry Fedchun, president of the Canadian Automotive Parts Manufacturers' Association, as long as it's using the right measure of success: profitability. "The government should be a profit-oriented organization," he says. "If you invest tax money and you get more tax dollars back, that's a good deal for taxpayers." It requires a fundamental shift in government philosophy, one that until now has been preoccupied with wealth distribution rather than wealth creation and with guaranteeing jobs over the long-term sustainability of business.

"Industrial policy can work if you are smart about it. The Finns had a vision—the government did its part and industry did its part," says Avrim Lazar, president of the Forest Products Association of Canada. "In Canada, industrial policy is really social policy; regulations are developed around creating an industry where there is no market. I'm not sure an industrial policy was ever tried in Canada where the idea was to make money. While other countries focus on making a buck, we try to right a wrong."

NO MORE MANURE

The ultimate irony of the National Policy is that nearly 130 years later, free trade still does not exist in Canada. In the United States, where they seem to take these things a little more seriously, it is illegal to bar trade within the Union; Canada should follow their example. The Conference Board of Canada makes a direct connection between the tangle of conflicting provincial regulations and Canada's productivity gap with the United States. The bureaucratic overload not only costs business an estimated $33 billion annually, but fragments the Canadian marketplace, leaving companies smaller and less competitive.[133] "When you've got business owners spending huge amounts of time filling out paperwork for government, you know they aren't going to be thinking about going to other markets," says Catherine Swift, president of the Canadian Federation of Independent Business. "It's not rocket science."

According to Brian Lee Crowley, president of the Atlantic Institute for Market Studies, it's high time the federal government flexed its muscles and instilled some discipline. Until now Ottawa has avoided imposing its will in the name of national unity, but it's time the federal government reclaimed its responsibility over national economic policy, he says. Ottawa should give the provinces one year to remove interprovincial trade barriers, or bring in federal legislation to outlaw them. The feds should take a similar stance with a national securities exchange, as well as insisting that any individual professionally qualified in one province is qualified for the entire country. If the provinces balk, says Crowley, Ottawa should go to the Supreme Court for a reinterpretation of the trade and commerce clause in the Constitution Act, which clearly states that the national economic space falls within federal jurisdiction.

Canada is in dire need of national strategies in a range of sectors, from forestry and energy to the education sector, but if the country is to make any headway it will have to grapple with the issue of Quebec. Until now, Ottawa has preferred to placate the provinces by offloading more powers and spreading the wealth around. Sylvia Ostry, a former deputy minister under Pierre Trudeau and a distinguished fellow at the University of Toronto, calls it "the manure policy." "You spread it across the country and hope something springs up," she says. "I said that to Trudeau, and his response was, 'But what about Quebec?' You can't run a country like that. If we had the political will and were determined, there is a policy way. It would require a huge cultural mental shift. The business of Quebec has overshadowed our ability to do this."

A good place to shore up the country's increasing balkanization is abroad. While I understand Stephen Harper's desire to court Quebec, his decision to allow the province to have a seat at UNESCO was a mistake, as was his approval for turning Quebec's Washington bureau into a full-fledged political and economic delegation. The "have-not" province already boasts twenty-eight delegations in eighteen nations and is aiming for close to three hundred around the world. These delegates not only enjoy cushy diplomatic packets, but are often unapologetically separatist.

I don't know how many times I've come across a Latin American whose only knowledge of Canada is "the plight of Quebec." It not only makes Canada look ridiculous, but as Derek Burney, Canada's former ambassador to the United States, wrote, provincial delegations "diminish, if not confuse, Canada's voice in the world."[134]

CULTIVATE INTERESTS, NOT FRIENDS

In 2000, Parliament's Commons Committee on Foreign Affairs and International Trade undertook a review of Export Development Canada (EDC). A thorough assessment of the agency's continued viability was long overdue, yet the exercise largely revolved around whether the EDC was upholding Canadian standards on human rights and the environment in its dealings abroad. "EDC has demonstrated its effectiveness in bringing economic benefits to Canadians and plays an equally vital role in promoting Canadian values globally," declared International Trade Minister Pierre Pettigrew, in response to the hopelessly misdirected review. "We are taking steps to ensure that [EDC] is able to continue to evolve as an effective agency dedicated to supporting exporters with a clearer focus on working to support Canadian values in the areas of human rights and the environment."[135] Huh? What about the value of having as many Canadians exporting as possible? Apparently that wasn't on the agenda.

If it were up to Michael Hart, he'd scrap EDC tomorrow. Others are more forgiving; they'd break it up and privatize its different lines of business. "Instead of five major banks promoting export finance, we've got one obscure bureaucracy," says Hart. "How's that good for the country?" That's not to say there isn't a role for an export credit agency, but it should be to fill in the gaps where the private sector won't go, rather than crowd out the banks altogether. In reconfiguring EDC's role, readjusting its guiding principle would also help. Whether the agency is "self-sustaining" is immaterial. The purpose of EDC is not to be profitable, but to get as many companies as possible successfully exporting, and if it can get the banks involved, all the better.

At the same time, EDC should not be another fiefdom unto itself, but part of a one-stop shop that encompasses the gamut of government trade services. What those services should be must also be reconsidered. While some observers have high praise for the trade commissioner service, others, like Hart, question the need for government to provide free market intelligence when the information is readily available in the private sector. "Why should government do that in today's world?" he asks. "I can see that a hundred years ago, but with today's communications and transportation, do we need to hold the hand of a potential exporter?"

Jim Sherry, a veteran trade commissioner now working in the private sector, agrees that providing market intelligence is not the way to go. In many cases, he says, the embassies hire local companies to gather market information, removing the bureaucrats from a more intimate involvement with Canadian companies. Many of the embassy commercial officers are local hires with a very narrow understanding of Canada and are little more than "glorified interpreters." Sherry advocates a much more hands-on approach, especially with notoriously complex countries like China. "If the Canadian government gives a hoot about small and medium-sized companies internationally, then it has to have a completely dedicated trade commissioner service that helps individual companies succeed and prosper internationally," says Sherry. "It's those guys who need the trade commissioners holding their hands, because let's face it, they need the help."

Kam Rathee, president of the Canada–India Business Council, would go one step further. He argues Ottawa could put Canada's countless ethnic business associations to good use by hiring some of their members as independent trade advisers to guide neophyte Canadian companies going into new markets. It would help tackle the two biggest weaknesses plaguing the trade commissioner service: that bureaucrats are not businesspeople, and that with only a three-year posting in each country they barely get comfortable before it's time to leave. An Indo-Canadian adviser would already know the lay of the land in India, says Rathee, and being a businessperson, would have the skills to go beyond collecting business cards to actually clinching a deal. "Companies need to be able to get to the next step, and civil servants do not close deals," he says. "It's like driving a car when you have no experience in how to get the best mileage out of it. Business is done by businesspeople."

Ultimately, just like any company, the government needs to come up with an international business plan that identifies clear goals and strategies and establishes rates for success. For it to work, the underlying rationale should not be to wean Canada off its dependence on the United States, but to broaden the country's global reach as an end in itself and as a matter of survival for any self-interested country. Canada needs to ask itself, "Where can I get the best bang for the buck?" and then target those markets for promotion and trade-facilitating agreements.

The plan must also be coordinated; that is, don't tell Canadians to do business with China and then have the embassy in Beijing deny business visas to potential Chinese investors who have been invited to government-sponsored trade fairs. Even worse, don't encourage them to invest in a corruption-riddled environment without the support of investment-protection agreements. The plan must be consistent, pragmatic and focused on the real barriers to real trade, such as anti-competitive practices, double taxation and exorbitant Japanese tariffs on canola oil. Whatever markets the government targets should be chosen in coordination with the business community, and like any good company the government should promote only its best products, whether they are wood-frame housing or auto parts.

Above all, when it comes to handling trade, Canada must be *impressive*. Spouting hollow platitudes about Canadian values is not impressive, and neither was Pierre Pettigrew as trade minister. The government cannot afford to name anyone other than the absolute best person to the post; to do otherwise tells the rest of the world that Canada doesn't take trade seriously. And that goes for ambassadors too: when you hand out plum posts to MPs with no qualifications other than loyalty to a political party, it diminishes the entire country. Ambassadors are Canada's most important calling card internationally, which means they need to be sharp negotiators equipped with a strong business sense. "The commercial activism of American and Japanese diplomats is everywhere—they are always selling," says European trade consultant Boris Rousseff. "Canadian diplomats in Europe talk about everything but trade. You need more people with corporate experience."

Diplomats should also be evaluated on their social skills and entertaining prowess. Throwing a great party is infinitely more critical to boosting trade relations than is the ability to inundate your potential business partners with bureaucratic paperwork signed in triplicate. All too often, Canadian ambassadors are unbearably dull, distant and not tapped into local communities. In India, for example, the High Commission invites the same hundred people to every function, says Pradeep Sood, former president of the Indo-Canada Chamber of Commerce. Perhaps that's why, when Paul Martin visited New Delhi in 2005, hardly anyone attended the press conference (including Sood and Kam Rathee, both of whom were in town but failed to receive an invitation).

Networking needs to be the new modus operandi, and everyone from ambassadors to trade commissioners should focus on cultivating influence and access to the real power players. It might help if the federal government tapped into the country's rich multicultural resource when it comes to appointing ambassadors. As Richard Liu, an entrepreneur who has worked closely with the government, notes, while countries like Mexico, Malaysia and Mauritius all have ethnic-Chinese ambassadors to China, Canada has never named a Chinese Canadian to the post. "Everybody knows that when Chinese deal with Chinese, you gain," says Liu. Instead the Beijing embassy and federal bureaucrats seem more concerned with whether embassy staff speak French rather than Mandarin.

If Ottawa were truly tapped in, it would replace the government lobbyists and representatives from Atomic Energy of Canada who normally crowd the junkets to China with members of the Chinese Canadian community who have serious contacts on the mainland and are doing a lot of business below the radar. "Our trade marketing efforts aren't very sophisticated," says David Pecaut, senior partner with the Boston Consulting Group in Toronto. "We need to be much more adept at getting ourselves connected to these markets at the level of the people who are the real movers and shakers. Our trade policy model is still back in the 1960s and 1970s—we haven't moved into the world of networks, connectivity and government and the private sector working together."

INVEST IN A ROLODEX

The good news is that Canada already has a network of worldwide contacts; it just needs a Rolodex to store them in. There are an estimated 2.7 million Canadians living abroad, representing 8.8 per cent of the population and on a per capita basis one of the largest expat communities worldwide.[136] Although the majority reside in the United States, 644,000 are in Asia. While many have returned to their country of origin because they felt professionally stunted in Canada, they would be powerful allies in attracting investment and boosting commercial ties. Harvard professor Michael Szonyi argues the émigrés should be treated as a "net overseas asset." He observes, "Now that they have gone back, we have to ask ourselves, how can this be good for Canada? Rather than think of this as a failed policy, we've dispatched Canada boosters to countries around the world where there is lots of mobile investment capital."

One way to keep émigrés in the Canadian fold is to remove the tax on worldwide income that Ottawa currently levies on Canadian residents or Canadians living overseas with assets in Canada. Like so much of Canadian policy that has the reverse effect of its desired intent, the tax actually *encourages* émigrés and expats to cut all ties to Canada. To avoid paying tax, Canadian citizens living abroad must close their bank accounts and sell their assets and can no longer pay into registered retirement savings plans (RRSPS). Forced to choose between living tax-free or cutting up their Royal Bank credit cards, it's a no-brainer and only Canada ends up losing out. Instead, Ottawa should follow the American lead, which taxes income above a certain threshold regardless of where a U.S. citizen resides. In that way, overseas money would continue to flow back home and Canada would get something back for giving out its passport like lollipops on Halloween.

The government should also come up with a database to track Canadian émigrés as well as all foreigners who come to study at Canadian universities. David Pecaut suggests making the students part of a global "Friends of Canada" network and treating them like alumni, even bringing them back to Canada occasionally for specific events. "You'd be amazed," he says, "once it got going, how much affinity there really is and how much benefit you'd get from influencing them for very modest amounts of money."

As for the immigrants who are already here or on their way, the government should pre-approve their professional credentials before they arrive in Canada, and their qualifications should be accepted across the country. The government should also raise public awareness of the potential benefits of hiring immigrants to break into international markets. It could spread the message through television commercials and make the campaign part of its one-stop trade-promotion shop.*

EMBRACE YOUR INNER ENTREPRENEUR

"Foster a culture of entrepreneurship" was one of the most common recommendations made to government by individuals interviewed for this book. That's a touchy one, considering that many of the people elected to Parliament have generated much of the anti-corporate vitriol that has become gospel in Canadian society. William Lyon Mackenzie King, Canada's longest-serving prime minister, who racked up twenty-one years in power, believed that capitalism spawned wars and debased society. He wrote that industry was "a monster so demonical as to breed a terror unparalleled in human thought."[137] Not surprisingly, "there isn't a businessman in government," says Alvin Segal, chief executive of Montreal clothing manufacturer Peerless Clothing. "You should hear the questions they ask. They don't have a clue." Adds Avrim Lazar: "They're almost innocent of business, as if it exists in a different universe and it's not their problem."

---

* The government of Ontario has launched a television campaign highlighting the benefit to companies of hiring new Canadians to expand internationally.

Which leads to the obvious question, How do you devise industrial strategy, trade policy or a tax regime when you don't understand how business works? From the results gleaned to date, the answer would seem to be, not very well. If the government wants to encourage Canadians to be more entrepreneurial, it's first going to have to add a few entrepreneurs to its own ranks. Businesspeople should be encouraged to enter government, as they are in the United States and France, says John Hancock. "You see it everywhere in the U.S. government. Of course you get the bagmen and the cronies, but you also get Larry Summers and Robert Rubin, the best of the best," he says. "Bureaucrats have no interest or sensibility for what business is looking for because they've never done it. In the U.S., it's part of their DNA."

If there's any hope of coming up with a strategy, business and government are also going to have to work together. "We need a greater partnership between the Canadian government and Canadian business," says Neil Tate of BMO. "A strategy can't just be devised by the government; it must be done together with business. There needs to be a joint commitment." In Australia and New Zealand, notes Tate, senior business executives volunteered a year or two of their time to take a leadership role in developing an Asia strategy for their countries and in some cases were seconded to specific government ministries. "By the time you've become a senior executive of a large or medium-sized corporation, you're committed to this country and you want to give back. We need to create a forum where we can develop a plan that will keep Canada open for business."

A number of executives suggested starting off with a two- or three-day brainstorming session with the prime minister and business representatives. Derek Burney, a long-time bureaucrat who has also worked for Bell Canada and aviation manufacturer CAE, recommended creating sectoral advisory groups like those established to negotiate NAFTA. An overarching business committee would provide the link to government. "In Finland," notes Avrim Lazar, "government and industry got together, and they were shameless about it."

Dollars to doughnuts, one of the first things businesspeople would tell government is to lower taxes. Successive governments have tried chipping away at the country's oppressive tax burden, including Stephen Harper's Tories, who pledged to ratchet down Canada's taxes on business investment to the lowest among the G8. But that depends, of course, on the minority government staying in power. Meanwhile, as of 2006, Canada had the sixth-highest marginal effective tax rate on business out of thirty-six industrialized countries, and it is the only member of the OECD whose tax rate is now *higher* than it was in 1982.[138] Some governments, like Quebec's, try to offset the burden by offering huge tax breaks to entice companies like French video game giant Ubisoft to establish its North American beachhead in Montreal. They've been promised two thousand jobs out of the deal, but it's like biting off your nose to spite your face. How does it help all the would-be Quebec entrepreneurs who opt to join the province's swelling union ranks rather than pay exorbitantly high taxes to start their own company?

The high taxes, whether on business or personal income, mean there is little incentive to work longer hours or to take a risk when an individual would do just as well working nine to five as a bus driver. Why would people from Newfoundland get a full-time job, never mind start their own business, when they can work for two months and then qualify for welfare for the rest of the year? "We're a society where the government says 'We'll look after the risk for you,'" says Michael Hart. "In the end, it dulls your entrepreneurial capacity." Adds one long-time bureaucrat: "'The government will provide' is our mantra. But the point was to provide a safety net—it's not supposed to be a hammock."

Many of the people snoozing in that hammock are the 3.2 million, or roughly 20 per cent, of the Canadian workforce employed in the public sector. There are a lot of places where government needs to bolster its ranks; Ottawa definitely needs more trade negotiators, and as Beijing consultant John Gruetzner suggested, MPs should have foreign-policy advisers just as U.S. members of Congress do. But during the three years I spent researching this book—whether speaking to Deszö Horváth, the Hungarian-born, Swedish-raised dean of York University's Schulich School of Business, or Francesco Bellini, the Italian-born pharmaceutical entrepreneur—I rarely came across a native-born Canadian with the kinetic drive that distinguishes the globally minded. I became convinced that all the homegrown Canadians must be working in obscure government departments tasting new varieties of cheese to see whether they competed with cheddar.

Imagine if all these people were creating wealth instead of trying to leash it. Canada would have more entrepreneurs than it would know what to do with!

GIVE POWER TO THE PEOPLE

Quick: what is Canada's most important asset? If you said oil or natural gas, you'd be wrong. It's people. So why is it that we put so little stock in them? Canada boasts one of the most educated populations in the world, but educated for what? The OECD notes that an "usually high" number of Canada's post-secondary students attend community college and trade school, which is good for the automotive industry. But while we seem to focus on churning out workers, what about leaders?

Only 30 per cent of Canadian managers have university degrees, compared with 46 per cent of Americans. Headhunters routinely recommend that Canadian companies recruit senior-level executives from the United States. The Americans not only invest close to double, per capita, on post-secondary education, but churn out 87 per cent more business graduates on a weighted basis than do Canadians.[139] As a consequence, Canadian CEOs are less well trained, says Rotman's Roger Martin, and are "not as capable as they should be in setting strategies that will enable their firms to compete as effectively as they could."[140]

Part of the problem, he argues, is that there are not enough spaces available for business education. Martin notes that business undergrads and MBA students face among the longest waiting lists and lowest acceptance levels in the Canadian university system. He also points out that of the two thousand research chairs Ottawa aims to create, fewer than ten will be dedicated to business scholars. The reason, says Alan Middleton, executive director at the Schulich Executive Education Centre in Toronto, is that business and commerce are treated as specialty majors on the margin rather than as an integral part of a comprehensive education. As an example he points to Queen's University School of Policy Studies, Canada's premier training ground for future public administrators. The school doesn't offer a single commerce or management course, instead focusing on economic policy and analysis, and "brand is like a foreign word," says Middleton. "There's a point where you have to turn policy into plans and plans into actions—and that's where there is a lot of slippage," he says. "Commerce is not a separate entity. It's entwined with who we are as human beings and who we are as a contemporary society. You can't separate it."

Many observers believe that the education system should begin fostering a greater awareness, not only of business and branding, but of the world, long before university. "If kids don't demonstrate an inclination to be entrepreneurs or leaders by the time they are seventeen or eighteen, there's very small chance they will ever be," says Schulich's Dean Horváth. "Leaders and entrepreneurs, you develop early on." International business courses should be offered in high school, and international trade should be included in the curriculum as early as Grade 5, suggests SNC–Lavalin's Michael Novak. Schools also need to do a better job of teaching world history, and more emphasis needs to be placed on teaching a uniquely Canadian brand of marketing.

To make up for the shortfall in university-level business education, government should either lift tuition freezes or promote the creation of private universities.* Otherwise, business schools will have no choice but to stuff their rosters with higher-paying international students or open campuses in other countries, where they can charge higher fees. In an ironic twist that short-sighted politicians fail to see, tuition freezes,

---

* Until recently, private universities were *illegal* in Ontario, but although they've been decriminalized, no one's dared to pick up the gauntlet. British Columbia, on the other hand, does have a number of private institutions.

intended to ensure that education remains accessible, actually impinge on the universities' ability to help train homegrown business leaders.

Limited funding is not the only problem. Lorna Wright, the former assistant dean of Schulich's international MBA program, admits that only five hundred students have graduated from the highly regarded program in fifteen years. Of those, most have been new Canadians and foreign students. Why? Because Canadian-born students are unable to fulfill the requirement for a second language. Official bilingualism is evidently not working and seems to have turned Canadians off a second language altogether. The policy is also increasingly archaic in the wake of the rise of new global languages like Mandarin and Spanish. "The major business machine of the next 30 to 40 years is going to be China," says Leo Seewald, who spent summers as a teenager working in a Chinese toy factory and now, fluent in both Mandarin and Cantonese, works as a lawyer in Hong Kong. "If we start learning Chinese now, it will create a natural bond and in fifteen or twenty years we'll be so ahead."

The government should follow the lead of the Edmonton public school system, which offers seven bilingual programs and is widely considered one of the best school systems in the world. Unfortunately, the prospects aren't promising. According to Ontario provincial legislation, it is illegal to offer bilingual programs in languages other than English and French. When the Toronto school board was asked whether it was open to introducing a similar program, the answer was that it would be "difficult," because it wouldn't be fair to the hundreds of other world languages that weren't chosen. "Equity is a big thing at the school board," said one rep. "Which language would you choose?"[141] (Gee, maybe the one parents ask for?) That's almost as much of a disservice as the one done to Quebecers who are denied the right to learn English, which is still the world's predominant business language. Several Quebec entrepreneurs I spoke with told me that their lack of English-language skills had been a huge disadvantage, and as a result they had made sure to send their children to English Canadian universities.

"We need a better education system. We need to celebrate multilingualism. You should be able to learn the language you want, not the one dictated by the school system or by politics—it creates an awareness of the world, and it will create competitiveness," says Pierre Alarie, a Quebecer who is trilingual, as are his children. "We messed up as a society because we decided everybody had to be bilingual, while in Quebec there was no quality English teaching available for so many years. Unfortunately, it is still too often the case, so you can't compete."

At its core, the system needs to do something it has never done before: prepare a new generation of internationally oriented, culturally fluent, strategic-thinking *leaders*. "When what you want to change is the export culture, you need a new breed of leaders," says Victor Garcia, a manager with Hewlett-Packard Canada. "How do you fix that? Education. You need to start preparing a new generation of leaders so that the next level of CEOs, leaders and managers has an ingrained sense of globalization."

THEY ARE DOING IT DOWN UNDER

Does all this sound pie-in-the-sky? Do you read these recommendations for changing the way Canada operates and think, there's a better chance of pigs flying or a woman being elected prime minister again? Well, before dismissing these prescriptions altogether, you should know that there's a country very much like Canada that has already taken most of them to heart. Dubbed the "Lucky Country," Australia also suffers from an embarrassment of riches—a sprawling, resource-rich territory and a small population—that seemed to seal the country's fate as a commodity producer with few world-class multinationals. Up until a few decades ago, one could hardly distinguish between Canada's and Australia's industrial policies, they were so similar. But then, Australia woke up.

It didn't have much of a choice. With several states teetering on the brink of bankruptcy in the 1980s, Australia was forced to revisit many of its protectionist policies. The federal government essentially privatized large swaths of timberland, got rid of supply management in the dairy industry, opened up the banking sector to foreign competition and allowed the domestic banks to buy insurance companies. The Australian Wheat Board was largely deregulated and listed on the stock exchange (although it still has an export monopoly),* and the export credit agency was reformed. As Australia gets set to scrap foreign-ownership restrictions on media companies, it boasts the most deregulated economy in the Western world, according to the OECD, with the least amount of government ownership and fewest restrictions on markets.

At the same time, it has doubled the annual rate of immigration and attempted to speed up the integration process by pre-approving professional qualifications before new entrants arrive. It promotes multilingualism as part of an aggressive trade strategy, encouraging government officials to learn an Asian language, while companies like Qantas airlines fund scholarships to study Chinese and Japanese. More people now study Japanese in Australia than anywhere else in the world outside Japan and South Korea. Arguably the world's leading proponent of free trade, Australia in recent years has clinched a number of high-profile deals and is expected to ink an agreement with Japan in 2007. In 2005, it rang up US$25 billion in exports to the world's second-largest economy, compared with US$9 billion for Canada, which is physically closer to Japan than Australia is. Even more notably, Australia, with its twelve trade offices in China, saw its merchandise exports to the mainland jump 45 per cent year-over-year in 2005, compared with a 6 per cent increase for Canadian exports. Australian prime minister John Howard has been to China nine times in the past ten years.

"Australia is beating Canada to the gun in China all the time, and yet we are a Pacific Rim nation, we have a larger Chinese population and a larger economy than Australia," says BMO's Neil Tate. "It doesn't seem appropriate that we should be playing second fiddle." But we are, and in

---

* The corporation was expected to be further restructured and its export monopoly possibly scrapped in the wake of revelations that it paid $260 million in kickbacks to the former Iraqi regime of Saddam Hussein.

more ways than one. The Australians' growing trade might in China, combined with their heightened profile in the United States, has turned the Aussies into the new kids on the block that everyone wants to be friends with. Thomas d'Aquino, president of the Canadian Council of Chief Executives, came to that realization during an APEC summit in 2003. After the meeting, Chinese president Hu Jintao flew to Australia, marking one of his first official visits since assuming power the year before. When d'Aquino asked a senior Chinese official why Hu had chosen to call on Australia, the answer was that "if Australia was a close friend of Washington, then it was a close friend of China."

But beyond influence, the reforms introduced under Howard and his predecessors have also brought Australia unparalleled economic growth and prosperity. Considered one of the "miracle economies" along with Finland and Ireland, since 1992 it has averaged an annual GDP growth of 3.5 per cent, representing the longest period of uninterrupted expansion in Australian history. It has outstripped Canada in productivity growth, while net household income has more than doubled in the past decade. According to the OECD, Australia edged past Canada to claim the world's ninth-highest GDP per capita in 2005, up from seventeenth spot in 1990. At the same time Australia has become one of a handful of privileged countries to eliminate its net debt. Perhaps most importantly, according to Prime Minister Howard, "the country is more assertive and confident."[142]

So how was Australia able to do it? It comes down to a few key factors. Most importantly, Australia, adrift as it is, a massive island marooned in the middle of the South Pacific, doesn't have anyone to rely on but itself. In other words, it does not have the United States, the world's richest and most dynamic economy, at its doorstep, ready to snap up whatever it dug up or cut down. Second, it is has a more powerful federal government, which allows for more concerted and coherent strategies. "Australia doesn't have the luxury of coasting, so they have to work at it more coherently than we do," says Derek Burney. "They don't allow individual states to peddle their products; they have a single Australia focus, while we're willy-nilly all over the place."

Australia also has political leadership in the persona of John Howard, an unapologetic free marketer who has not shied away from confronting politically delicate reforms head-on. As he noted in an interview with the *Financial Times*: "I have a profound revulsion for political correctness."[143] Lastly, the Aussies seem to have a much greater sense of who they are, which allows them to trumpet their own unique brands, whether they are bikinis, shampoo, steakhouses or shiraz wine.

IT'S UP TO US

Jeff Swystun isn't often flummoxed, but he was a few summers ago in New York, when an American MBA student asked him a seemingly innocuous question: "What is Canada all about?" The branding executive, who usually has an answer for everything, stuttered. (He admits, "I don't stutter often.") It's a question Swystun still grapples with, as do many Canadians, and it's at the heart of our ability to confidently take on the world. Pablo Breard immigrated to Canada fifteen years ago and went on to a successful career as an executive at Scotiabank; yet, after all these years, he admits: "I don't know what being Canadian is." It has made him question not only his own future in Canada, but the country's future. "In order to understand how to compete, you have to have a massive overhaul of what Canada is and what it means to be Canadian," he says.

To do that, Canadians need to come to terms with what, until now, have been the two defining features of the national psyche that ultimately prevent them from claiming their rightful identity. On the one hand, for most of its history Canada has been a reactionary and defensive country, reacting to and defending itself against the United States. Canadians define themselves by what they are not—American—which is not only disingenuous but also destructive. Canadians have more in common with Americans than with any other country in the world. They share many of the same values: freedom, democracy, rule of law, a Judeo-Christian ethic and an (at times grudging) belief in a market-driven economy. With all that great inheritance, why focus on the negative? Doing so creates the impossible task of trying forge an identity in a vacuum that inevitably leads to feelings of inferiority.

It's equally difficult to say what you stand for when your country promotes the cult of "middleness" as if it were a religion. From Canada's choice to become a Dominion, which is neither a fully independent country nor quite a colony, to its willingness to sacrifice a strong central government on the altar of national unity, the nation has attempted to present its middle-way approach as an act of virtuous compromise, something to be admired. But this reflects nothing more than a patent inability to make a decision or take a stand, and what we end up with is a country of fence-sitters and a watered-down identity that eschews boldness in favour of blandness. No wonder Canadians suck at branding. "Branding Canada is about branding people, and that is hard," says Jeff Swystun. "Especially if you don't know who you are, but who you aren't."

That seeming lack of identity, in turn, has serious ramifications for Canada's ability to project itself into world markets. Think of Jamaican rum or Italian leather—exports are closely tied to their country of origin, and a national brand confers a certain reputation, either for excellence or for knock-off schlock. Right now, Canada's image is "completely flat, like a jellyfish," says one European observer. Schulich's Alan Middleton agrees: "Canadians are invisible." The Asia Pacific Foundation of Canada came up with similar findings in its surveys of Asian businesspeople. "Nothing about Canada stood out," says former president John Wiebe. "We're seen as this bland country. We're nice people, we have beautiful scenery, but we don't stand for anything." And that is a pretty hard sell. "I'm sorry, but how many times have you visited a nice but boring country?" asks Middleton. "Canadians are in danger of boring the entire world to death."

Marketing gurus Swystun and Middleton argue that Canada needs to go through a major rebranding exercise to develop a "master brand" that not only patents our uniqueness, but also clearly defines what we want to accomplish as a country. If Nazi Germany and Fascist Spain can remake themselves, so can Canada, which begins with a tremendous head start. According to the 2005 Anholt-GMI Nation Brands Index, Canada came second behind Australia, with the best brand reputation for liveability, landscape and investment. "It's a demonstration of market potential. What the survey points to is that there is the potential, the goodwill on the part of consumers around the world to buy a lot of stuff from Canada," said survey co-author and branding strategist Simon Anholt. "Canada could be playing a much more significant role in world affairs on many, many fronts."[144]

A great place to start would be a television ad celebrating some of Canada's greatest business successes and most internationally renowned exports. It could showcase an array of innovators, entrepreneurs, workers and artists, from the originators of the Blackberry handset to scenes of Cirque du Soleil's dazzling acrobatics and the opulent luxury of Isadore Sharp's Four Seasons hotels (even if the company is no longer Canadian-owned). I'd juxtapose hardrock miners and Prairie ranchers with Bombardier planes and Céline Dion. It would be all about what Canada is, instead of what it isn't, and it would introduce the world to what Canadians can do. More importantly, it would show *Canadians* what they are capable of.

Ireland has done something similar, hiring Bono, the lead singer of the rock band U2, as the country's spokesperson for attracting foreign investment. But while Ireland has taken out full-page ads in the *Wall Street Journal* to promote itself as an ideal manufacturing hub, it has also backed its glitzy campaign with a fundamental restructuring of its economy. Canada is very good at talking the talk without walking the walk, though, and any attempt at rebranding will be a fruitless exercise in semantics unless the federal government is able to unplug the country's economic bottleneck and unlock its potential. Otherwise university graduates and internationally trained executives will continue to migrate abroad in search of opportunities, and companies will continue to transfer their headquarters south.

There's just one catch. For Canada to embark on such an ambitious endeavour, it needs something that for most of its history it has sorely lacked: leadership. In many ways, the vacillation and defensiveness that has plagued Canadian leadership is a product of our history. Canada is a nation of workers and labourers, and since most of its big companies are owned or managed by foreigners, there is little opportunity for Canadians to learn to think strategically. We have largely abandoned the top spots to foreigners, and as a result our government is like an oversized union chief with the keys to the till. It's preoccupied with making sure its members have decent pay and benefits, even contracting out some jobs to sympathetic "brothers" in the banking, media and telecommunications sectors, but it couldn't come up with a forward-looking tactical strategy to save its life.

That's why the government is constantly caught up in interminable interdepartmental consultations, white papers, Royal Commissions and policy reviews. It's not about seeking compromise—nobody knows how to make a decision. And that can be dangerous. If you stand in the middle of the road long enough, you're liable to get run over, warns Kimon Valaskakis, Canada's former ambassador to the OECD. As a Texas senator once explained to him: "The only thing in the middle of the road is a dead armadillo."

China, India and others are barrelling down the highway, with their economies at full bore; Canada's time to act is now. And that action must begin with its leaders. If Canadians don't believe in themselves, it's largely because government is sending them signals that it shouldn't. If Canadians think big business is bad, it's because government is confirming their suspicions. If Canadians glorify the middle of the road, it's because that's what government espouses. If Canadians are indecisive and risk-averse, it's because that's how they see government behave. If Canadians don't know their place in the world, it's because their government is lost.

Everybody has to grow up sometime. Either we cut through the mythologies we have spun around ourselves, or we risk being ensnared in them forever. If we need any proof, look no further than Argentina, a country that, like Canada, once brimmed with potential. "Argentina was the one country in Latin America that should have succeeded," says Victor Garcia, an Argentinian-born manager with Hewlett-Packard Canada. "What failed was at the top. Like Canada, it lacked strategy and leadership.

Just as a company is a reflection of a president, a country is a reflection of its prime minister." And vice versa. A government is nothing more than the sum of its parts, and ours is a direct reflection of who we are; how far it is able to peer out ultimately depends on the vision of the Canadian people. "If we aren't careful, we'll end up a country that's so watered-down, there'll be nothing to save," says Eamon Hoey. "There's a lack of leadership in government, a lack of leadership in our corporations. We need a revolution in thinking. If not, Canada will end up a broken country."

In Argentina, an entire generation has been robbed of the opportunity to dream, strive and aspire to a better life. Those who could leave have done so, in search of a new beginning, flooding cities like Miami and Toronto. Canada still offers that promise, as evidenced by the many immigrants who have reached the pinnacles of success in their adopted country. Canada has all the makings of a global leader. The question is whether it wants to be one. "I think we live in one of the best nations in the world," says Francesco Bellini. "We are very privileged with what we have here, but we really could be the best."

SOURCES

INTRODUCTION

1 Derek DeCloet, "Perils of a Grand Old Brand," *Report on Business*, May 2004, 60.

2 Andy Hoffman, "Imports Frothing Up Beer Market," *Globe and Mail*, February 16, 2006.

3 Andrew Willis, Sinclair Stewart and Andy Hoffman, "Inside Teck's Bold, Frenzied Inco Play," *Globe and Mail*, August 17, 2006.

4 Andy Hoffman and Elizabeth Church, "Munk Rants: Where's Miners' Courage?" *Globe and Mail*, September 13, 2006.

5 Paul Brent, "Canadian Brand Sags, Agency that Created Famous Rant Loses Flagship Beer Business," *National Post*, November 2, 2004.

6 Derek DeCloet, "The Deal Is Done, But O'Neill's Molson Legacy Comes into Question," *Globe and Mail*, January 29, 2005.

CHAPTER 1: TIME TO WAKE UP

7 International Trade Canada, "Canadian Direct Investment Abroad," Trade and Economic Analysis, Source: Cansim Table 376-0051, May 2006.

8 François Lavoie, "Canadian Direct Investment in 'Offshore Financial Centers,'" Statistics Canada, March 14, 2005.

9 Micro-Economic Policy Analysis Branch, Industry Canada, "Special Feature: Canada's Trade and Investment Linkages with Brazil, China and India," *Trade and Investment Monitor*, 2003, 52.

10 Jacqueline Thorpe, "Canada not ready for new trade powerhouses," *National Post*, April 19, 2004.

11 United Nations Conference on Trade and Development, *World Investment Report 2006, Developing and Transition Economies: Implications for Development*, United Nations, New York and Geneva, 2006, 51. Also Chinese government figures.

12 Saeed Rahnema and Michael Howlett, "Impediments to Industrial Policy: Overcoming Path Dependency in Canada's Post Staples Transition," *Journal of Australian Political Economy*, June 2002, No. 49, 114–135.

13 International Trade Canada, Department of Trade and Economic Analysis, *Monthly Trade Bulletin*, Vol. 6, No. 9, November 2004.

14 Richard A. Cameron, "Intrafirm Trade of Canadian-based Foreign Multinationals," Industry Canada: Industry Canada Research Publications Program, Working Paper No. 26, December 1998.

15 Ibid.

16 Michael Hart, "What's Next?" Ottawa: Centre for Trade Policy and Law, 1994, 23.

17 As referred to in TD Economics, "Canadian Business Goes Global for Growth, Globalization: Peril or Panacea for Canadian Business," TD Bank Financial Group, June 14, 2004, 11.

18 Kindly furnished by William Polushin, president of Amaxis Inc., during an interview in Montreal in June 2004.

19 *Financial Post Business*, FP500 Special Issue, Canada's Largest Corporations, June 2006, 108.

20 TD Economics, "Canadian Business Goes Global for Growth, Globalization: Peril or Panacea for Canadian Business," TD Bank Financial Group, June 14, 2004, 11.

21 Referred to in a speech by James Wolfensohn, president of the World Bank Group, given at the Conférence de Montréal, June 7, 2004.

22 Dominic Wilson and Roopa Purushot-haman, "Dreaming With BRICS: The Path to 2050," Goldman Sachs, Global Economics Paper No. 99, October 1, 2003.

23 As quoted in a speech by David Emerson, minister of industry, at the National Manufacturing Summit of the Canadian Manufacturers and Exporters, Ottawa, February, 7, 2005.

24 Kindly furnished by William Polushin in a document entitled "Canada's International Trade Performance: 1994–2003," January 2004.

25 "State of Trade," International Trade Canada, 2004.

26 Carin Holroyd, "The Costs of Falling Behind: Canada's Economic Relationship with Japan," Asia Pacific Foundation of Canada, *Canada Asia Commentary*, No. 38, February 2005, 3.

27 *Canadian Business*, Investor 500, Special Investing Guide, Summer 2004.

28 Wendy Dobson, "Taking a Giant's Measure: Canada, NAFTA and the Emergent China," C.D. Howe Institute *Commentary*, No. 202, September 2004.

CHAPTER 2: STEEL DINOSAUR

29 Derek DeCloet, "Stelco CEO's Gloomy Corporate Picture Wins Points for Accuracy," *Globe and Mail*, May 4, 2004.

30 *Financial Post Business*, FP500 Special Issue, Canada's Largest Corporations, June 2006, 66, 68.

31 Ibid.

32 Canada came in number one in the 2004 KPMG study of the cheapest industrialized countries to do business in. The study, entitled "Competitive Alternatives: The CEO's Guide to Competitive Business Costs," was published in February 2004. The results are proudly posted on Industry Canada's website.

33 Geoff Dyer and James Mackintosh, "Next For the West Are Cars 'Made in China,'" *Financial Times*, May 31, 2005.

34 David Lin and Alison Leung, "Auto Parts Exports Set to Double," *The Standard*, February 18, 2005. Also John D. Wiebe, "Why China Is an Auto Solution," *National Post*, February 2, 2005.

35 Barrie McKenna, "Foreign Suppliers May Turn Out to Be the Winners of the Lumber War," *Globe and Mail*, October 24, 2006.

36 Kindly furnished by William Polushin, president of Amaxis Inc., in a document entitled "Canada's International Trade Performance: 1994–2003," January 2004.

37 Yuen Pau Woo, "The East Asian Automobile Industry: Opportunity or Threat?" Canada in Asia series, Asia Pacific Foundation of Canada, January 2005.

38 Greg Keenan, "Toyota Seen Overtaking GM as No. 1 Auto Maker by 2010," *Globe and Mail*, May 19, 2005.

39 Table: "Non-residential Machinery and Equipment Investment per Worker in the Business Sector in Canada and the United States," kindly furnished by Andrew Sharpe, executive director, Centre for the Study of Living Standards. Also, Andrew Jackson, "Free Trade's Leap's of Faith, Hard Landings," *National Post*, December 8, 2003.

40 Jeremy Grant, "Chinese Learning to Talk Contracts Not Contacts," *Financial Times*, March 11, 2005.

41 Steven Chase, "Put Out the Welcome Mat, Flaherty Told," *Globe and Mail*, April 24, 2006.

42 Micro-Economic Policy Analysis Branch, Industry Canada, "Special Feature: Emergence of India as a Global Economic Force—Opportunities and Challenges for Canada," *Trade and Investment Monitor*, 2004.

43 Tim O'Neill, "Macro Stability and Economic Growth: The Past 20 Years," in David E.W. Laidlaw and William B.P. Robson, *Prospects for Canada: Progress and Challenges 20 Years after the MacDonald Commission* (Toronto: C.D. Howe Institute, September 2005), 34.

44 TD Economics "In Search of Well-being: Are Canadians Slipping Down the Economic Ladder?" Topic Paper, TD Bank Financial Group, January 18, 2005.

45 Someshar Rao, Andrew Sharpe and Jeremy Smith, "An Analysis of the Labour Productivity Growth Slowdown in Canada Since 2000," Centre for the Study of Living Standards, *International Productivity Monitor*, June 2005.

46 The Institute for Competitiveness and Prosperity, *Rebalancing Priorities for Canada's Prosperity*, Report on Canada 2006, March 2006, 4.

47 Neil Reynolds, "The Unproductive Productivity Fix," *Globe and Mail*, June 22, 2005.

48 Greg Quinn and Alexandre Deslongchamps, "Firms Try to Cope with Rising Loonie," Bloomberg News in *National Post,* December 3, 2004.

49 Laura Ramsay, "As Currency Rises, Firms Reinvent Themselves," *Globe and Mail,* May 25, 2006.

50 Philip Cross, "Recent Changes in the Labour Market," *Canadian Economic Observer,* Statistics Canada, March 2005.

51 Simon Avery, "In Ottawa, It's a Low-budget Tech Rebound," *Globe and Mail,* November 9, 2006.

52 Cathy Gulli, "Canada Calling," *National Post Business,* May 2004, 57.

53 Institute for Competitiveness and Prosperity, "Strengthening Structures: Upgrading Specialized Support and Competitive Pressure," Working Paper 5, July 2004.

54 In an article by Paul Viera, "Canada to Suffer Slowdown, Analysts Predict," *National Post,* March 15, 2006, FP2.

55 Andy Hoffman, "Alcan Can't 'Justify' Smelter Deal," *Globe and Mail,* January 5, 2007.

56 Roger L. Martin and Michael E. Porter, "Canadian Competitive-ness: A Decade after the Crossroads," *National Post* series on Competitiveness, 2001, 51.

57 Gilles Rhéaume, "Open for Business? Canada's Foreign Direct Investment Challenge" (Ottawa: The Conference Board of Canada, June 2004).

58 Anne Golden, "Opening the Door to Foreign Investment," *National Post,* June 3, 2004.

59 Eric Beauchesne, "Conditions Ripe for Productivity," *National Post,* April 26, 2005.

60 Carl Gomez, "Who's to Blame for Canada's Productivity Woes?" TD Economics Topic Paper, TD Bank Financial Group, June 15, 2005.

61 Lionel Fontage, "Foreign Direct Investment and International Trade: Compliments or Substitutes," Organization for Economic Co-operation and Development, Working Paper 199/3, October 1999.

CHAPTER 3: TARIFFS AND TRAINS

62 Ben Forster, *A Conjunction of Interests: Business, Politics and Tariffs, 1825–1879* (Toronto: University of Toronto Press, 1986), 190.

63 Michael Bliss, *Northern Enterprise: Five Centuries of Canadian Business* (Toronto: McClelland and Stewart, 1987), 251.

64 Ben Forster, *A Conjunction of Interests* (Toronto: University of Toronto Press, 1986), 190.

65 Gordon Laxer, *Open for Business: The Roots of Foreign Ownership in Canada* (Toronto: Oxford University Press, 1989). Also Tom Naylor, *The History of Canadian Business 1867–1914,* Volume I, The banks and finance capital (Toronto: James Lorimer & Company, 1975).

66 Glen Williams, *Not for Export: Towards a Political Economy of Canada's Arrested Industrialization* (Toronto: McClelland and Stewart, 1987), 21.

67 Ibid., 19.

68 Ibid., 48.

69 Ibid.

70 Ibid., 27.

71 Gordon Laxer, *Open for Business* (Toronto: Oxford University Press, 1989).

72 Ibid.

73 Glen Williams, *Not for Export* (Toronto: McClelland and Stewart, 1987), 70.

74 Michael Bliss, *Northern Enterprise* (Toronto: McClelland and Stewart, 1987), 510.

75 Ibid., 580.

76 Roger L. Martin and Michael E. Porter, "Canadian Competitiveness: A Decade after the Crossroads," *National Post* series on Competitive-ness, 2001.

77 Elizabeth Church and Keith McArthur, "How to Raise Your Game," *Globe and Mail*, October 17, 2005.

78 Glen Williams, *Not for Export* (Toronto: McClelland and Stewart, 1987), 20.

79 Michael Bliss, *Northern Enterprise* (Toronto: McClelland and Stewart, 1987), 311.

80 Interview with Joseph H. Hirshhorn, conducted by Paul Cumming, New York, December 16, 1976, Smithsonian archives of American art.

CHAPTER 4: THE MILK MAFIA

81 Frederic Tomesco, "Saputo Hints at Expansion to Boost International Sales," Bloomberg News in *Globe and Mail*, November 18, 2005.

82 International Trade Canada, EPM TRQ Imports Summary Control Year: 2006, APRMT61, November 15, 2006, 5.

83 "The Top 1000 Banks," *The Banker*, Vol. 155, No. 953, July 2005.

84 Sinclair Stewart, "Cash-rich BMO Boosts Dividend Pay-out," *Globe and Mail*, May 25, 2006.

85 Andrew Sharpe, "What Explains the Canada-U.S. ICT Investment Gap?" Centre for the Study of Living Standards, *International Productivity Monitor*, Fall 2005.

86 Eric Reguly, "HSBC a Shining Example of How We Missed the Boat," *Globe and Mail*, December 8, 2005.

87 Michael Bliss, *Northern Enterprise* (Toronto: McClelland and Stewart, 1987), 277.

88 The Senate Committee on Banking, Trade and Commerce, "Competition in the Public Interest: Large Bank Mergers in Canada," Sixth Report, December 2002.

89 John Turley-Ewart, "The Problem with Merger Hype," *National Post*, July 26, 2005.

90 Peter C. Newman, "Towers of Power," *Report on Business*, November 2005, 85.

91 Peter C. Newman, *The Canadian Establishment: The Acquisitors*, Vol. 2 (Toronto: McClelland and Stewart, 1975), 300.

92 Allan Levine, *The Exchange: 100 Years of Trading Grain in Winnipeg* (Winnipeg: Peguis Publishers, 1987), 19.

93 SPARKS Companies Inc., *The Canadian Barley Industry in Transition: A Study for Alberta Agriculture, Food & Rural Development*, December 2003.

94 Steven Chase, "Income Trusts: Party's Over," *Globe and Mail*, November 1, 2006, A1.

95 Eric Reguly, "Feds Don't Have the Will to Halt Income Trust Train," *Globe and Mail*, September 10, 2005.

96 Robert Bothwell and William Kilbourn, *C.D. Howe: A Biography* (Toronto: McClelland and Stewart, 1979), 220.

97 Allan Levine, *The Exchange* (Winnipeg: Peguis Publishers, 1987), 79.

98 Ibid., 31.

CHAPTER 5: WHY MEXICANS DON'T DRINK MOLSON

99 Robin Taylor, "BCI's Misadventures in Latin America," *National Post*, August 8, 2002.

100 Ibid.

101 Tyler Hamilton, "Retreat from Brazil: How Montreal Entrepreneur Charles Sirois Got a Close-up Look at the 'Seamy-underbelly' of Brazil's Telecom World," *Toronto Star*, April 5, 2003.

102 Paul Brent, *Lager Heads: Labatt and Molson Face Off For Canada's Beer Money* (Toronto: HarperCollins, 2004) 160, 163.

CHAPTER 6: TEAM CANADA AND TEQUILA

103 Glen Williams, *Not for Export: Towards a Political Economy of Canada's Arrested Industrialization* (Toronto: McClelland and Stewart, 1987), 77.

104 Richard Fahey, ed., *Report on Trade*, Canadian Federation of Independent Business, 2003.

105 Andrew Griffith, "From a Trading Nation to a Nation of Trades: Toward a Second Century of Canadian Trade Development," External Affairs and International Trade Canada, Policy Planning Staff Paper No. 92/95, 1992.

106 Ibid., 67.

107 Ibid., 64.

CHAPTER 7: DRAGON SLAYERS

108 Craig Wong, "Takeover Will Speed Growth, Intrawest Says," *Globe and Mail*, November 2, 2006.

CHAPTER 8: MULTICULTURAL MEAL TICKET

109 Asia Pacific Foundation of Canada, "The Role of Asian Ethnic Business Associations in Canada," *Canada Asia Commentary*, No. 35, April 2005.

110 Asia Pacific Foundation of Canada, "Vancouver as an Asian City," *Canada Asia Commentary*, No. 24, May 2002.

111 Michael Szonyi, "Asian-Canadians and Canada's International Relations," Canada in Asia, Foreign Policy Dialogue Series (Vancouver: Asia Pacific Foundation of Canada, November 2003), 7.

112 Shiboa Guo and Don J. DeVortez, "Chinese Immigrants in Vancouver: Quo Vadis?" Research on Immigration and Integration in the Metropolis, Vancouver Centre of Excellence, Working Paper Series No. 05-20, October 2005, updated February 2006.

113 Clifford Krause, "Some Skilled Foreigners Find Jobs Scarce in Canada," *New York Times,* June 5, 2006.

114 The Conference Board of Canada, "Performance and Potential 2004–2005: How Can Canada Prosper in Tomorrow's World?" (Ottawa: 2004).

115 Michael Posner, "The Invisible Man," *Report on Business,* June 2005, 34.

116 David Ley and Audrey Kobayashi, "Back to Hong Kong: Return Migration or Transnational Sojourn?" Research on Immigration and Integration in the Metropolis, Vancouver Centre of Excellence, Working Paper Series, No. 05-09, April 2005.

117 Ibid.

118 James Bagnall, "High Tech's Immigrant Success," *Toronto Star,* July 28, 1997, C5.

CHAPTER 9: THE MEXICAN LUNCH

119 TD Economics, "Canadian Business Goes Global for Growth, Globalization: Peril or Panacea for Canadian Business," TD Bank Financial Group, June 14, 2004, i.

120 KPMG, "Emerging Markets: The Canadian Experience in India," November 2005.

121 Kindly furnished by William Polushin, president of Amaxis Inc., during an interview in Montreal in June 2004.

122 Paul Brent, *Lager Heads: Labatt and Molson Face Off for Canada's Beer Money* (Toronto: HarperCollins, 2004), 159.

123 Laurel McLean, *Repatriation Practices in Canadian Energy Companies: A Case of Lost Opportunities,* University of Calgary, Faculty of Education, December 2003.

124 Michael Brick, "A Developer Back From the Brink," *New York Times,* February 21, 2003.

CHAPTER 10: A NEW APPROACH TO PARENTING

125 Don Martin, "Well-meaning Execs Not Wanted in Ottawa," *Calgary Herald,* May 18, 2006.

126 The Conference Board of Canada, *Death by a Thousand Paper Cuts: The Effect of Barriers to Competition on Canadian Productivity* (Ottawa: Conference Board of Canada, May 2006), 17.

127 Roger Martin, *The Demand for Innovation in Canada* (Toronto: Rotman School of Management, August 12, 2002).

128 Richard Harris, "Canada's R&D Deficit—And How to Fix It," C.D. Howe Institute, *Commentary,* No. 211, May 2005, 4.

129 Roger Martin, *The Demand for Innovation in Canada* (Toronto: Rotman School of Management, August 12, 2002).

130 Mirko Bibic, "Cable's 'False Modesty' Plan," *National Post,* April 22, 2006.

131 Heather Scoffield, "Defer to Market, Bernier Tells CRTC," *Globe and Mail,* November 16, 2006.

132 Greg Keenan, "GM Canada CEO Hitching Auto Maker to Knowledge Bandwagon," *Globe and Mail,* October 7, 2004.

133 Laura Jones et al., *Rated "R": Prosperity Restricted by Red Tape* (Toronto: Canadian Federation of Independent Business, December 2005), 10.

134 Derek Burney, "Foreign Policy: More Cohesion Less Pretence," for the Simon Reisman Lecture in International Trade Policy (Ottawa: Centre for Trade Policy and Law) March 14, 2005, 6.

135 In a press release by Foreign Affairs and International Trade, "Pettigrew Announces Government's Response to Export Development Act Review," No. 107, May 18, 2000.

136 Kenny Zhang, "Recognizing the Canadian Diaspora," Asia Pacific Foundation of Canada, *Canada Asia Commentary*, No. 41, March 2006, 2.

137 Neil Reynolds, "An Economist Takes the Helm of the Canadian Ship of State," *Globe and Mail*, February 8, 2006.

138 Jack Mintz, "The 2006 Tax Competitiveness Report: Proposals for a Pro-Growth Tax Reform," C.D. Howe Institute, *Commentary*, No. 239, September 2006.

139 Roger Martin, *The Demand for Innovation in Canada* (Toronto: Rotman School of Management, August 12, 2002).

140 Ibid.

141 Katherine Harding, "Bold Strokes on Language," *Globe and Mail*, May 20, 2006.

142 Sundeep Tucker, Victor Mallet and Kevin Brown, "Howard's Blend of Tenacity and Pragmatism," *Financial Times*, February 28, 2006.

143 Ibid.

144 Caroline Alphonso, "A Great Place To Do Business—Just No Beacon for Culture," *Globe and Mail*, August 2, 2005.

ACKNOWLEDGEMENTS

THIS BOOK WAS a three-year project, a passion really, and I have many people to thank in helping me realize it. I couldn't have done it without the countless Canadian businesspeople, consultants, lawyers, bankers, academics and civil servants who, without knowing me, took a risk and answered my unsolicited call to arms. I thank them for taking a chance on me, opening their minds and offices to me, and inspiring me with their determination and desires for change. While I simply write about the challenges facing Canadian businesspeople to be globally competitive, they live it every day.

There are too many people to thank everyone by name, but I am indebted to a number of individuals who went to extra lengths to support me in this endeavour, either with their time and patient explanations or by providing me with valuable contacts. I am grateful to Pierre Alarie and Ian Mallory for their insights, Boris Rousseff for his unvarnished dedication to Canada, and Roy MacLaren, for restoring my faith in government. I would like to thank Howard Balloch and John Gruetzner for sharing their valuable knowledge of China. Also a thanks to Gary Comerford for taking an unscheduled meeting with me when I showed up on the wrong day, and Rick Waugh, who, true to his Winnipeg roots, agreed to an interview over the initial objections of his minders.

I would also like to acknowledge Roger Martin, whose incisive analysis first planted the seeds for this book in my head, and Glen Hodgson and Jayson Myers, whose grasp of this subject matter provided rich resource material. A warm thank you also goes out to David Fung, Tim Plumptre and Stanley Hartt. I would also like to extend my appreciation to William Polushin for his support. Last but not least, I would like to express my gratitude to those individuals who shall remain nameless, but who agreed to tell their stories despite the risk to their own careers because they believed it was important to share their knowledge.

Of course, none of their stories would have made it to print without the support of my publisher, Scott McIntyre, an ardent booster of the Canadian cause. To my editor, John Eerkes-Medrano, thank you for the thoughtful suggestions. And I must doff my hat to my agent, Rick Broadhead, who, in true entrepreneurial spirit, cold-called me after seeing an article I had written and asked me if I'd like to write a book. It just so happened I had one on the go.

The journey that brought me here actually begins fifteen years ago in Flin Flon, Manitoba. I took my first job out of journalism school at the *Flin Flon Daily Reminder* and my time there taught me more about Canada than anything before or since. From Flin Flon, I made my way down to Chile, Argentina, and Peru, before settling in Mexico. Latin America taught me that the little stories are usually part of a much bigger one, and I am indebted to the *Financial Times* for tutoring me on the workings of international markets and helping to hone my analytical skills. This book is an amalgam of those two very different, but essentially intertwined experiences.

Writing this book was a journey in itself and I would like to thank my family and friends for not letting me lose my way. I would like to thank Michele Mani for always looking out for me and Carla Kearns for her thoughtful assistance. I am grateful to Franca Festa for her unwavering support. Scuby, thank you for keeping me company all those years, I only wish we could celebrate together. To my daughter, Isabella, you taught me what's really important. This book was a family endeavour and, above all, I would like to thank my husband, Andrea, for his unconditional support and faith in me. I couldn't have done it without you.

INDEX

Brazil, 3–4, 6, 20, 22, 41–42, 47, 49, 51,
57–58, 80, 89, 115, 116, 141–47, 149–55,
176–77, 179–81, 183, 246–47, 252,
256, 265–66, 268
British Columbia, 24, 93–94, 118–19, 123,
211
Bronfman, Samuel, 98–99
Business plans, 243–44, 246, 296
Business practices, 21, 212, 246–47, 254–56,
260–61, 265, 280

Canadian Wheat Board, 130–31, 138, 139,
289–90
Canbras Communications Corporation,
149–52
Cash-flow, 253–54
Chambers of commerce, 18, 22, 143, 278
Chile, 12, 21, 68, 171–72, 175
China, 3, 9–10, 23, 30–31, 40, 41, 43–50, 51,
54, 59, 68, 70–71, 111, 160–61, 170–71,
175, 176–77, 182–83, 215–18, 223–25,
235, 236–37, 245, 247, 250, 254,
259–64, 270, 273–74, 296, 297, 306–7
Choquette, Pierre, 203–4, 249, 257, 271, 279
Chrétien, Jean, 124, 170, 172–73, 174–75,
181, 274, 278
Cirque du Soleil, 198, 210
Clifford, Terry, 278–79
Clothing industry, 39, 52
Comerford, Gary, 10–11, 226–27, 258–59,
261, 272
Commitment, 168, 246, 247–48
Commodities, 26, 45, 55, 130–31, 139
Competition, 20, 28, 30–31, 33, 44, 46–47,
49, 53, 63, 69, 70–71, 80, 83, 86,
124–26, 132–39, 148, 189, 194, 204
See also tariffs, protective
Complacency, in Canadian business, 5,
32–33, 36, 52–53, 93, 116, 197
Conference Board of Canada, 36, 61
Confidence, lack of, 9, 58, 138, 190, 222

Contracts, 250–51, 263–64
Corruption, 19, 61, 142, 155, 178, 219,
239–41, 265–69, 271
Cosmetics industry, 205–8
Creo, 71–72, 199
Crown corporations, 84, 187, 190
Culture, corporate, 16, 58–59, 152, 162–65,
215–16, 219, 223–24, 226–29, 250–53,
257–69
Customer service, 147, 203–4, 250

Dairy industry, 105–13, 135
Dantas, Daniel, 153–55
D'Aquino, Thomas, 307
Deregulation, 126, 306
Development programs, 85, 97, 103–4, 136
Diefenbaker, John George, 85, 128
Distribution, 143, 147, 148, 156, 159, 203–4
Diversification, 33, 139
Dofasco, 5, 39–41, 92
Doha negotiations, 175–76
Domtar, 114, 119

Economic decline, 10, 39, 61–62, 63, 66, 68
Education and training, 65, 68, 244, 275–77,
279, 284–85, 302–5
Electronics industry, 52, 54, 57
Émigrés, networking with, 298–99
Energy industry, 17, 29–30, 58, 66–67, 80,
81, 85, 92, 114, 155–59
Engineering and construction industry,
28, 61, 134–35, 198, 240, 244
Entrepreneurship, 53, 72–74, 83, 97, 137,
198, 299–300, 301–2
European Free Trade Association, 174
European Union (EU), Canada and, 21,
33–34, 173–75
Executives, 57–58, 65, 86, 95, 144–46,
165, 222, 263, 276–77, 302–3
Experience, international, 251, 275–77
Export credit finance, 187–94, 294